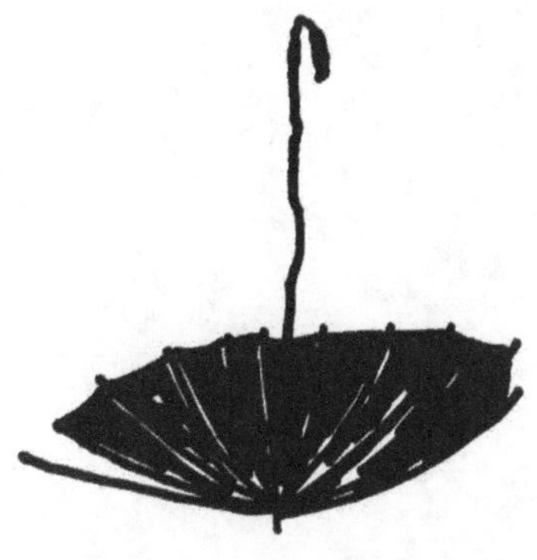

good deed rain

Go With the Flow: A Tribute to Clyde Sanborn © 2018
Allen Frost, Good Deed Rain, Bellingham, Washington
ISBN 978-1-64008-159-8

Cover painting by Clyde Sanborn, courtesy of Jan Sanborn
Back cover photograph of Clyde leaving La Conner by Joanne Zabik
Edited by Allen Frost
Production Assistance by Fred Sodt
Title page assistance by Maggie Feeney
Cover production by Katrina Svoboda Johnson

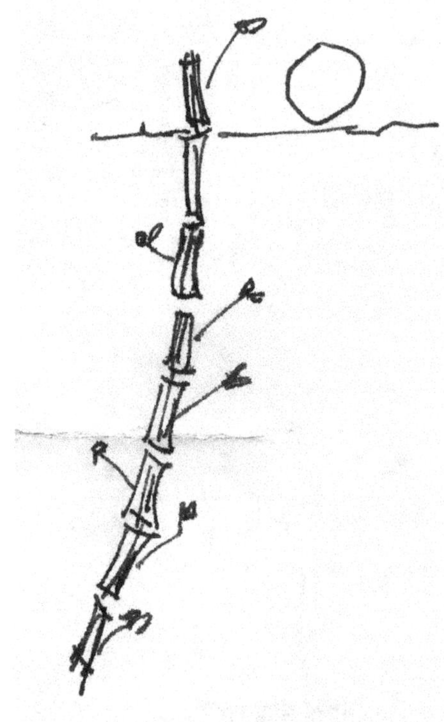

This book is especially dedicated to
Janet Saunders, Jim Smith & Michael Clough.

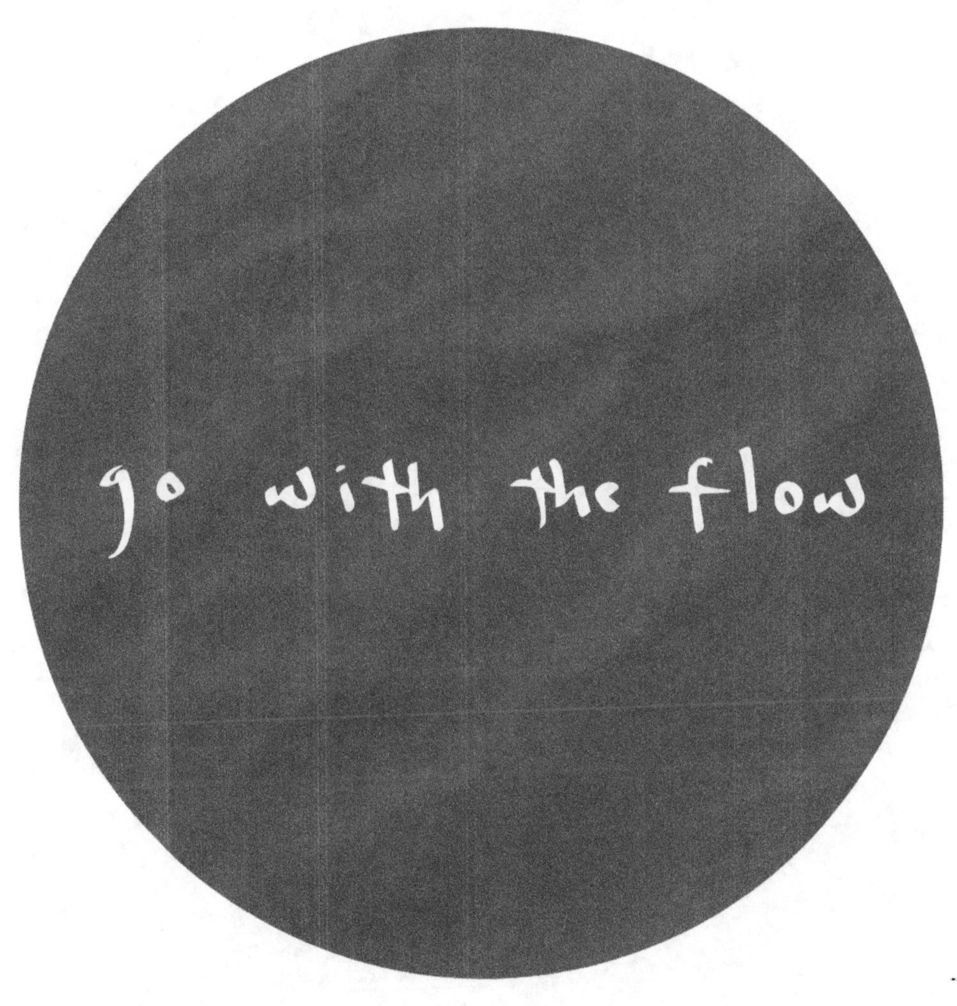
go with the flow

A Zen master was asked, "How does one enter the Tao?"
He answered, "Do you hear the sound of the stream?
There is the way to enter."

—Alan Watts

INTRODUCTION:

Late July, we were on Vashon Island out on the spit by the tall radio tower. The incoming tide was quickly pushing across the sandbar. The water moved so fast, you could stand there and see it eat the ground around you. Later that night, I was trying to sleep in the back of our car and all I could think of was Clyde Sanborn and Li Po. From the moment Charlie Krafft told me about Clyde, I immediately thought of Li Po, the Chinese poet who died when he reached overboard trying to catch the moon on the river. This shared fate was all I knew about poet Clyde Sanborn.

So I read Li Po for clues. David Hinton's *The Selected Poems of Li Po* was an excellent source. Words from this book read like telegrams from a mirrored river world 1200 years ago. Moonlight, mountains and valleys, rain, wine and rowing in the flow. Just switch the current of the Yangtze to the Skagit River.

Thinking of Clyde Sanborn in terms of Li Po helped me in these early stages where I knew so little about Sanborn. I wrote to translators David Hinton and Bill Porter/Red Pine. Mr. Porter responded: "I've never met Clyde Sanborn. Even in Port Townsend I'm often hearing about people I should have met but haven't. The hermit life style, I guess. Both Clyde's and mine…Not many Chinese lived as Li Po lived. If you're looking for someone like that, I suggest the Seven Sages of the Bamboo Grove, especially Juan Chi (also in *Finding Them Gone*). Nearly all of China's great poets were officials, which ruled out wild and crazy types." When a letter arrived from Tom Robbins, he also confirmed, "The reference to Li Po is probably not misplaced." Then, I received a book from Paul Hansen. In his poem "At the Grave of Li Tai-Bai" (Li Po) special dedication is made to Clyde Sanborn. So it seems natural there's a poetic transmission from China's mountains and rivers to Washington's Pacific Northwest.

But I really started to understand Clyde when Michael Clough wrote me. He provided some much needed biographical details, loaned me the incredible *rainbow city* coloring book, and all of a sudden I was seeing the picture come into focus. I include quite a few of the pages from that book as it gives you a good idea of the world Clyde found himself in, in the amazing 1970s Seattle. I was lucky to grow up then and remember the feeling.

Michael told me about Jay Carpenter and thanks to the internet I was able to track him down. Jay's stories and photos bring Clyde's Navy days to life and we're very lucky to have them. Clyde's sister Jan told me, "Clyde did NOT like to talk about that time. The only thing I remember him mumblingly relate at one juncture was the awful 'crossing ceremony' over the equator. He loathed it."

In my daily thoughts, more and more, Clyde even started appearing in my dreams. He's been so much on my mind, I'm sure it summoned an appearance at the grocery store when I ran into Crazy Carl. He makes blackberry wine in the woods. (In the included interview, Clyde says he does not like the name Crazy Clyde.) But meeting Crazy Carl and seeing him push his bicycle along Samish Way is a reminder that this is also the story of a person who lived far out on the fringes.

Having the support of the Sanborn family for this project was very important. Thank you to Jan Sanborn, Clyde's sister, and Sarah Sanborn, his niece. It's clear that Clyde is still very much with them. Jan wrote, "Life hasn't been the same since he left. He was my big brother, mentor, and always gave me that little extra push to stay with my creative side." And Sarah wrote that, "My uncle Clyde was a big factor in my life as a teen, and into my adult life. He was taken from us too soon. It's hard to live as a creative person with a poet's soul in this world, that is if you are living in the mainstream trying to make a living that way. I understand now why he wanted to live on the river, with his new family, his friends. The world needs more of his amazing life and light." Their comments encourage a deeper understanding of Clyde Sanborn.

The last week of August, I took a trip to La Conner. I walked along the streets Clyde knew, sought out a couple of the places he used to go. I even stopped in at the Chamber of Commerce and asked about him. Clyde's fading name is still painted on the pavement in a parking lot labyrinth by the post office. Then I followed directions out of town to visit with two of his longtime friends, Jimmy and Joanne Zabik. They live in a homemade cabin, in a beautiful spot overlooking Skagit Bay. Being there gave me a window into Clyde's world and I can easily see why he made this his home.

Summer was ending, I returned to my full-time job and work on the book slowed and then Jim Smith died. Jim Smith not only befriended and sheltered Clyde, he and his wife Janet Saunders were a huge help to me making this book. Jim's memorial was in early October, in the same shelter at Pioneer Park where Clyde's life was honored twenty years ago.

Many thanks to Steve Herold, Ben Munsey, Jim Smith and everyone who worked on *Flash Flood & Other Poems* (1997). Yours is a beautiful book, and I'm honored to be allowed the privilege to reprint it as Part 1.

Clyde's collected poems were never published in a book during his lifetime and like Cold Mountain who wrote his poems on trees and rocks, Clyde's poetry had to be saved, gathered from scraps of paper strewn in his wake.

Piecing together Clyde's life story, I couldn't have uncovered this much without the aid of many people. I asked to learn about Clyde and found a book. Thank you to everyone who helped. Your memories and treasures are a testament to the life of Clyde Sanborn.

Allen Frost
End of summer 2016, into winter 2017
Bellingham, Washington

Part 1:
FLASH FLOOD

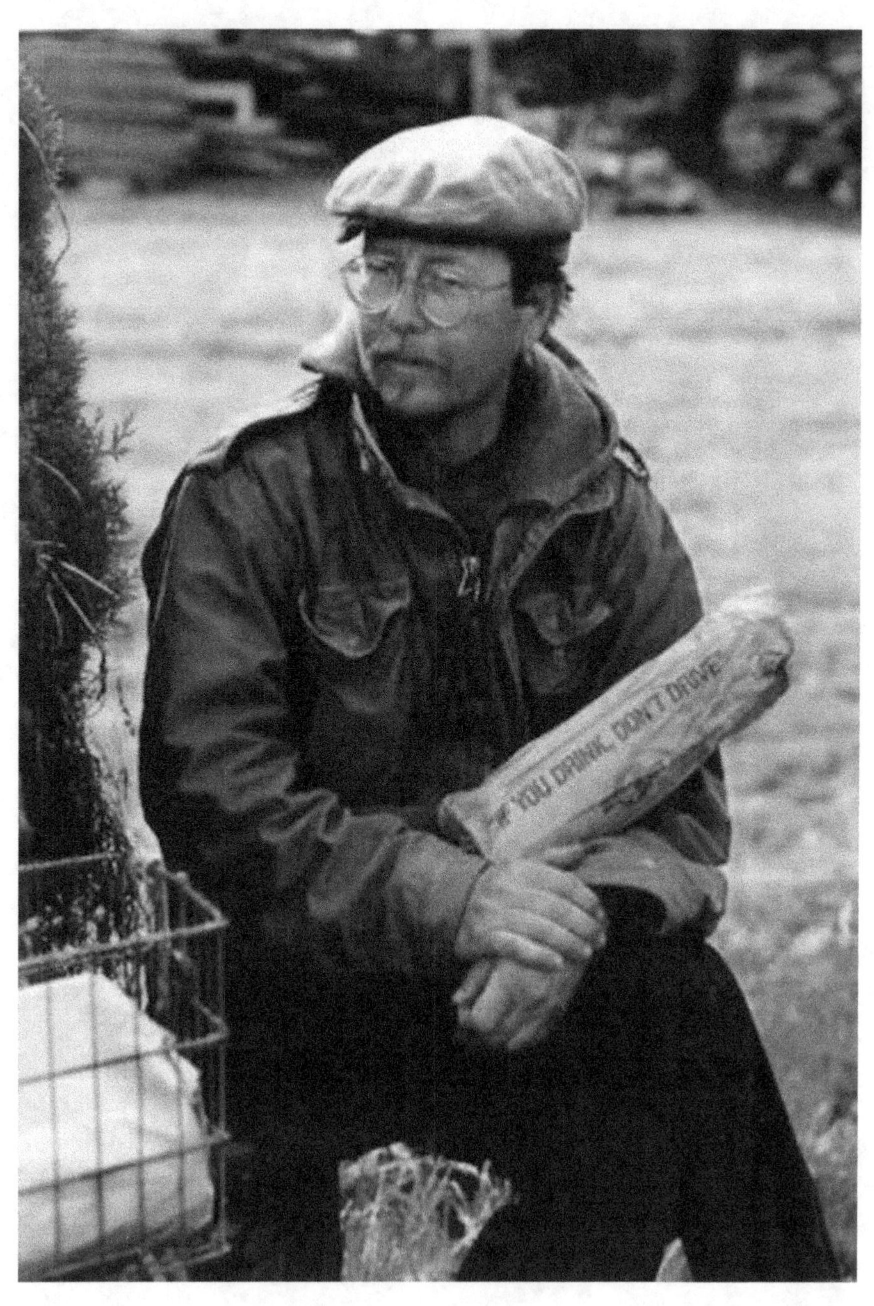

CLYDE SANBORN, 1948-1996

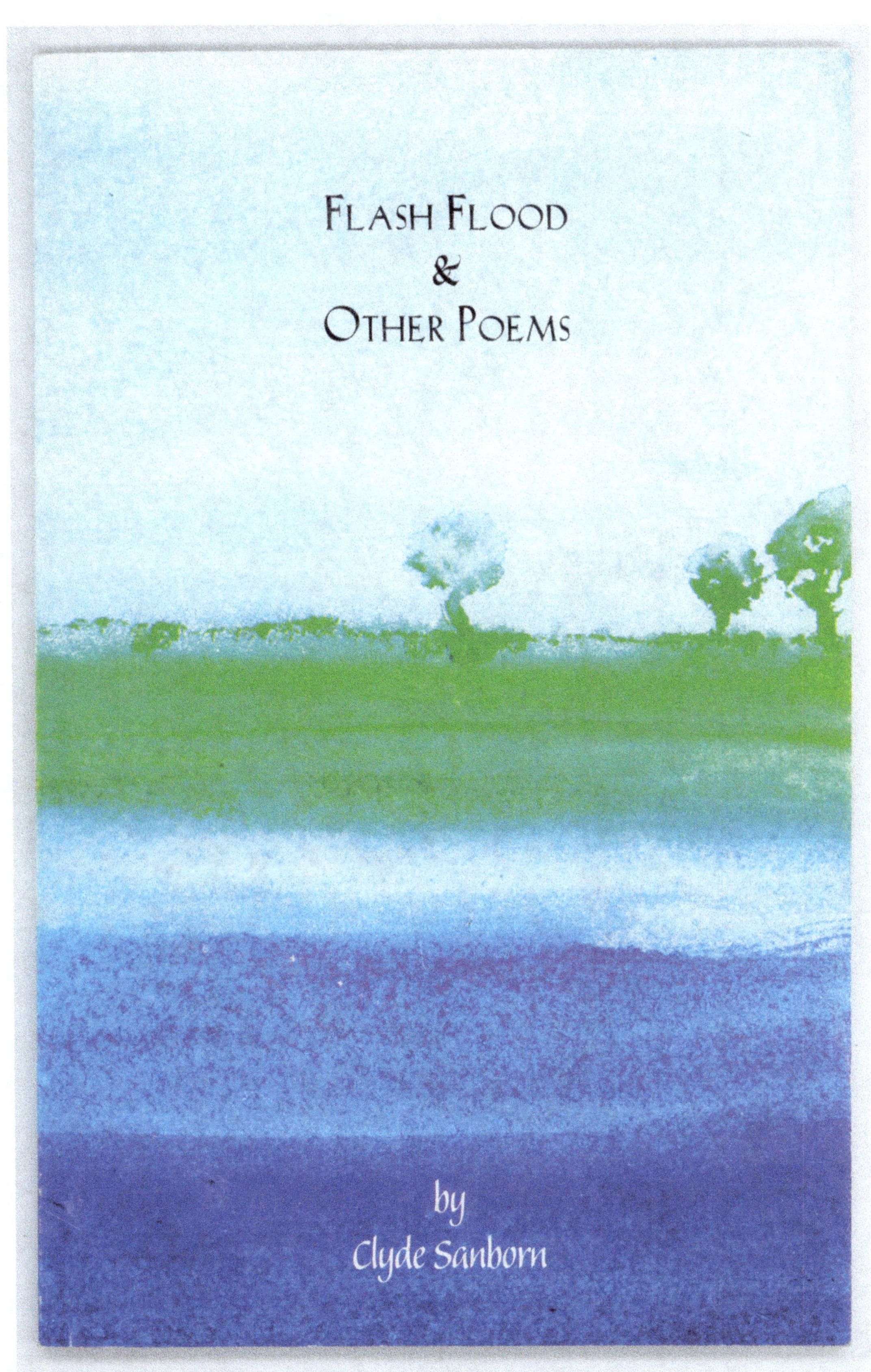

Flash Flood
&
Other Poems

by
Clyde Sanborn

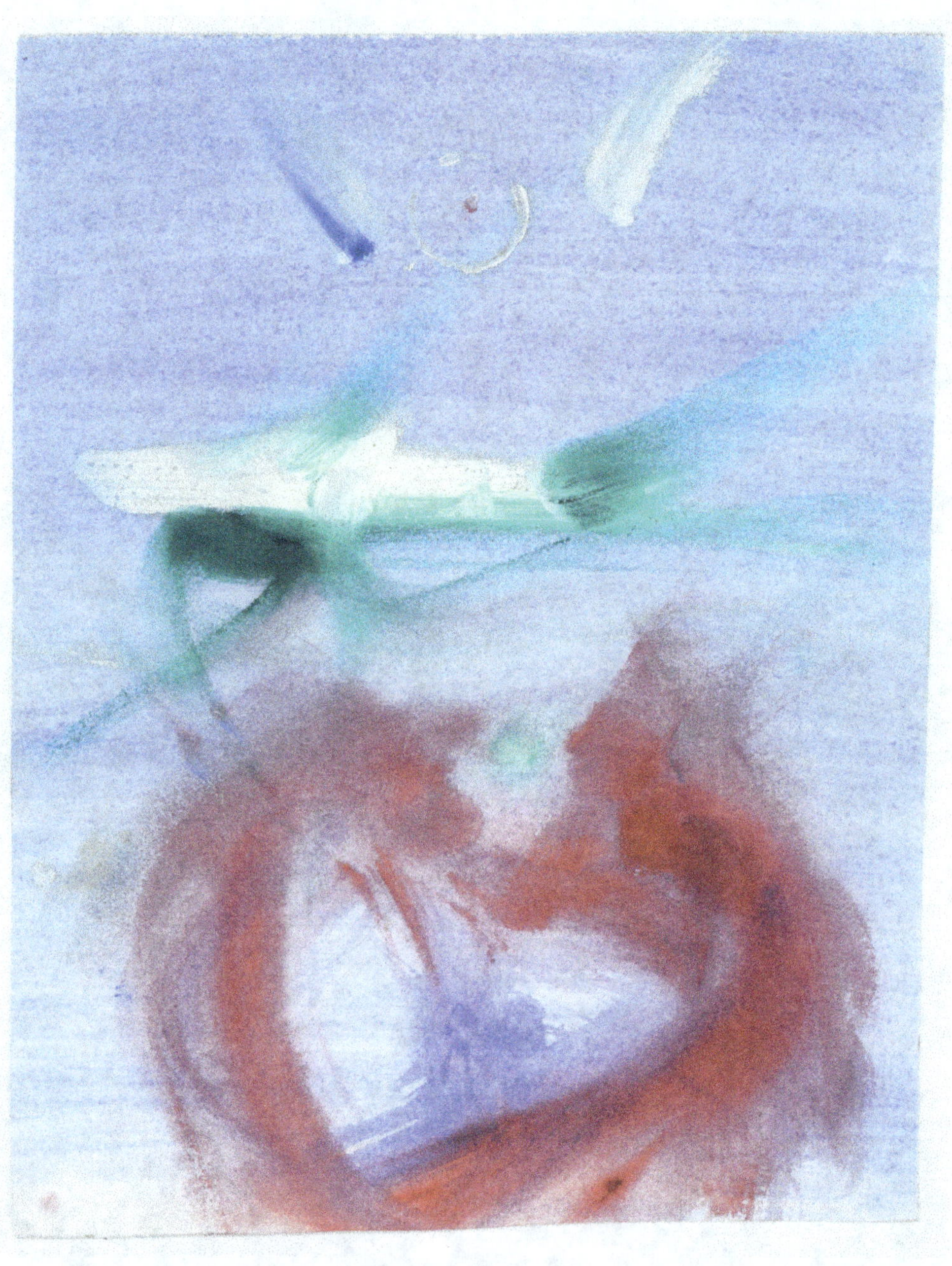

Artwork by Clyde Sanborn.

INTRODUCTION

After reading aloud his poem "Flash Flood" Clyde
once said, "Sometimes I write a poem and sometimes
one writes me. That poem wrote me." Clyde wrote a lot
of poems in his life, usually on scraps of paper and
cocktail napkins, which he would give away as gestures
of friendship. This book is a collection of those poems,
assembled by his friends.

Born and raised in Stockton, California, Clyde served
in the Navy in Japan, where he was introduced to Zen
Buddhism. In 1977 he settled down on the banks of the
Skagit River, living quietly and simply in houseboats,
sheds, tents, floatshacks. He painted and wrote poems,
observed nature and visited with his many friends, both
riverrats and townsfolk. On March 15, 1996, at the age
of 47, while rowing, he drowned near his home on the
river.

No poet could have lived his poetry more faithfully
and naturally than Clyde. His natural spirit made us
mindful of the failings of the modern age.

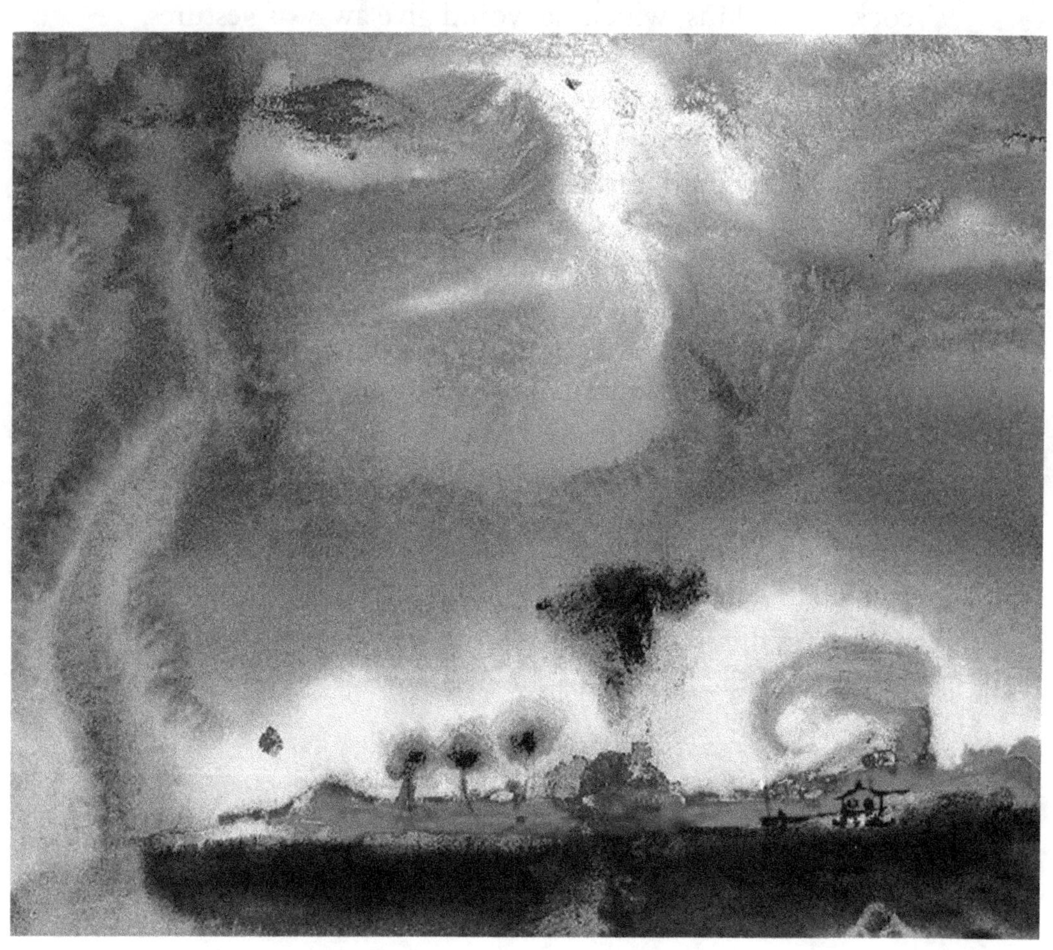

Flash Flood

Trout fly looping lazily.
Line slicing air, then landing,
Barely breaking surface tension.
The ponderous river, kinda huge and quiet,
Molding mud in silence.

Some dogs bark.
Horses restless.
Birds in frenzy, miles downstream.
Funny rumble felt in the bones.

Then, past the bend upriver,
Like the suddenness of an instantaneous elephant,
Thirty thousand buffalo, in fury red, stampede.
A water-wall of thirty feet
Of wood, rock, grasses, outlined in the sun,
Of flailing humans, soggy mattresses,
The homes of a thousand creatures.
Zany karma on the loose,
The queen of tragedy.

Then, scrambling to higher ground to escape
The raving tip of nature's tongue,
I reach the ridge
And while turning to watch,
I start to fade
And time slows,
And I reawake in the darkened room.

I reach to your arm and
Remember that you also have faded
To another dream.
And then, again, the tears begin
Like tiny flash floods,
But quiet,
Quiet.

Many Springs

There are many Springs today —
One is a new bird, another a warm stone.
One is a marshhawk flying upside down.
And the last is the last
Fall leaf that lived way up. Just landed.

Spring

The earth belched,
     and
     flowers were.

Spring, 1992

Perhaps the gravity
was too clear, or the
moon shown too much. It was
a gentle life until my socks stank,
the bitch said hello again, the flat tire... !
But on curious spring days it overrides —
     one color chasing another.

Spring / Sitting

The barn swallows and wild roses
arrived together this year.

Watching the river today. Water inside
water; clear to dense, fast to still —
Hey! My minds the same! I go in
and make tea.

Spring, Again

Spring can be tedious
when one has
        not been sprung.

Ode to Spring

Ah, to
    be in love —
when the skunk cabbages
    are in bloom.

Pond

The more one remembers
    the pond, the
clearer it becomes.
As we watch the descending
    flower petals
wrinkle it.

She

If one can handle the
     unfounded emotional
     bombardment — and
     still maintain a vast sense
of humor, . . .
          might work.

To Jack Dow, 1981

Love is torment
Whenever we hide it.
Why not lay it bare
     like the man coming up
Over the mountain? Large.

Breaking the Ice

When I wanted to meet
you, did I have to be a
400,000 ton ice breaker?

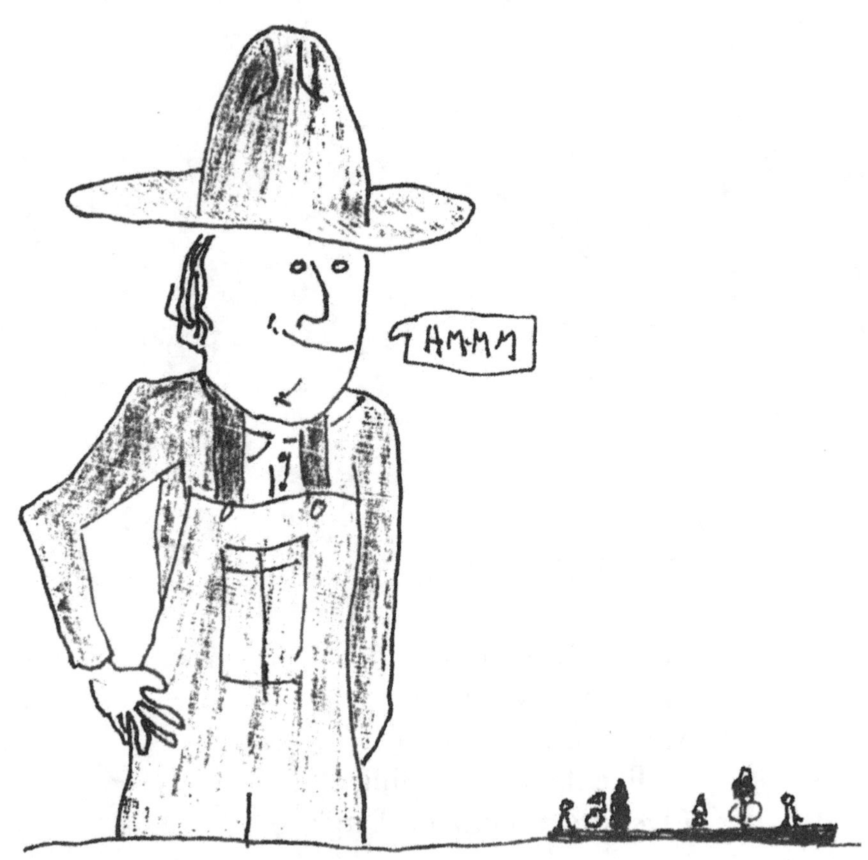

Hmm...

...it's just one of those lives —
the pretty girls live here. Hmm...?
    and the plants, hmm...?
And life lives here with
    Sylvia cat, hmm...
Well...

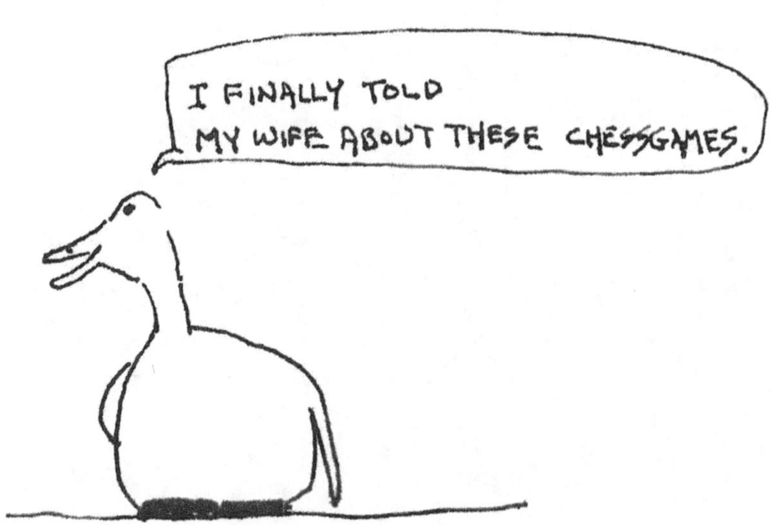

I'm Moving Towards the
Sound of Her Name

The wind knows her
But speaks a strange language.
The white owl saw her
On
The other side of the moon and
Will not make a sound.
Her shadow of violet
Breathes slowly in the night and somewhere
She wobbles with a half-crock'd soul
Along the continents of the world.

Valentine for Janet

Candy is dandy
but
Poetry's cheaper

Untitled 1

Pure love —
          enter laughing.

Autumn

The prince of leaves
    turns over, towards
        the princess.

Clouds

Clouds are hearts, without end.
After many lifetimes,
    I remember your eyes.

First Time at Black Dog Allen's

After June and July,
during the first summer day —
I met the giving earth bliss mother,
    on the backporch.
The gods,
came for lunch
naked.

Poem to Allen's Relatives

Hey! This boy knows the stars.
When you all are concerned about
new half-assed Buicks
he is singing his best song!
When you all are struggling thru a
diaper, or how the lawn might
be mowed, this boy falls upsidedown to heaven!
    You all must be trying to fool me.
But if you're not, let us simply go to sleep,
    and then wake up.
Oh, it is so difficult to keep up with
    the Jones's — or ourselves,
        for that matter.

Bex's Last Annual Bar-be-cue
        8-1-92

What is beyond the gateless gate?
A windy greenfield & swallows
    catching windy bugs,
And it's like the dateless date —
One just dates universe.

The Road to John Hahn's House

The road to John Hahn's house
    is very difficult.
Twists and turns,
    twists and turns.
The road to John Hahn's house
    is very difficult.

A Bird Talks to a Flower
       for Dana & Toni

Every Saturday morning
    at 8:00 a.m.
on every Sept. 25th, 1993
10 million birds
    sing in Edison.

X-Country Running
    for Tim

    Doing cross-country,
    the birds are with
    the sky. Funny how mind
works . . .

Untitled Fragment

What is the sound of one clam happening?

Sailing
    for the Sylvia

Jumping up and down on
the toy boat,
    Les and Sandy sometimes
inhale
to create
    fair winds.

("the situation is hopeless,
    but not serious").

When her keel was laid,
    the hurricanes and waves
kissed her gently.

Dear Sue

Helping people die is a grace.
    Even on hard days, it
    takes a gentle touch.

Two birds flew over, when
you weren't looking.
    They said, happy
    birthday too.

Sarah Dancer

... so she decided to dance.
She would sit by trees
for hours watching the
wind move the leaves — and
cats, when they pranced, and birds
as turned in the air.
Yes: to move, to move all around.

Roger
     Poem to Deanna

What is this Love of which
the poets sing — that it can
burn so brightly on such meager fuel?
A word, a glance,
a touch, are things that are
sufficient to sustain its glow.
And we pray they do not understand
its meaning.

Limerick

There once was a carver named Conta.
Who could sculpt both the back and the fronta.
        The chips they would fly,
        From his hair to his thigh,
As he hummed to the wood a sweet mantra.

To Amadeo

You big, and small.
        The air breathes thru you.
        Clouds too.

Slight Ode to Touristhood

Exquisite tweeds
    soft leather purse, the
tourist girl
squints in the sunshine
    and local color
        and Indians —
so cute
    she probably
has an
    eclair somewhere.

Oz Died

Oz died, but got to live somewhere else
    and still IS — as I think of it.
    And Oz died — but not much.
He's probably asking, "what's for lunch?"
    and meeting new people by now.

Poem to a Flower

With earth and air
    around you,
tyfoons and such —
    bugs, humans stomping,
animals and birds
    always wanting to eat you —
        you still stand.
A gift for someone.

Untitled 2

Even a
flower has
to wake.

How a Flower Travels

Pollen, kissing
        the air.

A Flower

A flower
     touches
you,
     without
     knowing it.

Flowers at Night

The night has its own flowers.
And flowers live at night.
        The moonbow at Shi-Shi
            walks the beach.
Which one it was,
        I don't know.
The ocean sounds, with or without us.

Nero Woof

Me ride with Paul.
Me smell and watch.
Me listen well and
    sit in car.
Me be good dog and
    wait. Me good big dog.
Me wait and rest.

Poem by Issa

Yes, the young sparrows
when you treat them gently
they will thank you
with their droppings.

Frog Jumps

Frog Jumps
Earth Moves

Roothe

Sometimes, far
out into the ocean,
a bumblebee sees
the sunset.

Applesauce in the Front Yard

Tarma is making fuzzy dreams on the frontporch.
Dreaming her tail is the wet fur of a dark comet.
She shakes the last drop off it,
Across the solar system.

New Bird

The new bird sits on the old volcano.
Mother earth rumbles.
Tossing girdles over the edge
    the dawn arrives.
Using a cane that is used by an angel friend,
    we think, and think about our thinking.

Talent Feline
        for Rosie Cat

This is your poem, purr pure pure purr purr purr cat, and
        rub against the leg.

Now we're outside, with the morning birds.

        R.

The silence
        of snail dream.

Peg

The cool lioness, sits
    in the shade of the world —
Growling, and then an
occasional purr. Having seen
everything, and watching
    the little birds.

Today

Today's a lazy planet
sunlight
shadows stroll with trees
over the horizon.

The wind plays with dust
in little dances
as birds do bellyflops.

A fading train whistle is a
kite string
and pulls it all up.

Weather

A bird wing
   and
      cloud loves.

Saturday Morning

Rocking gently in the breeze,
By the dock, in its slipper
In red and white and blue
Number III, Victoria Clipper.

Fall is a puzzle

Fall is a puzzle,
The leaves are the pieces.

Untitled 3

The Ocean is just
a wide spot in the
River.

Ash Wednesday

The first day of Lent —
    In the air,
        angels like square-dancers,
    skirts raised high, and laugh,
    and a wink.

Untitled Fragment
    Autumn 92

Leaf it Fall

To a Tourist Lady

Your golden earrings
and
diamond bracelet
cost more than I'll earn
mowing Lowell and Libby's lawn
in 10,000 lifetimes

Clyde's Principle of Poetics

    ONE should always
    carry a pen
    ONE never knows
when ONE
  may Run
    into a poem.

Wanted: For Rent

Nice, newer, new, or modern
2 bedroom mobile home. All
electric. Near new malls. Near
busline. Far from fear. In court.
485./monthly. References required.
Note from mom. All cement, no
sun, stars, or wind. Floral carpet.
Drinking pets, smoking children
only. No people need apply.
P.S. First 3 mos. cleaning deposit.
2 months dirty deposit. Deposit on
the deposit, $35.00. Deposit on the
deposit deposit, no extra charge.
Teflon bib for rude volcanoes.

Untitled 4

It's always windy.
    But sometimes
        the air and I
   are together.

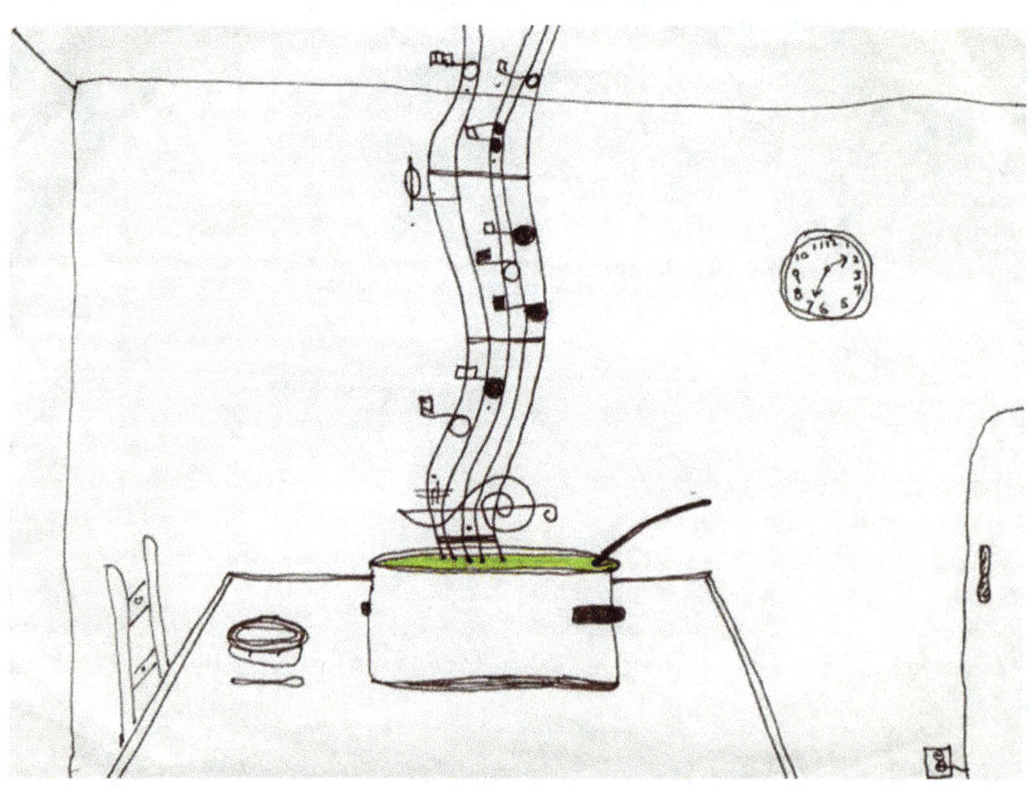

The Final Eye

     when the final eye
          seez it, the rest
of the universe will
     appear

Silence

As silence is
     born in an egg —
     It hatches and
          gets all over you.

Imagine

Words come out
    as ancient soldiers.
And the earth, as an
    ancient soldier.

War

Perhaps
    one day —
bullets will forget.

N.F.S.
    for la-la land

This poem is not for sale.
    And if it was, I
wouldn't
sell it, much.

Christmas Wishes

Less military-industrial thinking.
Calmer people.
Bigger angels.
More talking with trees and animals.
More respect for insects and stones.
And more Santas from the minorities and parades
    of silly Santas from the 3rd world and U.S.A.
and...
    an exchange program of Santa Clauses
    from all nations and, no nations thanks.

Quick hurricanes of mistletoe, devil in a head lock.
And an Oak for President, a Redwood for Governor,
        roses for the mayors of cities, thank you.

For Christmas I'd ask the world
        for enough love to give me goose bumps.
Homosapiens sitting in a ring of joy,
        their hats on backwards.

86'd

After 12 year i've
    finally made it.
Perhaps, if they discover
    that there is no edge
        to the world,
they will stop trying
    to push us
        off it.

86'd

After 12 years i've
~~finally made it~~ —

Perhaps, if they discover
that there is no edge
to the world,
they will stop trying
to push us
off it.

/s.

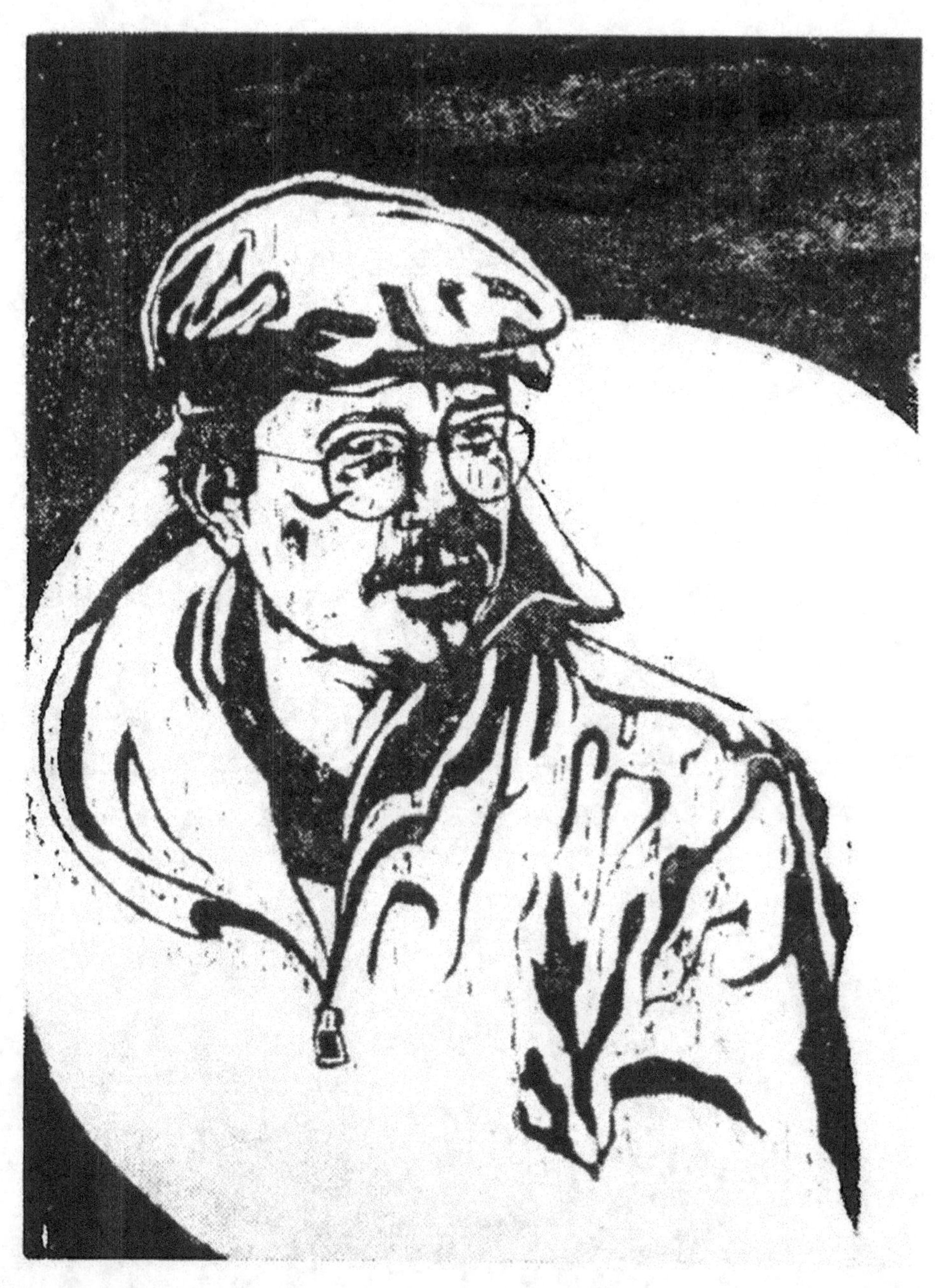

Woodcut by Claudia Gjertsen.

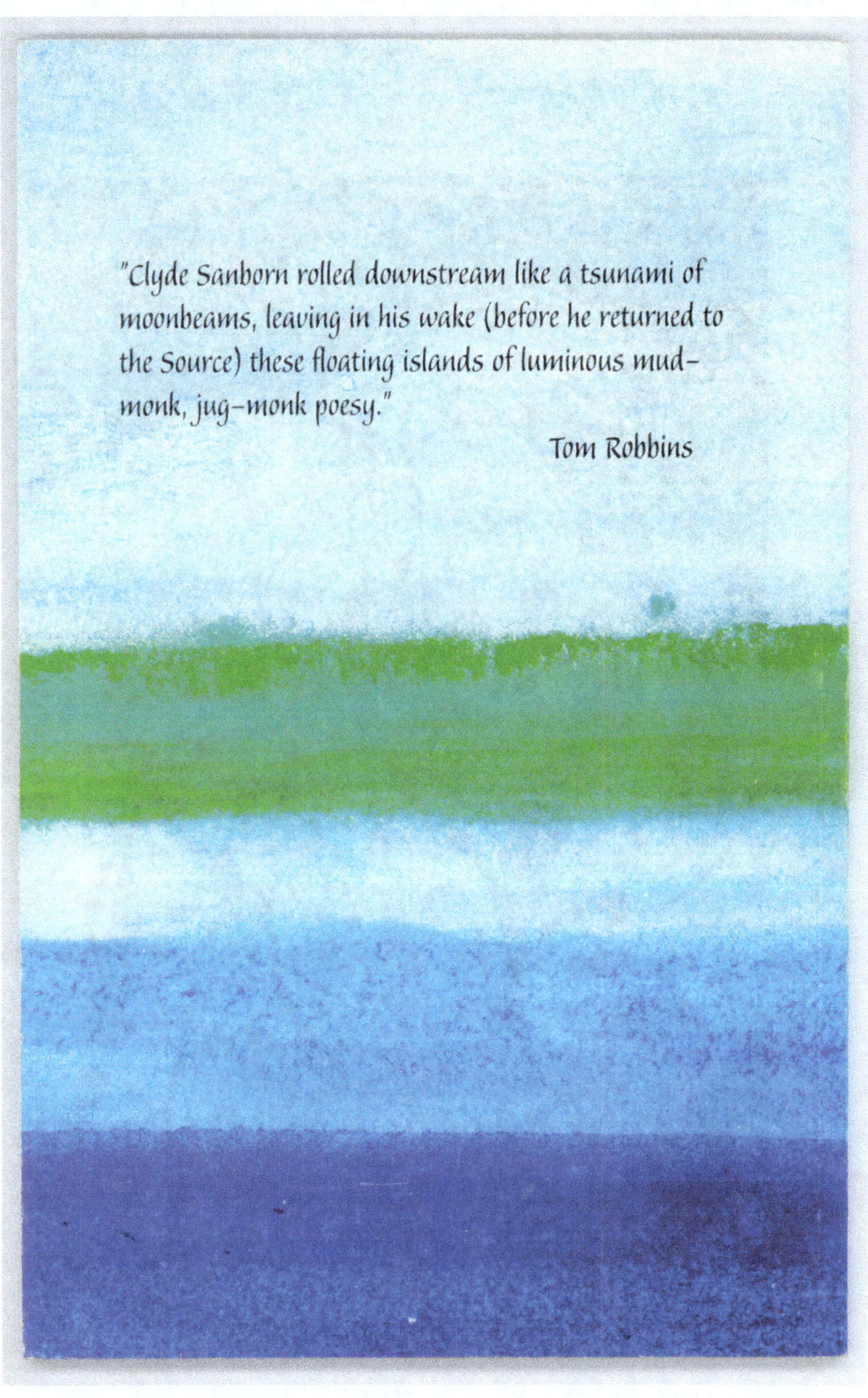

"Clyde Sanborn rolled downstream like a tsunami of
moonbeams, leaving in his wake (before he returned to
the Source) these floating islands of luminous mud–
monk, jug–monk poesy."

Tom Robbins

Part 2:
WAKE

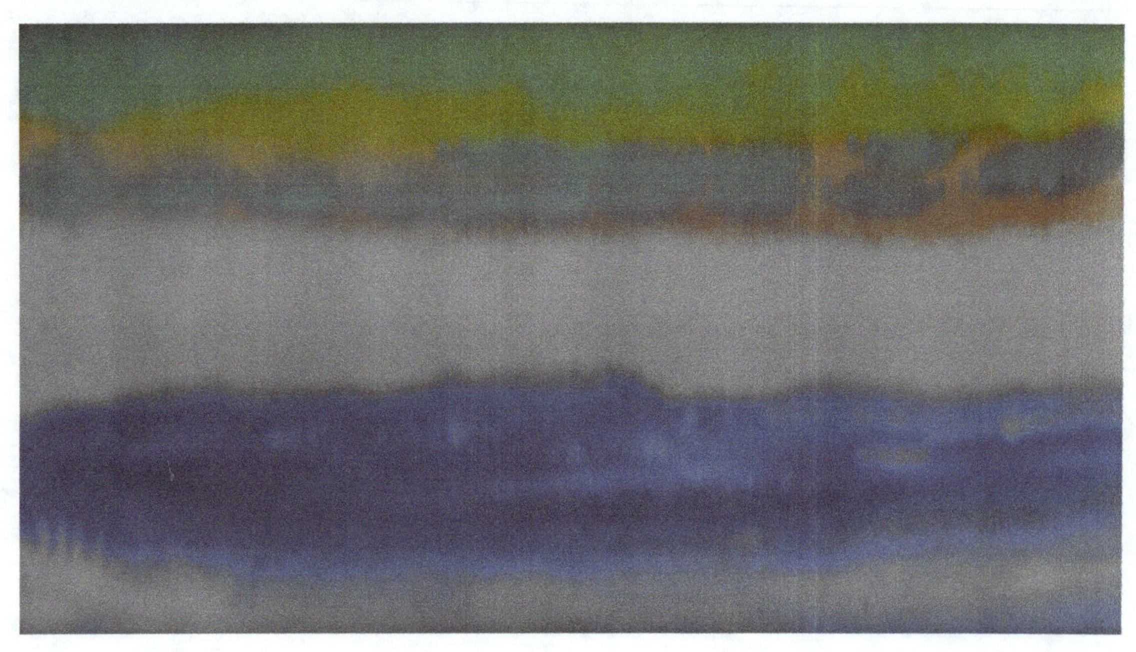

Clyde painting courtesy of Joanne Zabik.

MICHAEL CLOUGH:

As to how I met and got to know Clyde, I will have to tell some of my own story. He was in the Navy about the same time I was in the Air Force, 1967-70. I was stationed in Japan after a year in Thailand loading bombs on fighter jets (the Vietnam War). After I had been in Japan awhile, I decided to go on leave to California, San Francisco, to see what the psychedelic revolution was about. While waiting at the airport (several days) for a space available flight, I met two sailors who had been on a ship in the Philippines for the last year. They were being stationed in San Diego and were flying there ahead of their ship. They invited me to San Diego to hang out and meet their fellow crew members when they arrived. One of the sailors, Jay Carpenter, had a place there that his girlfriend had set up. So I went to San Diego to visit. The ship arrived. Along with the crew, we had a party and took mescaline. Strange how chance events or meetings can create the path of your life. One of the crew was Clyde and we became pals for the rest of his life. The next day after the party, Clyde and I walked together downtown, he to buy an engagement ring for a woman he met in New Zealand. Clyde was wearing a pair of those leather Indian sandals with the big toe ring that attached them to your feet. He was also wearing socks, which was a strain for the toe ring. It soon broke. Clyde removed the sandal, stuck it in his back pocket and continued to walk wearing one sandal and socks on both feet. When we got downtown he found a shoe repair shop, got the toe ring repaired, went to a jewelry store and bought a wedding ring. I liked the way this guy thought and he became my friend. I went to San Francisco. The scene had turned ugly by then. I returned to my duties in Japan, friend Jay and Clyde to theirs in San Diego. Clyde got married. I kept in contact with Jay and a year later got out of the Air Force. I went to stay with Jay and his girlfriend in San Diego. I didn't see Clyde, he was married and out of the loop. I stayed at Jay's and did some hitching in California until Jay got out of the Navy and moved back to Seattle where he grew up. I stayed in San Diego mostly slumming on the beach. Jay drove down and brought me to Seattle. Around Christmas he got a call from Clyde: he was splitting with his wife and wanted to come up. A week later he showed up, and the next week he went back for another try at his wife. A week later

he came back. Thus began Clyde's life in the Pacific Northwest…
Seattle life and on to La Conner.

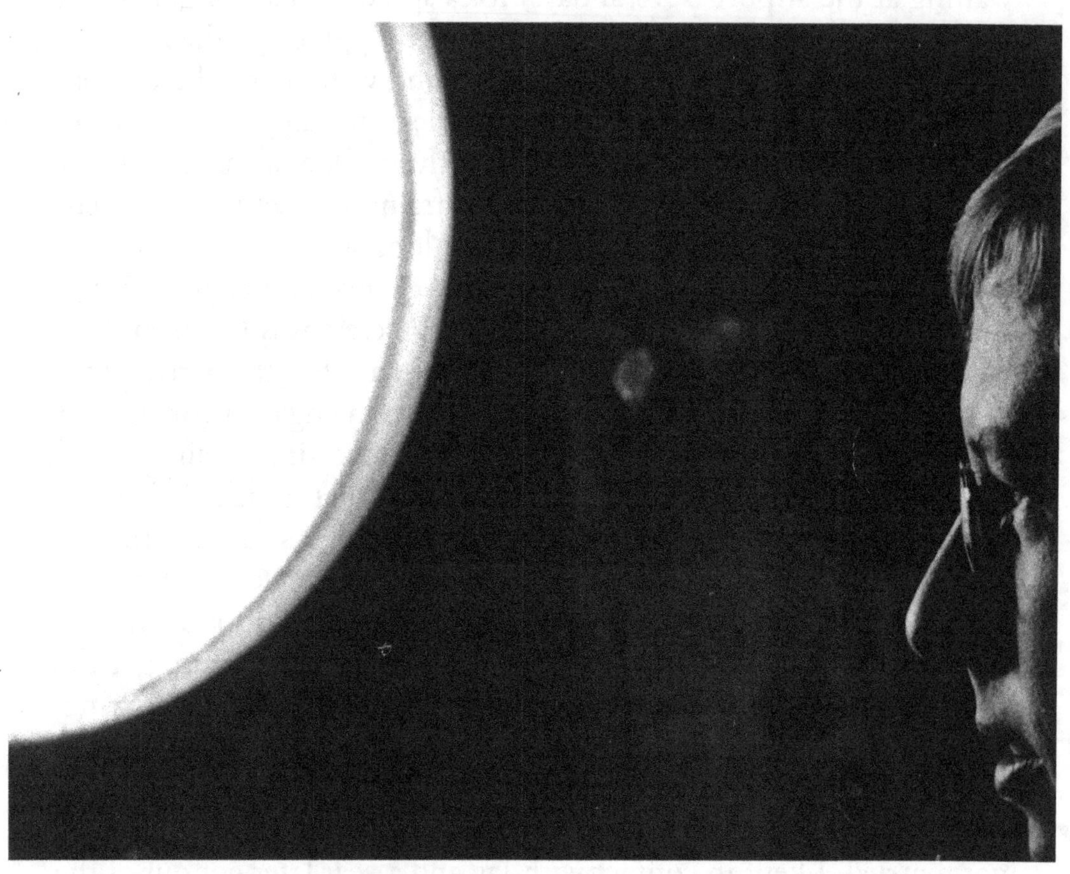

Clyde at porthole of USS Prairie, photo by Jay Carpenter.

JAY CARPENTER:

Clyde was one of the first people I met on the Navy ship I was assigned to, and we spent about 18 months onboard in San Diego and overseas. When I got out and returned to Seattle he decided to see if he would like it there, so when he was discharged he came to Seattle and roomed with me for awhile. He and I were pretty close friends from '69 to around '74-'75.

I had met Mike Clough in Japan when I was waiting in an Air Force transit terminal trying to get a free hop back to the States from Japan. He was an airman working in that terminal. We struck up a good conversation and he decided to take some leave and give me a one week tour of the area and Tokyo. When he was discharged he also came to Seattle and moved in with Clyde and me. Eventually they moved to an apartment in town together and stayed close friends until Clyde's death.

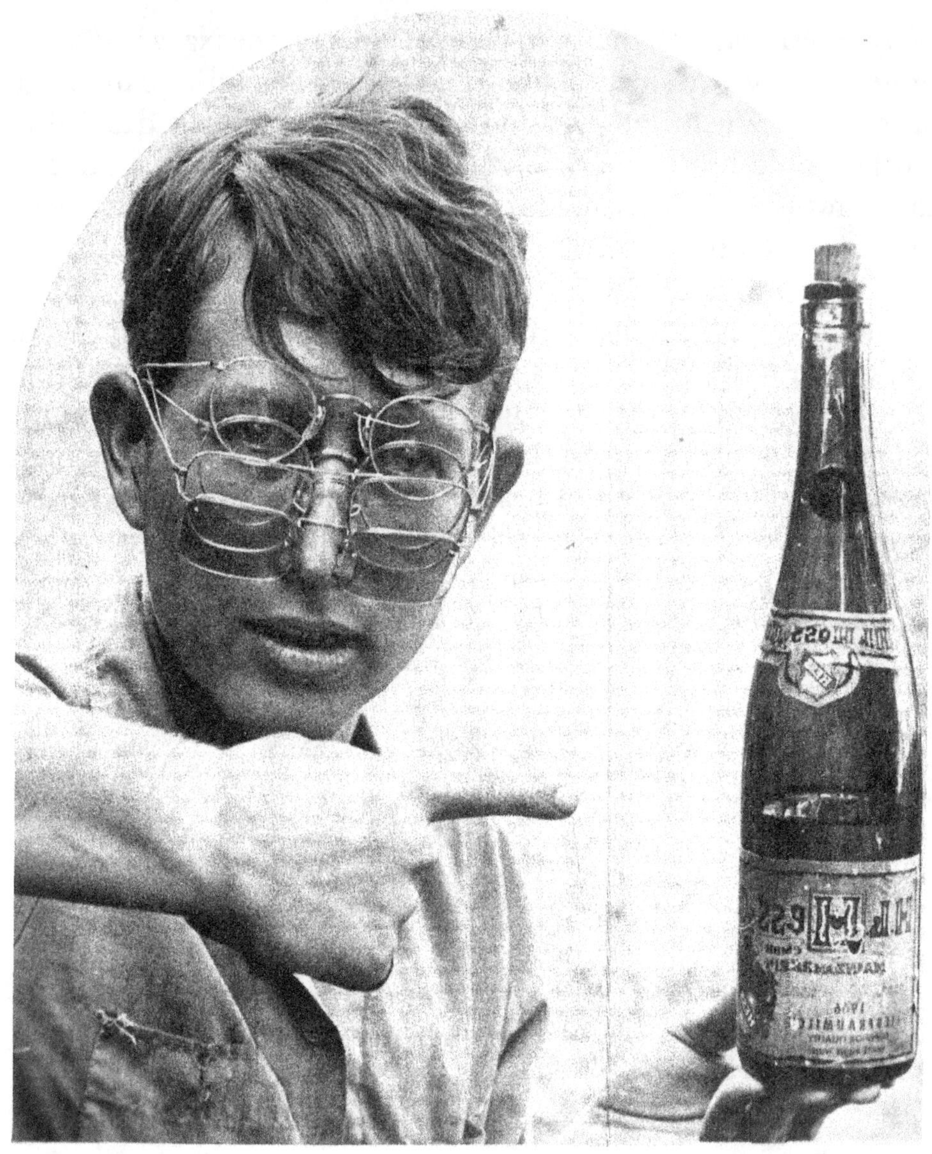

Photo Clyde

JAY CARPENTER:

I think this picture of Clyde was taken when our "gang" was all together at the recreation beach which the Navy operated at Subic Bay. At the bar you could either buy a beer or a sweet German wine.

Clyde preferred the wine. I recall we all gave him our eye glasses and he held up the wine bottle while I took the picture. I was a Navy photographer so I always had my camera on hand. This picture really reflects his sly humor. Never over the top or boisterous, but always very funny.

We met in October of 1969, the first week I came aboard the USS Prairie, AD-15. It was a destroyer tender, and the oldest ship still active in the Navy. I think it was launched in 1938 or 1939, and it was a floating supply and repair ship designed to service destroyers when they came in from active operations. In addition to repairing them and re-supplying them, we had medical and dental facilities, food service, a barber, a photo lab, a computer center, a store, and a number of other services for destroyers. It was also an antique ship in many ways, with very 30s design features, old engines, teak decks, and a real WWII feel. I liked it.

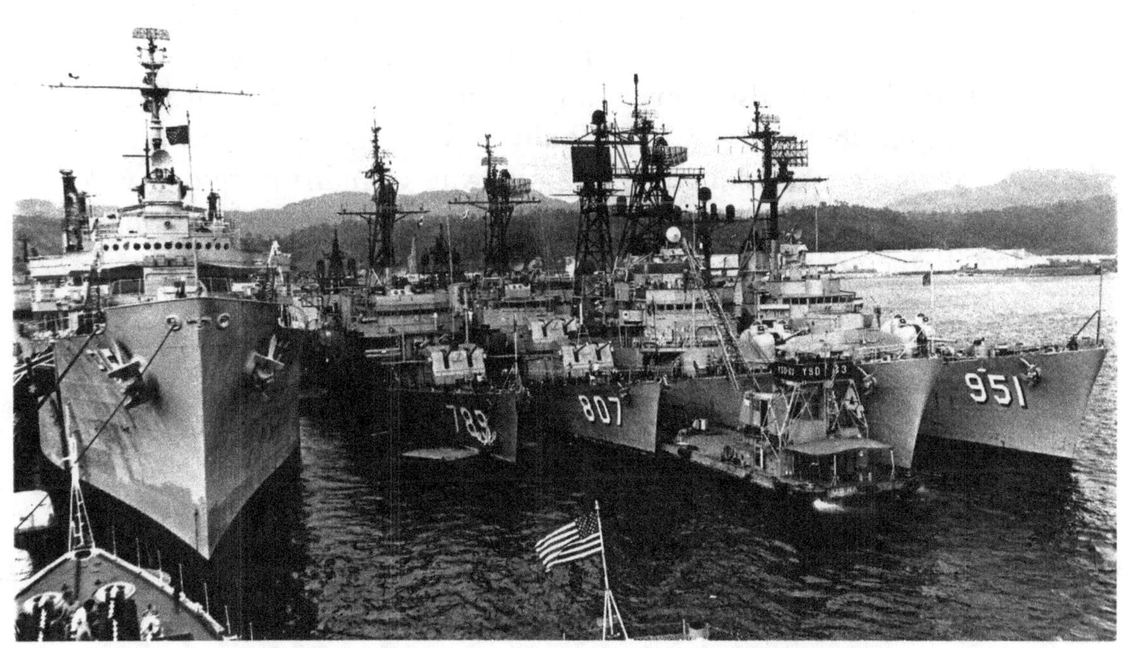

USS Prairie on left, at Subic Bay with destroyers alongside, 1970, photo by Jay Carpenter.

The ship had a crew that operated it and maintained it and sailed it to wherever it was assigned to go. It also had a repair crew who just serviced the destroyers, and, in my experience, had very little interaction with the crew who operated the ship itself. The operating crews of surface ships were referred to back then as the Black Shoe Navy. They berthed in separate areas and ate at different times. It may be like a carrier, where the ship operating crews are separate from the flight crews. I don't know if that is still the case. And I don't know what they called us, the repair divisions on board, and I probably don't want to know.

When I had checked into my assigned area, the photo lab, and had met my division officer, I had to go to the division clerk and give him my paperwork and formally become part of the ship's company. That clerk was Clyde Sanborn. He was very open and friendly, and very soon when I saw him on the mess deck at meal time I would join him and we quickly became friends. I had been in college and at the end of my junior year was called up to active duty from the Navy reserves, so I was a year or two older than most of my peers in the Navy and was also a year or two older than Clyde. By the time we got to Subic Bay I was 23 and most of my group of buddies on the ship, including Clyde, were about 20 or 21. The only guys my age were either junior officers or higher ranking petty officers who wouldn't hang out with me, so I was pleased to know a group of very smart and fun younger guys. Remember, back then, with the mandatory draft, there were a lot of people with 2 or 3 years of college becoming enlisted to avoid becoming cannon fodder in Vietnam.

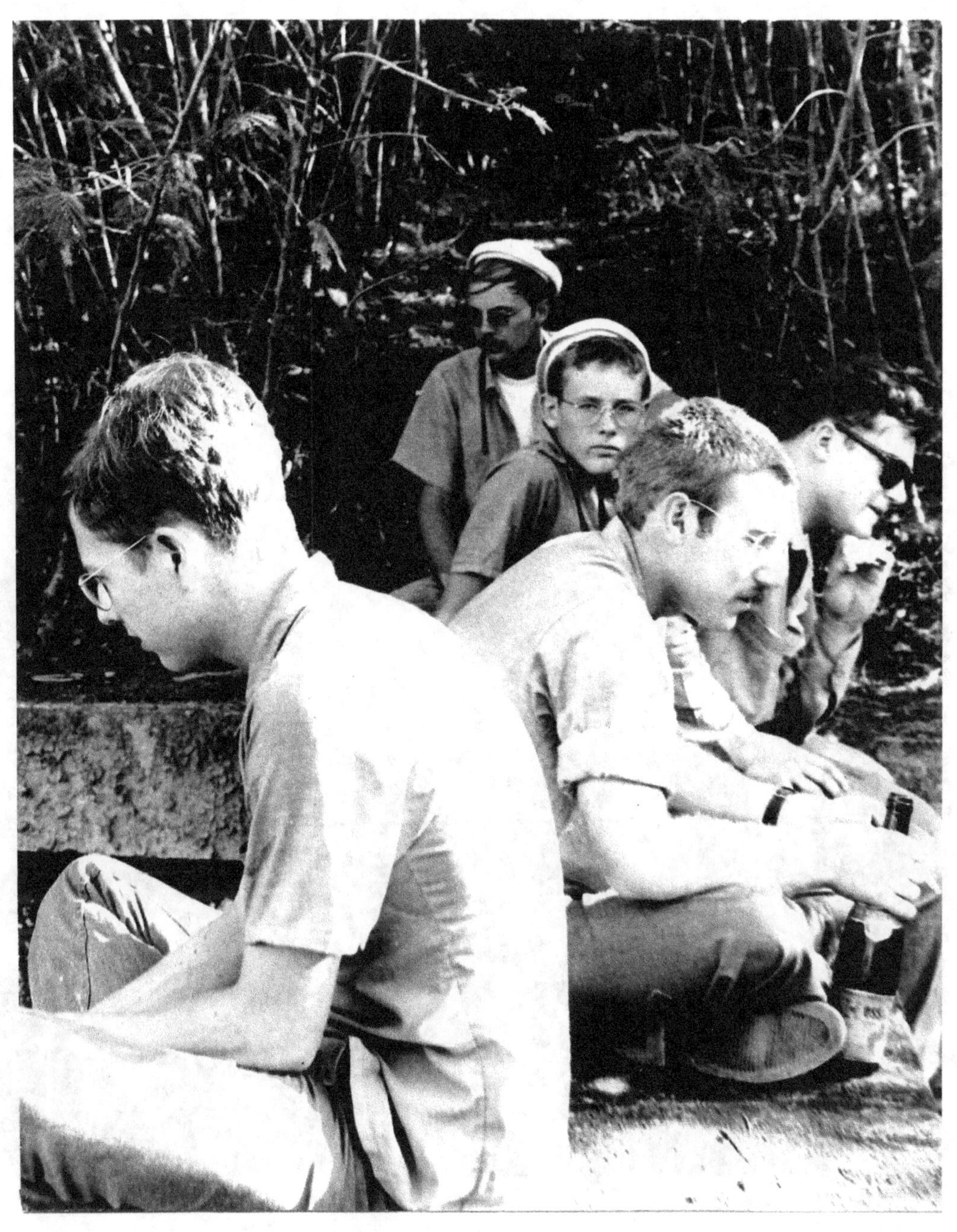

Clyde on left, and crewmates, photo by Jay Carpenter.

Pictures taken on Grande Island, the recreational island in the middle of Subic Bay where there was a dance hall, bar and grill, a shade structure, and playing fields for baseball, football, soccer, etc. I think it even had tennis courts. It was there to go to if you didn't like dealing with the Olongapo City bar and street scene.

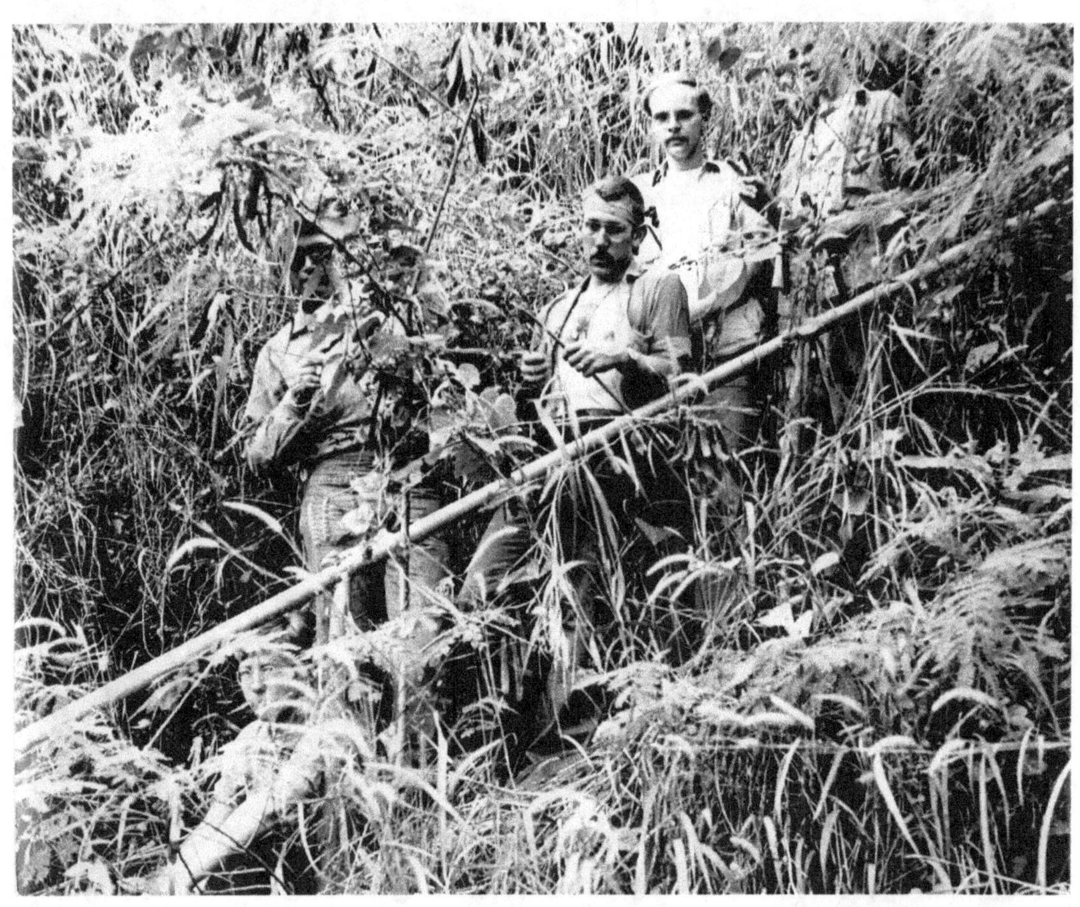

Left to right: Clyde, our ship's barber, one of our ship's electricians, Greg Milburn (The Hulk) at Grande Island, 1970.

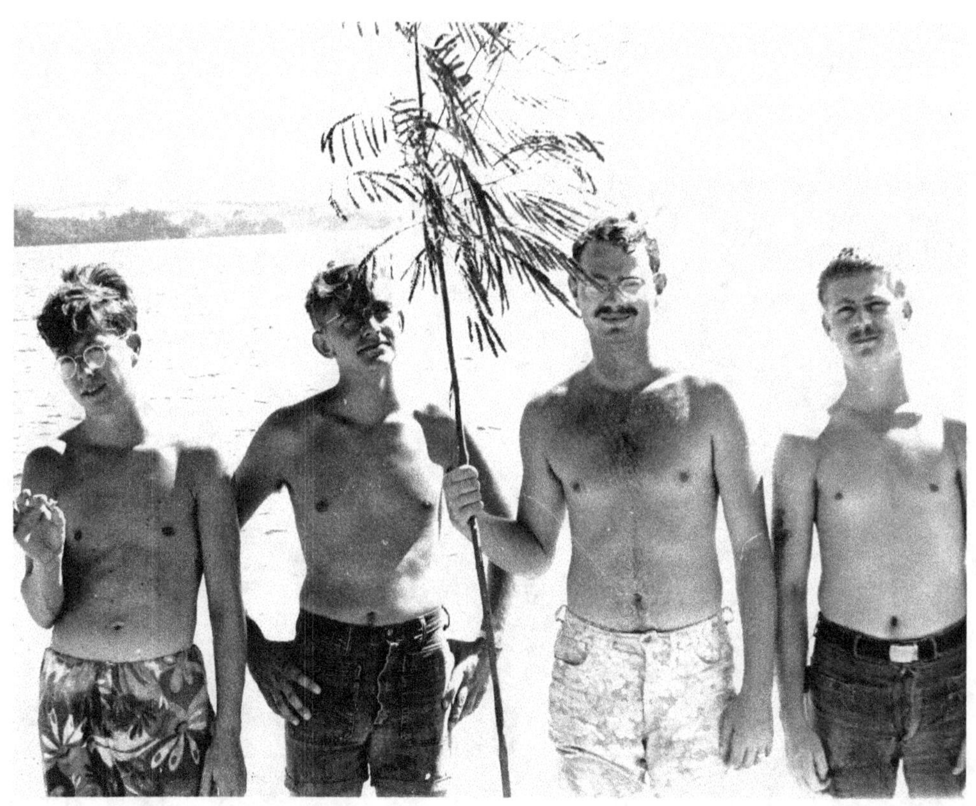

Left to right: Clyde, Steve Housel, Jay Carpenter, one of the ship's machinists. At Grande Island, 1970.

Also taken on Grande Island which you could only reach by taking a liberty launch from our dock out into the bay. It is a very large bay and our base there was quite pleasant—tropical and forested but also manicured. Many of the sailors stationed on the base brought their families, and so it had some large neighborhoods with nice homes. The beach there was amazing, consisting of tiny pieces of crushed coral and no sand. When you waded into the water even a few feet the living coral, smooth and not sharp, would start to sting you very lightly but after about 15 minutes your feet and then lower legs would start to go numb. That's when you returned to the dry beach. We used to snorkel there but one time we swam out to where the bottom just dropped away into a blue nothingness and we saw very large sharks, just huge dark shapes, cruising off of the shelf in the deep water. We never swam there again.

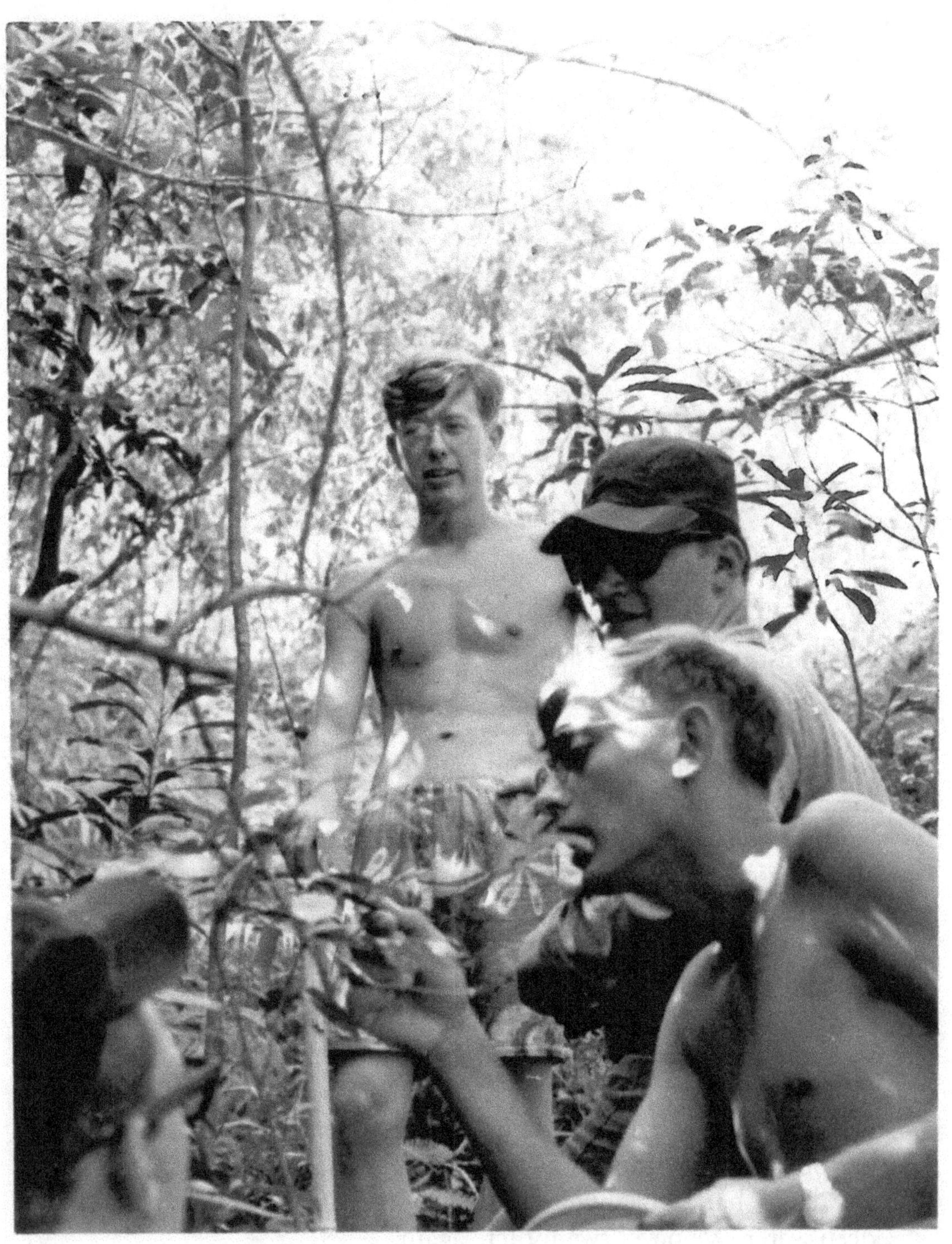

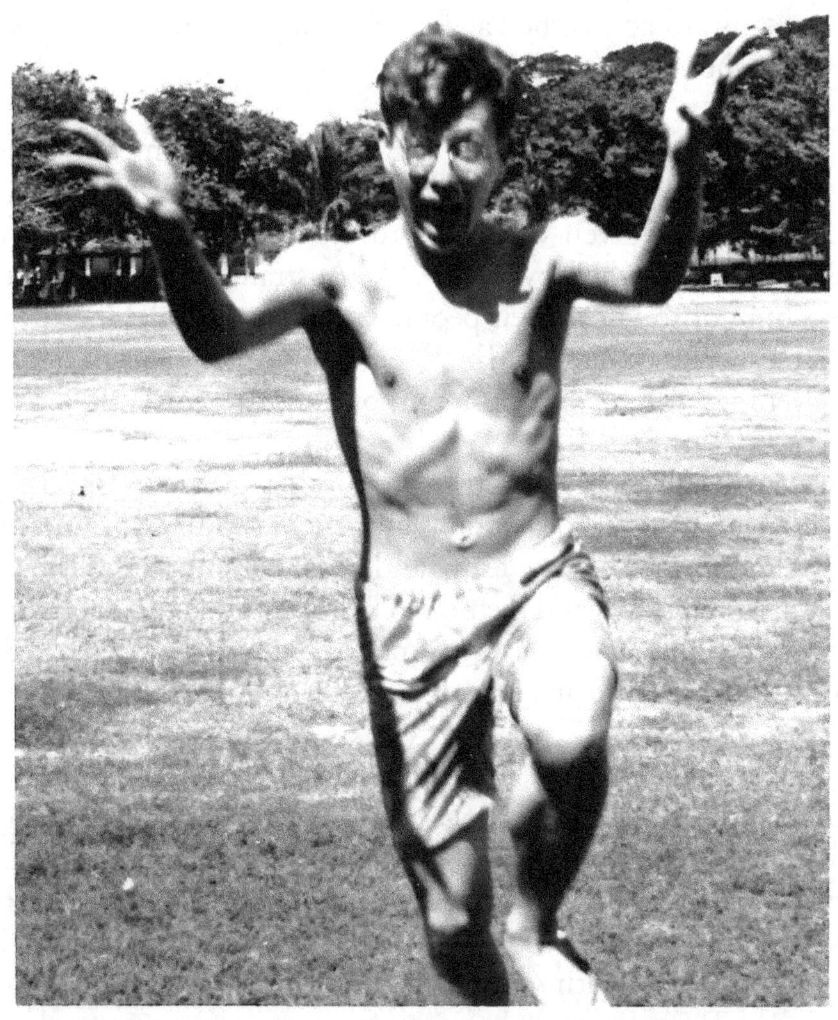

My first real experience of the benefits of being Clyde's friend was when my name came up, as does every new, low ranked Navy seaman on a ship, on the list of the next round of a 3 month assignment to mess duty. It didn't seem to matter that I was one of the photographers with a job I had trained for months to do, and an assigned duty station. Every new sailor on a ship then did mess duty first. Clyde quietly made my file card disappear when that rotation came up, and he became one of my best buddies. I did not have to do K-P and was probably one of the few who ever avoided it. Thanks Clyde, to this day...

So, on the way to Subic Bay our old ship lost a turbine and we limped onward across the Pacific, in stormy weather, for 3 weeks until we reached Subic.

Once in Subic we did what tenders do—repairing and re-supplying destroyers. We had our destroyers, and the ships of allied countries who we had given WWII destroyers to—Iran, Turkey, Korea—as well as allies with their own ships like Australia. We not only serviced them but got to know their people and enjoyed watching them have soccer and rugby matches. They were also fun to go into town with in the evenings. No further comment on those activities…

One adventure Clyde and I, and 2 other members of our "gang", experienced was our kidnapping by a small group of militia soldiers, President Marcos' private army and enforcement wing. They were a law unto themselves and seemed to be self-funded. They had to make their own wages, but Marcos armed them and I suppose fed them and gave them uniforms to look official.

Our small group of 4 was leaving our favorite Subic bar one night (our favorite because the house band could exactly duplicate any US or British band if we brought them the latest albums from those groups—they were called Freedom Highway and the USO eventually hired them to tour Vietnam with the USO tours as a backup band), when a large jeep with 4 armed soldiers pulled up and they ordered to get in. They demanded money from us, and we turned out our pockets and showed that we had nothing left after a night in the bar (we were making about $100 a month then). They drove us to the edge of town, made us get out and stand on the edge of the river at gun point, and demanded money again. We invited them to check our pockets again and then they just looked at each other (they were all 16-18 years old), and then loaded us back into the jeep, and drove us back into town. One of them turned back to us and asked where we wanted to be dropped off. We said—take us to the bar where you got us from—and they did. We scurried back to the ship.

While we were in Subic, our ship's Special Services department offered two different vacation trips for sailors with available leave. One was to Australia and the other to New Zealand. I didn't have enough leave, or spending money, to go. Clyde did, and he went to New Zealand and he met Kathryn. He came back telling us about her. He met her there, shortly after one of her friends was attacked by a shark in Wellington harbor while wading. The victim lost a leg and Clyde lost his heart to Kathryn. He came back to the ship and was full of Kathryn but he still had time left to finish with the Navy. I did not meet her until he was out of the Navy and had married her and brought her to Seattle.

But before that—Japan.

When our ship finished the deployment to Subic Bay we sailed to Hong Kong for R&R for a week. It was a great experience for us all but Clyde was smitten with Kathryn and stayed on board ship and, though many of our "gang" explored the city, I can't recall if Clyde joined us there on shore.

After Hong Kong we went to Japan to one of our bases there. I was eager to see and explore Japan since I thought I might never get there again. So I left the ship on leave, having to promise to be back to the ship in about 10 days in San Diego. I didn't see Clyde again after that until he came to Seattle. He had been transferred somewhere else in that short time off the ship while I was away.

JAY CARPENTER:

In the early winter of '71 I came off of active duty and went home to Seattle. I got an apt. and just kicked back for a few months, re-connecting with friends, and in the process meeting a woman through mutual friends and we started dating. As spring came around I enrolled at the UW for the summer session to begin my senior year, interrupted for almost three years by the Navy.

At that time Michael was discharged from active duty in San Diego. He didn't want to move back to wherever his family had ended up during his 4 years away, so I suggested that he contact a friend of mine in San Diego and crash at her place and I would drive down and bring him back to Seattle. We did that and very shortly after we returned I also heard from Clyde, not wanting to return to Stockton, asking if he could come to Seattle and stay with us while he checked out the town.

So, I now had two roommates. None of us had jobs, all three of us were collecting unemployment insurance from our Navy time, and I had GI Bill to pay for college. My apartment was free since my mother owned the building, and I became the manager for her. I only charged the guys for their share of utilities and we lived rent free so life was good. Clyde was still in close contact with the woman he had met in New Zealand, named Kathryn. Clyde was writing poetry at that time but I don't know if he was saving it yet or just experimenting.

As the summer wore on, I was in school, taking the bus into town. I left my car for them to use as they explored the city. I didn't have the time to really do a lot of things with them but they were meeting people and making new friends wherever they went. By Fall I was very involved with the woman I had met and we were both thinking about living together. When her lease was about to expire we agreed that it made sense for her to move in with me. Thus I had to tell the guys they needed to find another place on their own.

So, in January of '72 they moved out to an apartment in Capitol Hill and it was unique—not in an apartment building but on it. Sometime in the past a stand-alone house had been built on the roof of a 1920s or '30s era 6 story brick apt building. To get there you climbed 6 flights of stairs, opened the roof exit door and walked across the roof on a 4' wide wooden walkway to their front door. They had great views of the city and looked down onto the I-5 freeway. I think at this time Clyde had found a job and I believe it was washing dishes at The Deluxe Tavern on Broadway. It was, and probably still is, a major hangout and watering hole for the Capitol Hill crowd. Very bohemian back then and usually packed.

They threw some great parties at the roof top house with some fun and exotic new friends. My girlfriend and I tried not to miss them and my major recollection now about them was the abundance of large jugs of cheap red wine and clouds of smoke—legal and not. The house became kind of legendary on the Hill.

I can't recall how long they were in that house but at some point Clyde decided to bring Kathryn over from New Zealand and get married. He got an apt, also on Capitol Hill, and over she came. She was a very pretty, small and pale blond young lady with a delicious accent. We got together with them several times but Clyde was settling down to domesticity, as was I for that matter. And I was in the final push to graduate in Dec of '72. I can't recall what Michael was doing for work at that point, but he may also have been working in the kitchen at The Deluxe Tavern.

Immediately after I graduated my girlfriend and I gave up our free aptartment and took off in our van for a 6 month driving tour of the country, skiing wherever there was snow, and stopping for one month in Amish country where I took a temp job on a construction crew to replenish our cash. We worked our way up through New York, staying with several of her relatives, New England, staying with friends of mine, and finally entered Canada. We then slowly drove back across Canada and finally arrived back in Seattle, after many adventures, detours, and discoveries. In May of '73 I enrolled in graduate school at Western Washington University and we almost immediately moved to Bellingham. Shortly after that my girlfriend and I got married.

Through this all I had stayed in touch with Michael and Clyde, and Michael especially was very interested in visiting us in Bellingham and maybe moving out of the city and into a rural area. I can't recall the exact timing but either while we were on our road trip or shortly after our return, Clyde and Kathryn had split up. Clyde claimed it was because she wasn't as smart as he had thought she was, and was also boring and conventional. I suspect there was also the issue of his drinking which I am sure she frowned on. She went back to New Zealand and I never saw her again.

After one or two visits to Bellingham and the Skagit Valley area, both Michael and Clyde decided to leave Seattle and try to make a go of it out in the country. They initially settled in La Conner, and Clyde got another dish washing job there. I don't know what Michael was doing, but he soon relocated to a house way out in the delta of the Skagit River. For some time Michael had been making very large Japanese bamboo flutes-called Shakuhachi flutes. They are extremely difficult to play and Michael become quite good. His craftsmanship was so good that people started ordering them from him. When he moved into the house on the delta he also started painting exquisite mandala paintings on paper. I think those started selling well too. His house was so remote you couldn't get in or out at high tide so Michael had the peace and quiet that he was seeking.

He stayed close to Clyde in La Conner, and my wife and I visited him there several times. Unfortunately Clyde was consuming increasingly large quantities of wine and was difficult to be around. He was not belligerent or unpleasant but was just slow and groggy, not the sharp and funny wit that we had known. And it didn't matter what time of day we met him—he would be loaded. Since he didn't own a car and Michael was in a remote area and staying busy, we gradually lost contact with them, and especially with Clyde. The last time I saw Clyde I was in La Conner on a photo assignment and ran into him coming out of an alley behind the restaurant where he worked. He was pretty looped and barely coherent. It was mid-afternoon. I wish I would have had the chance to read Clyde's poetry during those La Conner years.

When did you know Clyde was writing poetry?

JAY CARPENTER:

He wrote, on very small scraps of paper, funny, short poems that reminded me of e. e. cummings
and James Thurber's small poems. The first ones I saw were on board our ship. Funny, sly, and sometimes rather naughty. I wish I had saved them, but they were often on strips of toilet paper or small notebook papers. They were all very clever. I think he didn't really show them to me, but instead he would write them and give them to me as gifts. Once he wrote a very witty and naughty one involving bathroom humor and just taped it above the toilet paper roll in the bathroom. It was clever enough, though somewhat juvenile, that I kept it there for several years before my wife finally said enough with the frat house toilet poetry, and it went away. I think it was centered on allusions to the "rump ramp" and the gravity involved. You get the picture. He was still pretty young at that point.

MICHAEL CLOUGH:

I am pretty sure Clyde was writing poems even in his Navy days. I don't know exactly when that bee got in his bonnet. But he had an old cardboard box full of poems that got lost before he made it to La Conner.

JAN SANBORN:

When he gave my mom the poem "Christmas Wishes," Christmas of 1981. Prior to that I can only remember his zeal for painting. I was so taken with the poem, that I asked him to make one for me as well (written out in his distinctive handwriting). He balked at first (he was funny that way), but then said okay. I now have both that one and the original he made for my mom.

Christmas Wishes

Less military-industrial thinking.
Calmer people.
Bigger angels.
More talking with trees and animals.
More respect for insects and stones.
And more Santas from the minorities and parades
    of silly Santas from the 3rd World and U.S.A. and ....
        an exchange program of Santas from
all nations, and no nations thanks.

Quick hurricanes of mistletoe, devil in a head lock.

And an oak for President, a redwood for Governor,
    roses for the mayors of cities, thank you.

For Christmas I'd ask the world for
    enough love
    to give me goose bumps.
Homo sapiens sitting in a ring of joy
        their hats on backwards.

for Mom, Christmas '81 / clyde

Clyde's "Christmas Wishes" 1981.

Christmas Wishes

Less military-industrial thinking.
Calmer people, bigger angels.
  More talking with trees and animals.
  More respect for insects and stones.
And more Santas from the minorities,
  and parades of silly Santas from
the 3rd world and an exchange
program of Santas from all nations,
  and no nations, thank you.
Quick hurricanes of mistletoe,
  devil in a headlock.

An oak for President
  a redwood for Governor,
  roses for the mayors of cities,
thanks.
For Christmas I'd ask the world
  for enough love to give me
  goosebumps.
Homo sapiens sitting in a ring of joy —
  our hats on backwards!

for Jan, me seester / 'mas '91 / clyde

Clyde's "Christmas Wishes" 1991.

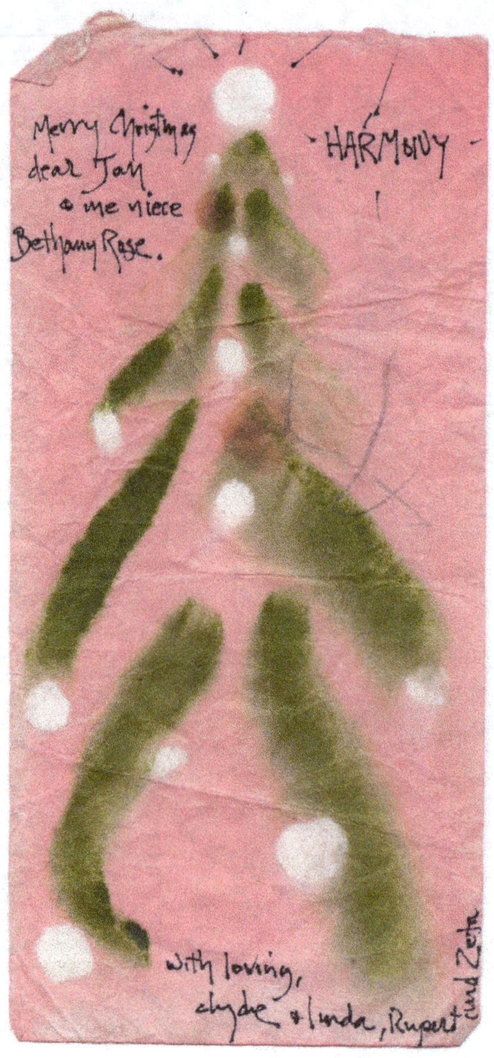

"Merry Christmas dear Jan & me neice Bethany Rose
With loving, Clyde & Linda, [& cats] Rupert & Zeta."

JAN SANBORN:

Clyde came to visit almost every Christmas, he didn't miss very many. Those visits were the glue to our relationship through the years, along with the many letters. Christmas was a fun time, with Clyde playing chef, baking, and making of music (Clyde on various percussion and guitar, Mom on piano, and me, either singing or playing the flute).

MICHAEL CLOUGH:

Not too long after Clyde moved to Seattle, our pal Jay took us on a camping trip in the mountains. As per usual on any trip, an acid trip was prerequisite. I took a hike with myself and when returning to camp saw Clyde sitting at the bank of the river. He was holding a long stick the end of which was stuck in the current. "This is life," he said, "You can't fight the current." He released the stick into the stream. "You should go with the flow."

JAY CARPENTER:

We used to explore Whidbey Island and the San Juan Islands together. This picture is my favorite—his Navy haircut has grown out and he had his ubiquitous camera—he always explored with a camera. Wish I knew where the pics ended up.

JAN SANBORN:

My parents were photography hobbyists, and had their own dark room for many years, which I believe was the root of his interest. He got a nice Nikon camera and lens when he was overseas (may have been in Thailand) and wanted to improve his skills.

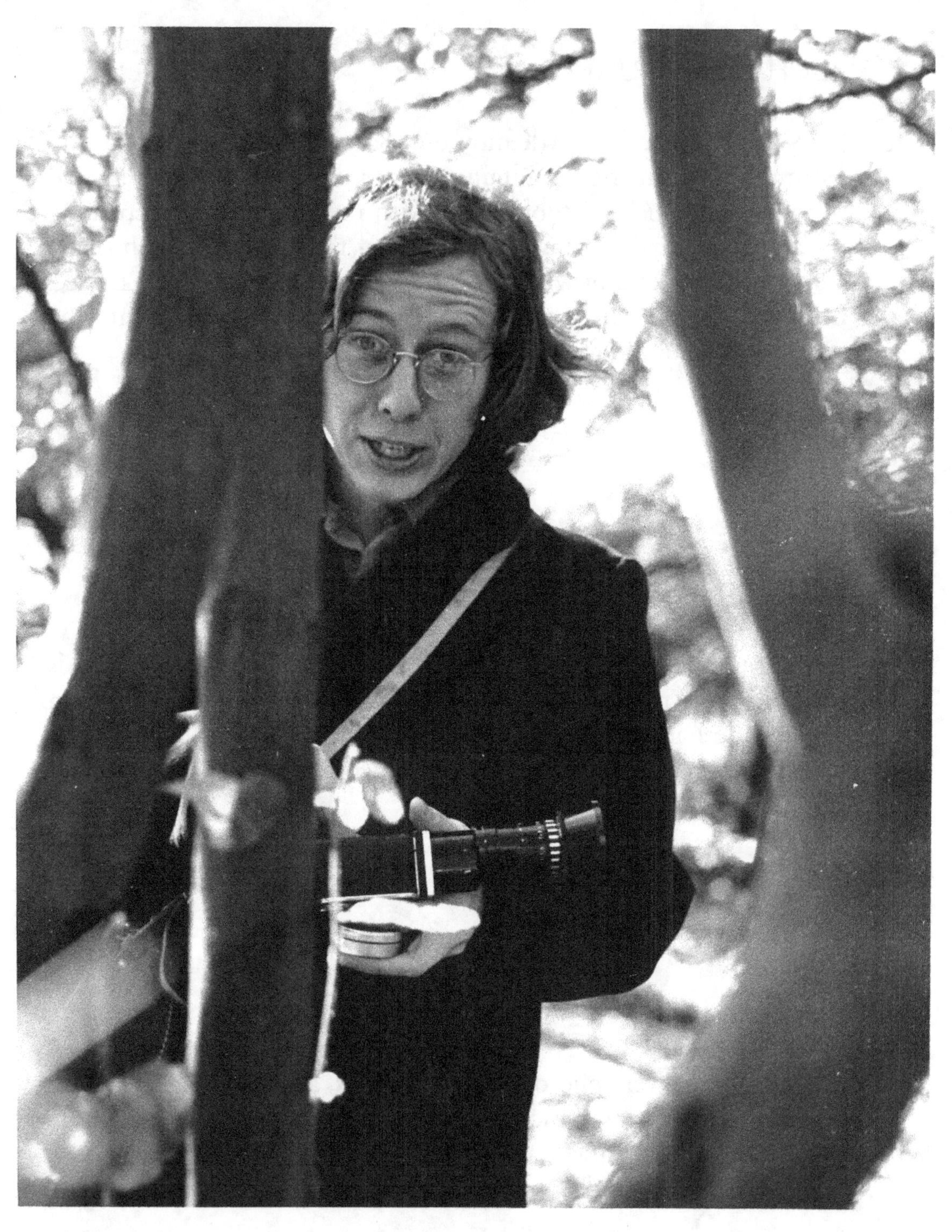

Clyde exploring. Photo courtesy of Jay Carpenter.

MICHAEL CLOUGH:

So Clyde shows up at Jay's December 1971 in West Seattle. We stayed with Jay for awhile then became roommates on Capitol Hill, in a penthouse apartment in an old brick building overlooking the freeway and Lake Union. It was owned by a strange old guy who taught a class on Tibetan Buddhism and claimed he parachuted into Tibet when he was in the Air Force. Studied the Secrets. It was a cool apartment. But Mr. Lavalley eventually got on our nerves trying to make us think he knew what we were thinking and his Siamese cat was always hanging out in our place and we were convinced it was spying on us. The 70s were strange times in Seattle.

I moved into an old house converted into small apartments behind Seattle Community College. Clyde moved into a similar one next door. I attended the College on the GI Bill; the Government paid a living wage. Clyde registered, got his first check, and didn't attend. We palled around. There were willing young women and an active neighborhood. At the Masonic Temple at the corner of Broadway and Pine they held various events like wrestling. There was a large banner that said *Faith Healing!* Clyde and I and my female friend went.

MICHAEL CLOUGH:

We were on a walk, Clyde and I, up Broadway then around the corner Roy Street. Clyde says that looks like an interesting place. Turns out we would both spend a lot of the next years in that place. It was the back end of The Deluxe, at the counter, maybe six stools facing the kitchen, the cooks, dishwasher, where regular coffee drinkers hung out. We later called it "the Counter Culture" the rest of the building was The Deluxe Tavern Steak House.

The city that Seattle was no longer is there. In the 1970s Smith Tower was the tallest building. A few historic remnants still remain between the High risers, parking garages, and Bistros; like Pike Place Market, Pioneer Square. That's the physical city. There was also a psychological cultural spirit in the 70s. People were exploring, experimenting, experiencing, seeking, protesting, the Vietnam War was still on, Nixon got impeached. There was great music, Happenings, art poetry, protests. Every variety of Guru, Spiritual, mystical, religion, cult, diet, that exists and then some.

There was also a lot of taverns in Seattle. Some had live music. Many neighborhood taverns where friends hung out or met new friends after work or on into the night. There were some that were the watering holes of the Artist intellectuals, writers, hippies and assorted characters. The famous Blue Moon that had a history that went back to the 'Beats' in the '50s. The Central in Pioneer Square. Place Pigale in the Market. The Deluxe on Capitol Hill where Clyde and I claimed our bar stools.

CHARLIE KRAFFT:

I got to know Clyde when he was working in the kitchen at The Deluxe Tavern on Broadway around 1975. We used to close the joint and meet Clyde at the back door where he'd emerge with a shopping bag of baked potatoes he'd distribute. He was a dishwasher and worked with a short-order cook there named Kip who everyone knew and liked.

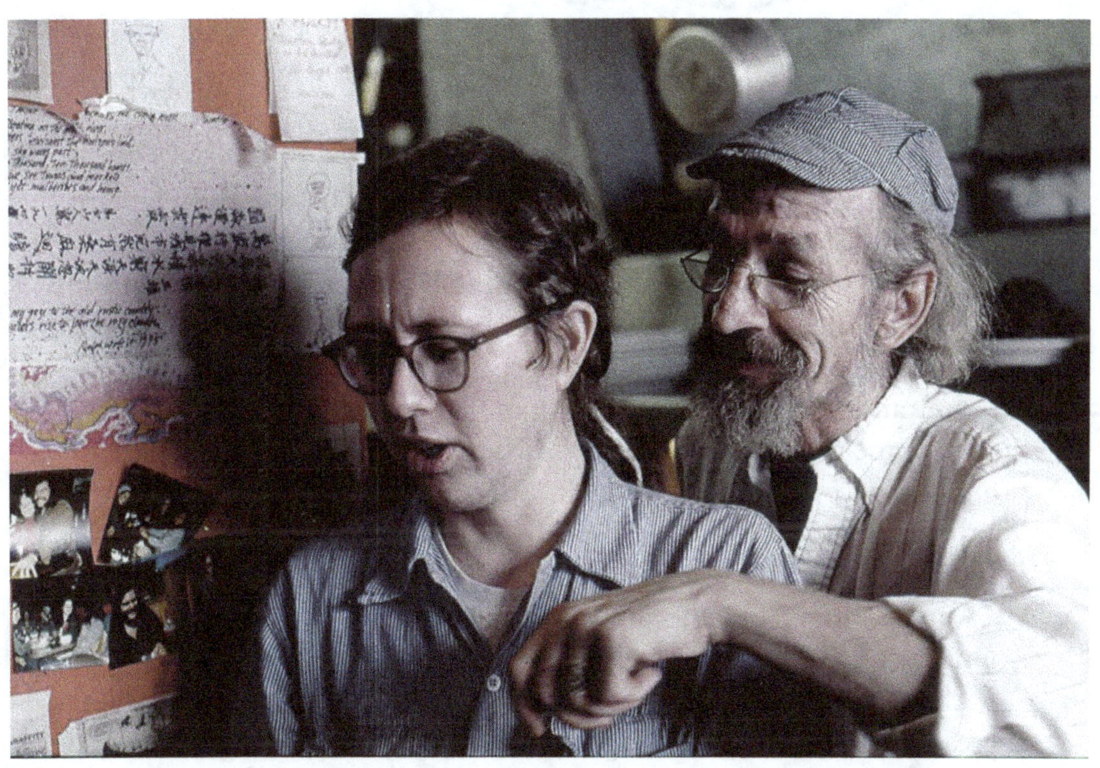

Clyde and Kip in The Deluxe kitchen, 1970s.

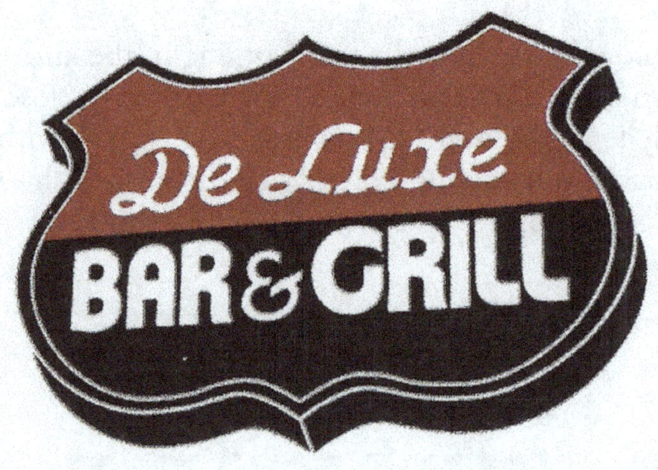

MICHAEL CLOUGH:

The Deluxe is on the corner of Broadway and Roy. The Harvard Exit Theater where they showed the great films and had some interesting parties was right next door. Cornish art school was down the block. The Theosophical Society and book store around the corner. The Jade Pagoda Cocktail lounge across the street (in case you needed one) and on down Broadway some small neighborhood grocery stores. Some more Taverns. Andy's Cafe for breakfast. Hadassah thrift store various other small stores, in other words a real neighborhood. Plus cheap rent back then in the surrounding streets.

And so The Deluxe became "the place." Friends, mentors, affairs, connections that mold one's life.

Clyde became dishwasher. I too at times over those years as it was a great job with not great wages but allowed you to hang out where you wanted to be, plus a meal and 3 glasses of wine or beer after the shift. Many times hanging out all evening till closing time, 2 A.M., then to The Dog House, or some other all-night dive for breakfast.

Clyde's "Sheil's Poem" early 1970s Deluxe Tavern, Seattle courtesy of Sheila Farr.

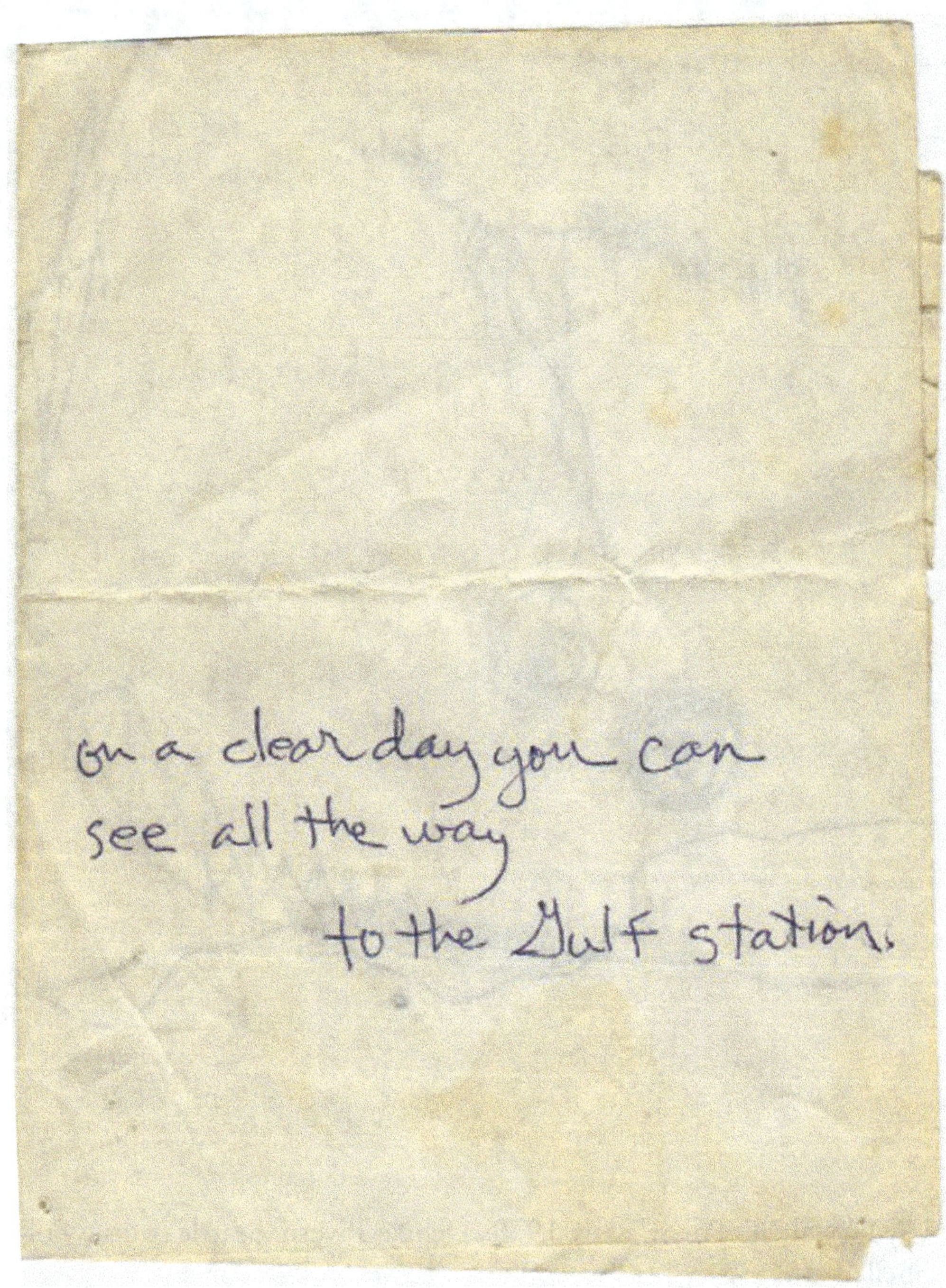

Written on other half of folded page, opposite "Sheil's Poem."

SHEILA FARR:

Clyde. He slipped into my life with barely a ripple. His habitat was The Deluxe Tavern on Broadway—a hangout for artists in those days. Aside from an occasional encounter on the street, I never saw him anywhere else.

When I first met Clyde—around 1970 I think—his gentle side-kick, Michael Clough, was always nearby. But later Clyde could often be found alone, on a barstool, beer in-hand, waiting for someone he knew to drop by. Then he'd drift over and float on the outskirts of conversation, hoping for an entry. Or he might just observe, scribbling a poem or drawing on whatever scrap of paper was available. To pay his bar tab and whatever other life expenses he peripherally accrued, he sometimes worked in the kitchen, washing dishes.

(A quick aside about The Deluxe: I was under the legal drinking age and worked next door at the Harvard Exit Theater—taking tickets and selling candy by night and taking ballet classes at the UW during the day. Often, when the movie was running, we "Harvard Exit girls," as we were known, would send over an order for salads and baked potatoes to our pals in The Deluxe kitchen. Our frugal, working-student supper was sometimes partially paid for in jellybeans. We were frequent customers and The Deluxe owners, Bernie and Joe, might neglect to check ID if we stopped in to have a drink.)

Anyway, time passed, and at the end of 1974, I moved up to the La Conner area with my former husband, the painter Paul Heald. Soon—how could it be?—there was Clyde, installed at La Conner's 1890's Tavern, the hangout of many Skagit Valley poets and artists, as if nothing had changed. Why did he come? How did he get there? Where did he live? What did he live on? I don't know.

I do know that Clyde styled himself after the great Chinese poets whose work he admired: Du Fu, Li Po. He thought an itinerant life of drinking and contemplation would lead to the composition of deep, lucid, eternal poems. But instead, drinking got the best of Clyde. After a while, when he sidled over to our table in La Conner, red-faced and bleary, he began to seem like a battered orphan who no longer hopes for love, but simply refuses to be abandoned.

Later in the '70s Paul and I moved back to the city and eventually parted. This time Clyde didn't follow. As life progressed, tales of Clyde occasionally sailed my way: He was living with a woman. He'd fallen off a barstool and injured himself. He was back on the streets. He was living in a shack by the river.

Then one-day word came that Clyde had drowned. As a surge of old memories rushed through me, I mourned for him and all the bright ideals we had followed. Maybe it was inevitable that such a liquid life would find its end in the river.

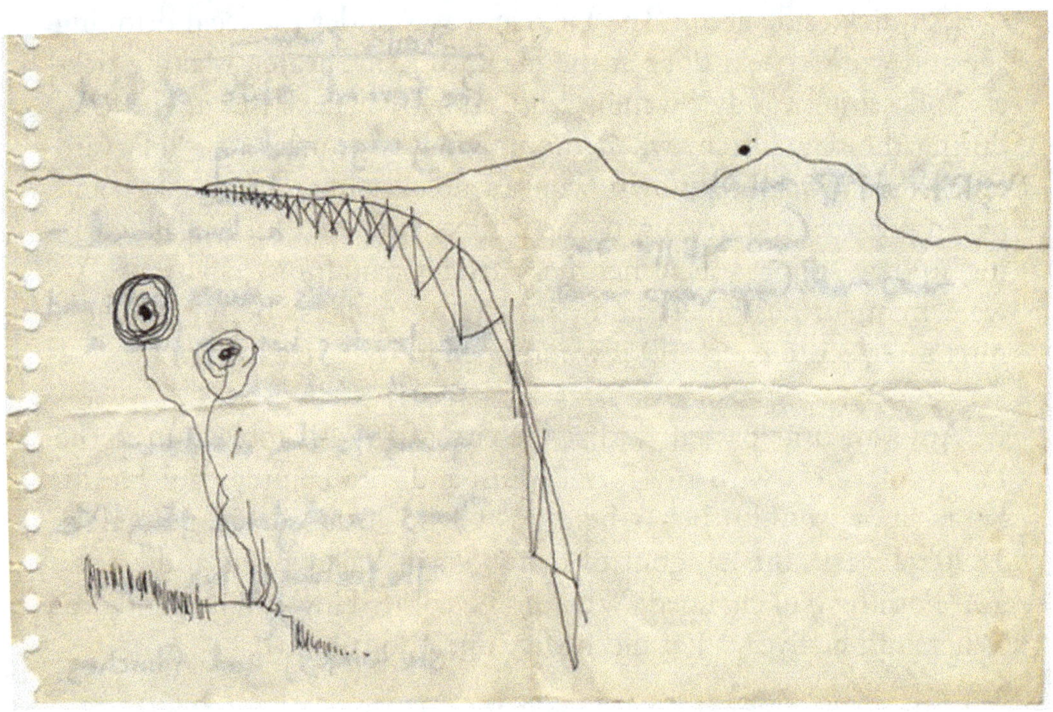

Drawn on reverse side of page from Sheila's poems.

MICHAEL CLOUGH:

The photo of Clyde in the Navy [on page 70] (he told me he had a chunk of hash in his mouth) was from a book *rainbow city: a deluxe coloring/poetry book*; put together in 1975 by a graphic art student who was hanging out at The Deluxe Tavern on Capitol Hill in Seattle. Clyde worked there washing dishes early '70s. The book was poems and such from the poets, thinkers and characters that hung out there. Robert Sund would even occasionally make an appearance there. Clyde had a cardboard box full of poems (many more than one liners) and other memorabilia that disappeared in one of his moves. Hence the only surviving poems napkins and bar coasters collected by friends.

EDITOR: Michael Clough mailed me a copy of this rare book, with bookmarked pages and notes from Michael (here in quotes). Amongst the illustrations are art by Ralph Aeschliman, "a great Sumi painter who lived in Fishtown awhile," a dot-to-dot by Michael and a couple poems by Clyde including, "Can of Worms or Oms. One of his Zen jokes." Also, Michael explained: "Clyde's Principle of Poetics was written by me. Clyde and I were at The Deluxe; I asked him if I could borrow a pen. He told me, 'A Poet should always carry a pen,' hence the poem. Doesn't matter to me, he deserves credit for it."

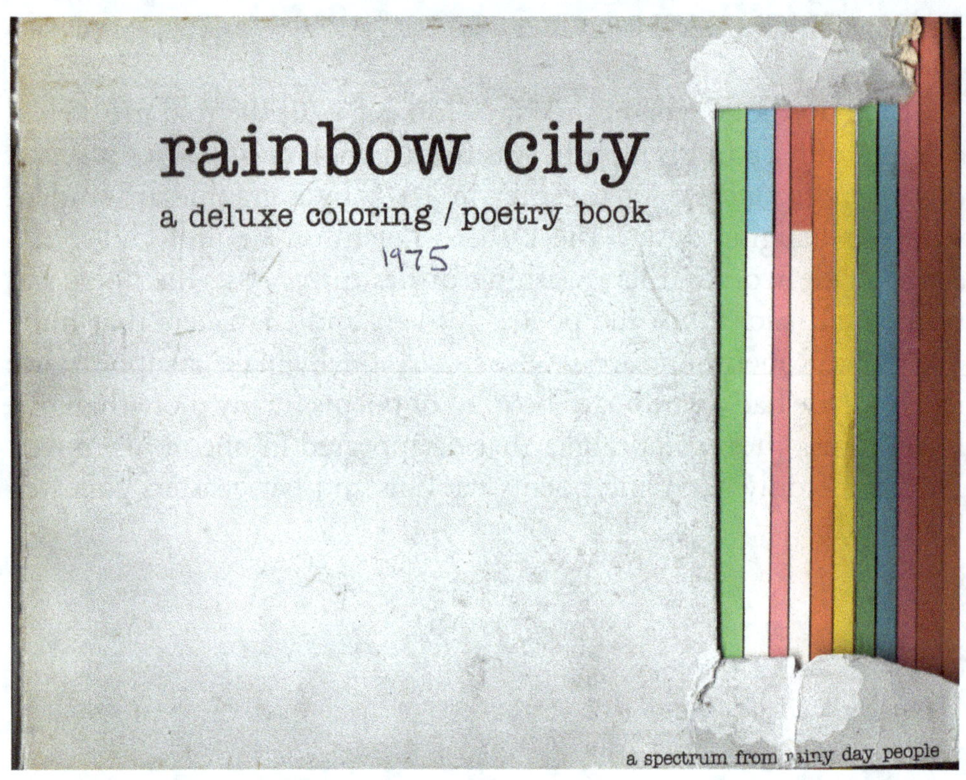

cover and title page

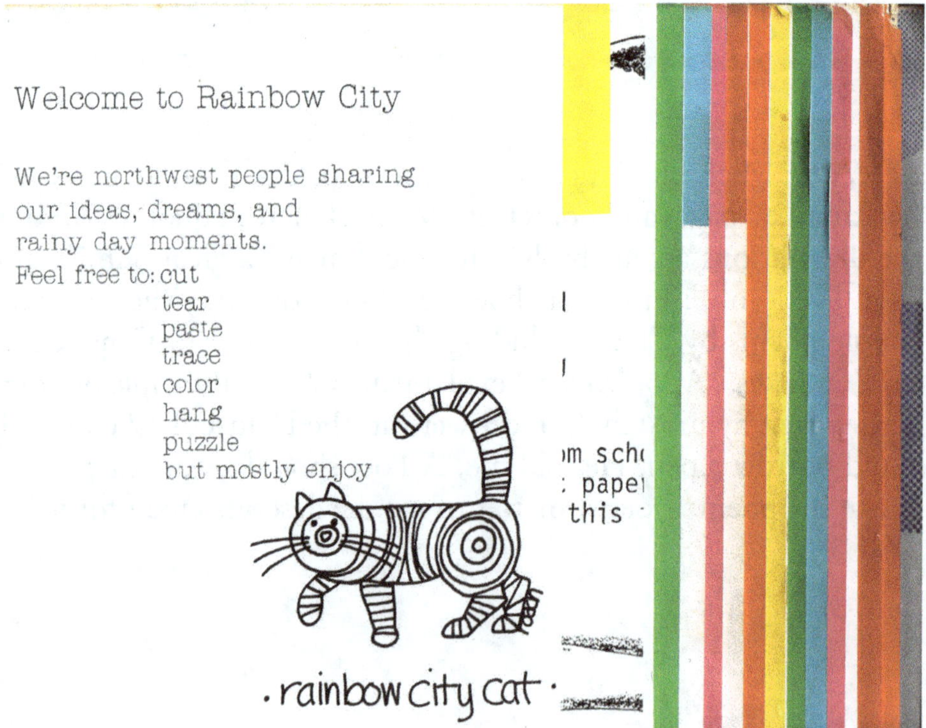

CONTRIBUTORS

Robert Beaty
Sarah Kay Barnett
Fred W. Briggs Jr.
Mikel Clough
Chris Emerson
Leslie Garrison
Don King
John & Sue Lager
Dennis Lovelett
Matt Lubic
Norma Bean Michaelini
Leslie Petty
Greg Peters
Ralph Aeschliman
Don Riste
Roach
Clyde Sanborn
Steve Schafer
Don Scott
Eric A. Zandbergen

Printing - Renick Litho
Brud, Mr. Best, Ralph and T.K. Roach

Publisher - Alley Graphics
159 Western Ave. W Seattle, Wn. 98119

CLYDE'S PRINCIPLE OF POETICS

ONE   should always

carry a pen

ONE   never knows

when ONE

may Run

into a poem.

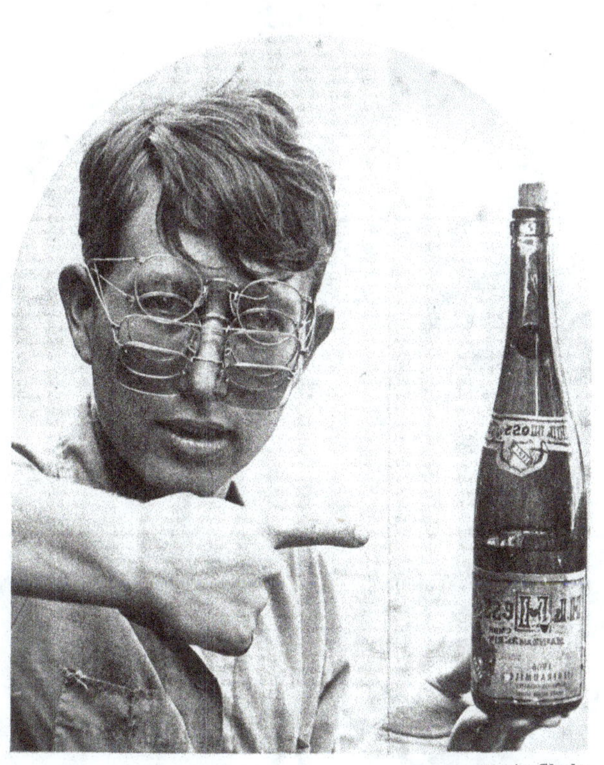

Photo Clyde

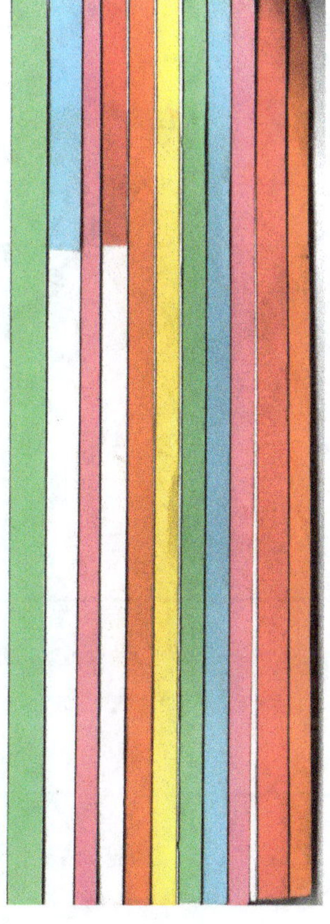

Dot to Dot
fill in the body

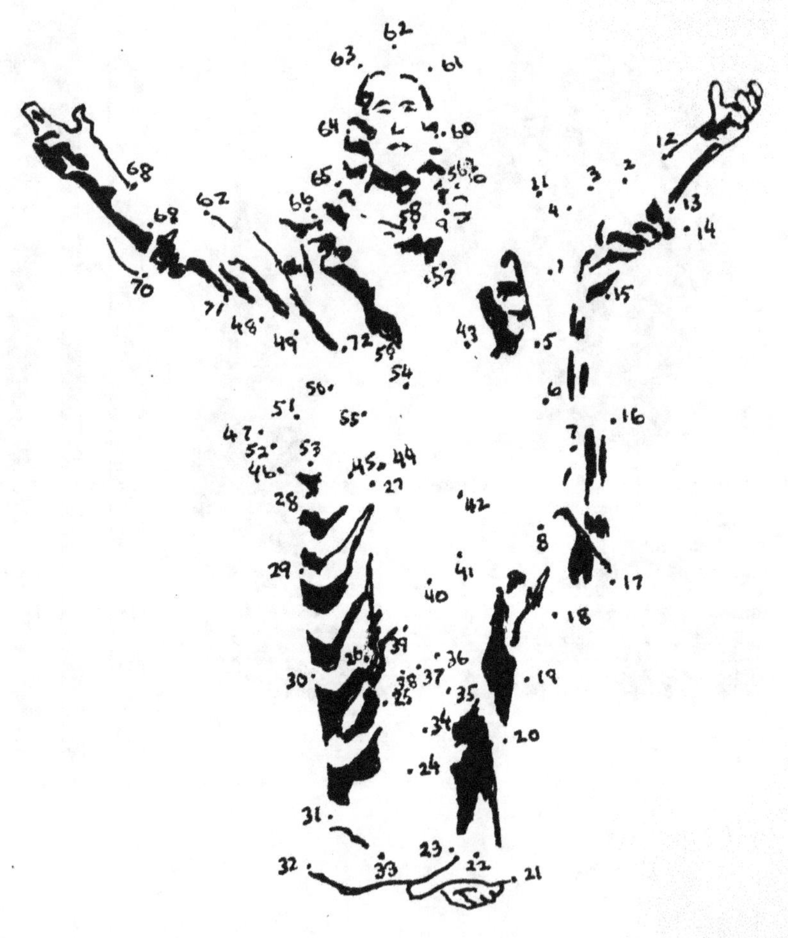

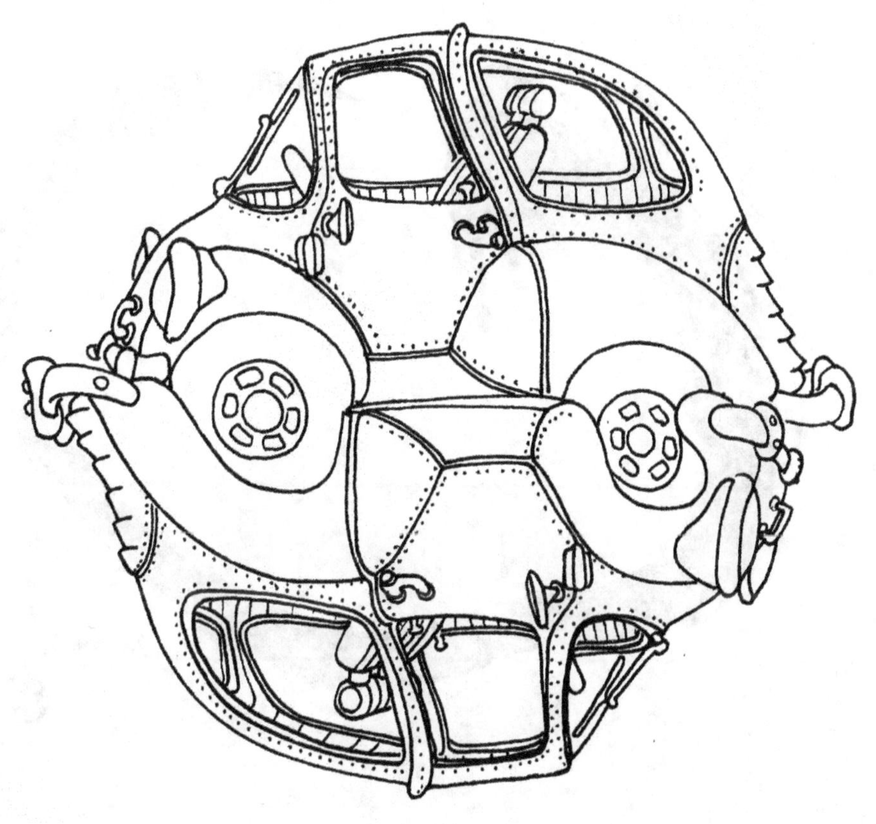

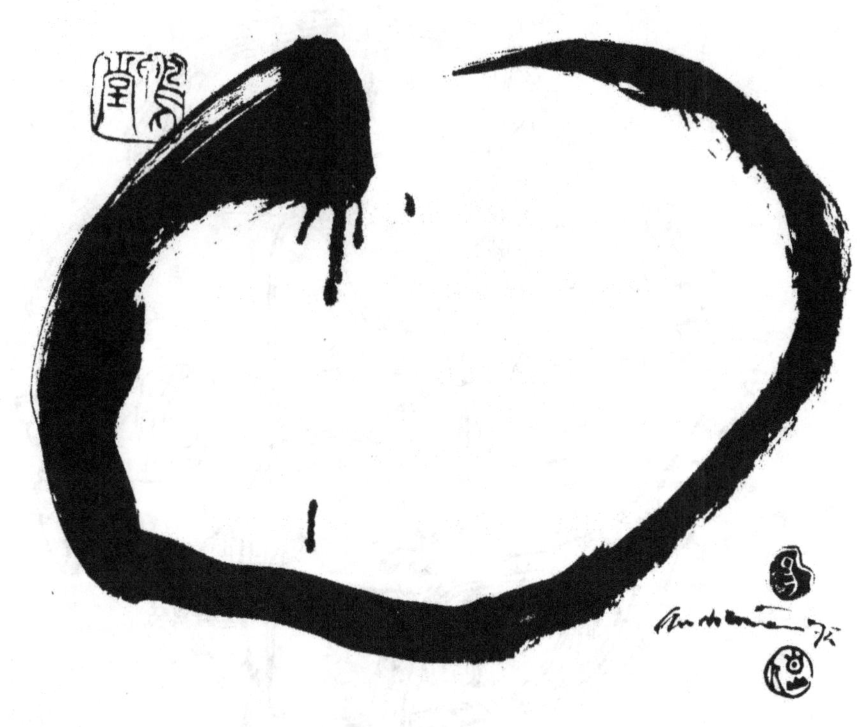

                    wavewave
                  wavewavewavewavew
                wavewavewavewavewavewavew
              avewavewavewavewavewavewave   e
            ewavewavewavewavewavewavewa
          avewavewavewavewavewavewavew
        wavewavewavewavewavewavewavew
      ewavewavewavewavewavewavewavew
    vewavewavewavewavewavewavewavew
  avewavewavewavewavearthwavewavewa
wavewavewavewavewavewavewavewavewav
ewavewavewavewavewavewavewavewavew
vewavewavewavewavewavewavewavewavewav
avewavewavewavewavewavewavewavewavewavew
wavewavewavewavewavewavewavewavewavewavewavewave
vewavewavewavewavewavewavewavewavewavewavewavewavew
wavewavewavewavewavewavewavewavewavewavewavewavewavewavewave
avewavewavewavewavewavewavewavewavewavewavewavewavewavewavewavewave
vewavewavewavewavewavewavewavewavewavewavewavewavewavewavewavewavewavew
ewavewavewavewavewavewavewavewavewavewavewavewavewavewavewavewavewavewavewa
oceanoceanoceanoceanoceanoceanoceanoceanoceanoceanoceanoceanoceano
ceanoceanoceanoceanoceanoceanoceanoceanoceanoceanoceanoceanoceanoc
eanoceanoceanoceanoceanoceanoceanoceanoceanoceanoceanoceanoceanoce
anoceanoceanoceanoceanoceanoceanoceanoceanoceanoceanoceanoceanocea
noceanoceanoceanoceanoceanoceanoceanoceanoceanoceanoceanoceanocean
anoceanoceanoceanoceanoceanoceanoceanoceanoceanoceanoceanoceanocea
eanoceanoceanoceanoceanoceanoceanoceanoceanoceanoceanoceanoceanoce
ceanoceanoceanoceanoceanoceanoceanoceanoceanoceanoceanoceanoceanoc
oceanoceanoceanoceanoceanoceanoceanoceanoceanoceanoceanoceanoceano
ceanoceanoceanoceanoceanoceanoceanoceanoceanoceanoceanoceanoceanoc
eanoceanoceanoceanoceanoceanoceanoceanoceanoceanoceanoceanoceanoce
anoceanoceanoceanoceanoceanoceanoceanoceanoceanoceanoceanoceanocea
noceanoceanoceanoceanoceanoceanoceanoceanoceanoceanoceanoceanocean
anoceanoceanoceanoceanoceanuniverseanoceanoceanoceanoceanoceanocea
eanoceanoceanoceanoceanoceanoceanoceanoceanoceanoceanoceanoceanoce
ceanoceanoceanoceanoceanoceanoceanoceanoceanoceanoceanoceanoceanoc
oceanoceanoceanoceanoceanoceanoceanoceanoceanoceanoceanoceanoceano
ceanoceanoceanoceanoceanoceanoceanoceanoceanoceanoceanoceanoceanoc
eanoceanoceanoceanoceanoceanoceanoceanoceanoceanoceanoceanoceanoce
anoceanoceanoceanoceanoceanoceanoceanoceanoceanoceanoceanoceanocea
noceanoceanoceanoceanoceanoceanoceanoceanoceanoceanoceanoceanocean
anoceanoceanoceanoceanoceanoceanoceanoceanoceanoceanoceanoceanocea
eanoceanoceanoceanoceanoceanoceanoceanoceanoceanoceanoceanoceanoce
ceanoceanoceanoceanoceanoceanoceanoceanoceanoceanoceanoceanoceanoc
oceanoceanoceanoceanoceanoceanoceanoceanoceanoceanoceanoceanoceano
ceanoceanoceanoceanoceanoceanoceanoceanoceanoceanoceanoceanoceanoc
eanoceanoceanoceanoceanoceanoceanoceanoceanoceanoceanoceanoceanoce
anoceanoceanoceanoceanoceanoceanoceanoceanoceanoceanoceanoceanocea
noceanoceanoceanoceanoceanoceanoceanoceanoceanoceanoceanoceanocean
anoceanoceanoceanoceanoceanoceanoceanoceanoceanoceanoceanoceanocea
eanoceanoceanoceanoceanoceanoceanoceanoceanoceanoceanoceanoceanoce
ceanoceanoceanoceanoceanoceanoceanoceanoceanoceanoceanoceanoceanoc
oceanoceanoceanoceanoceanoceanoceanoceanoceanoceanoceanoceanoceano

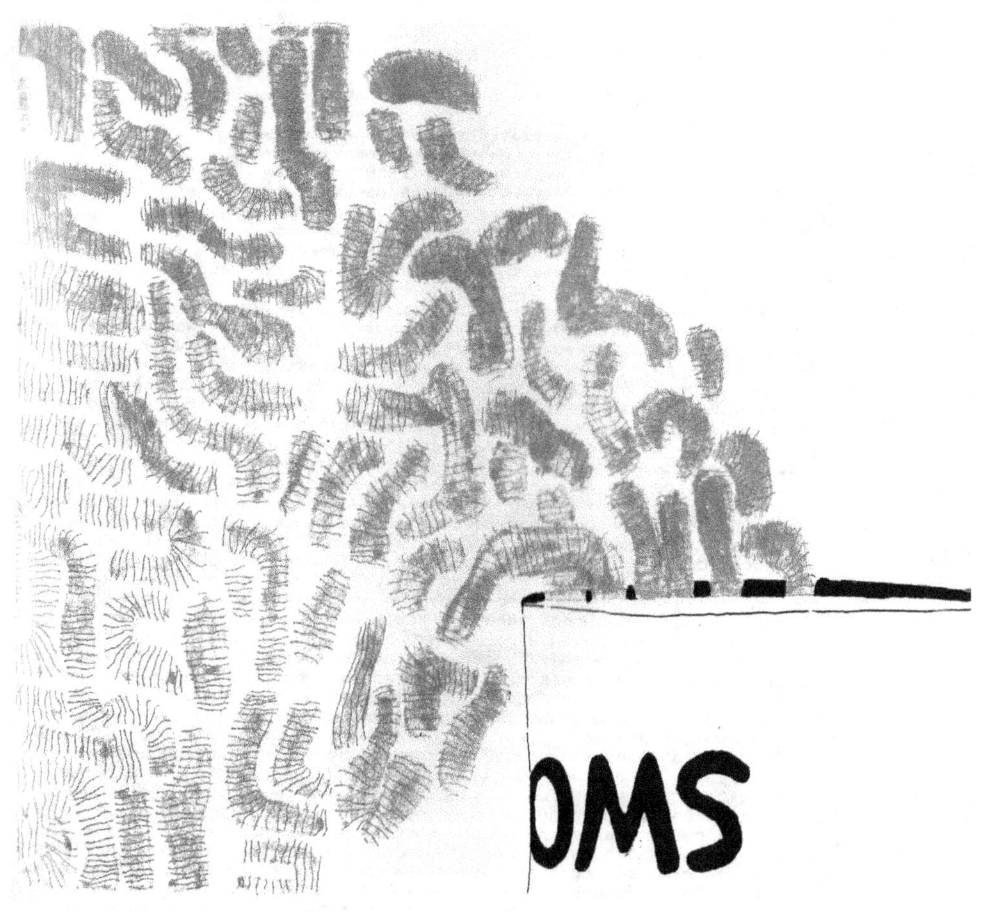

OMS

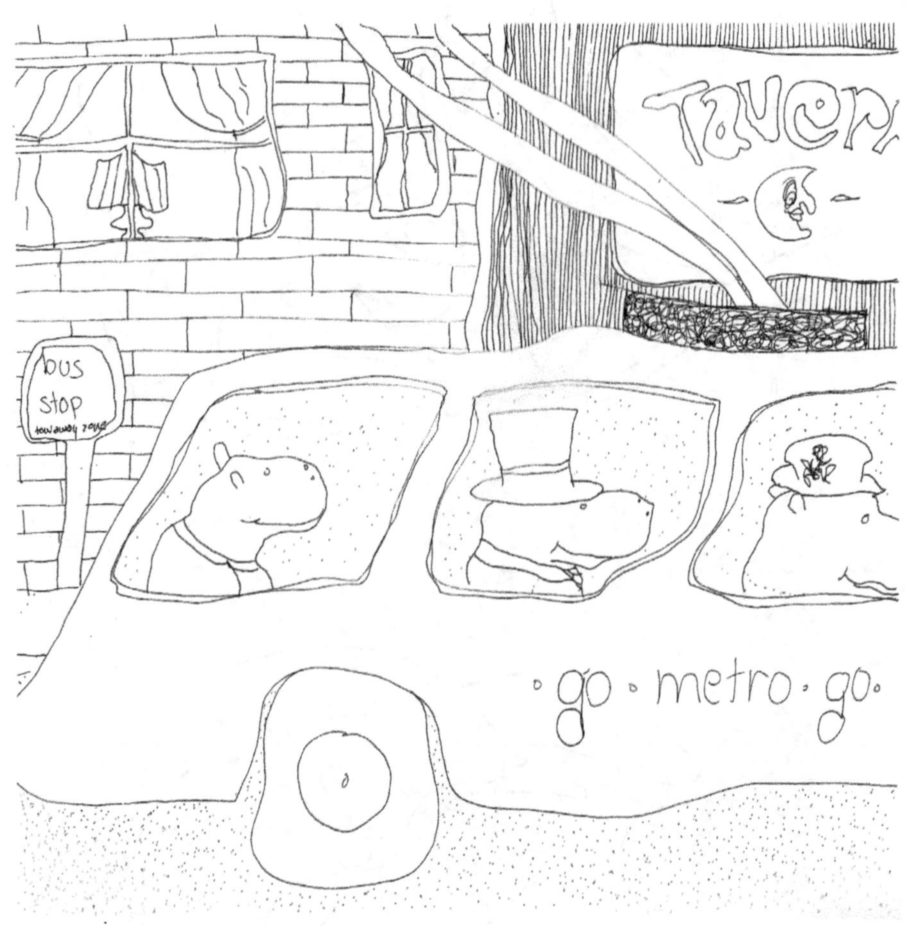

Tavern
bus
stop
tow away zone
· go · metro · go ·

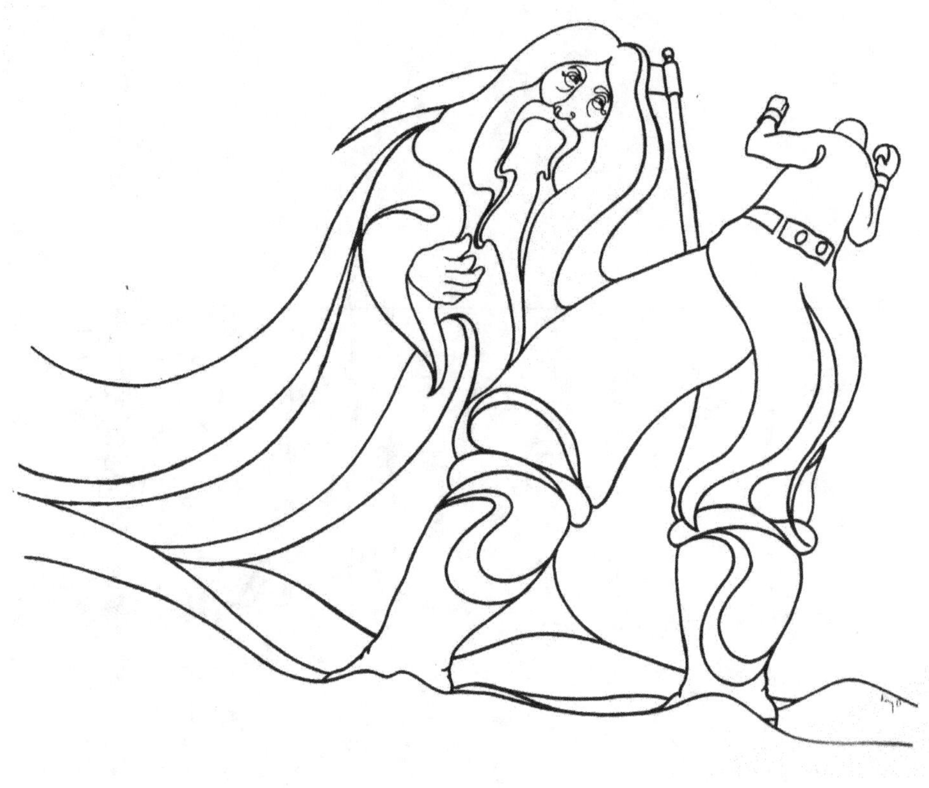

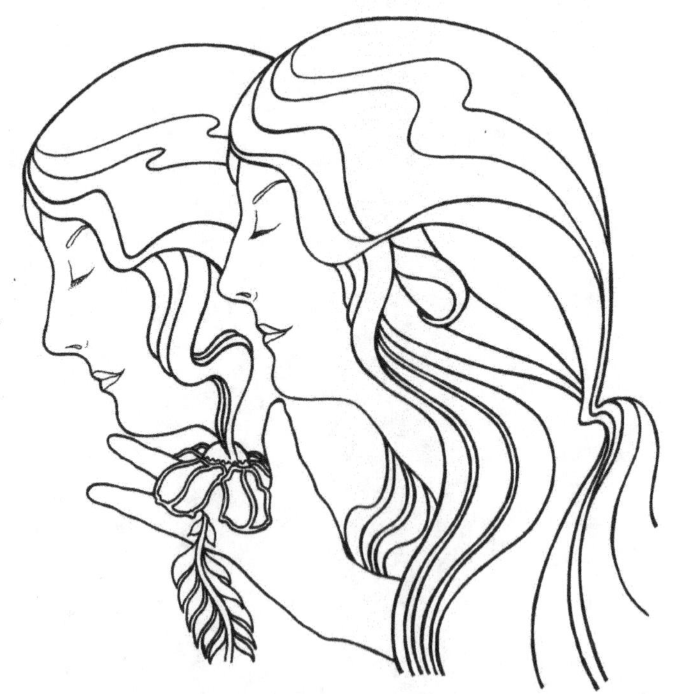

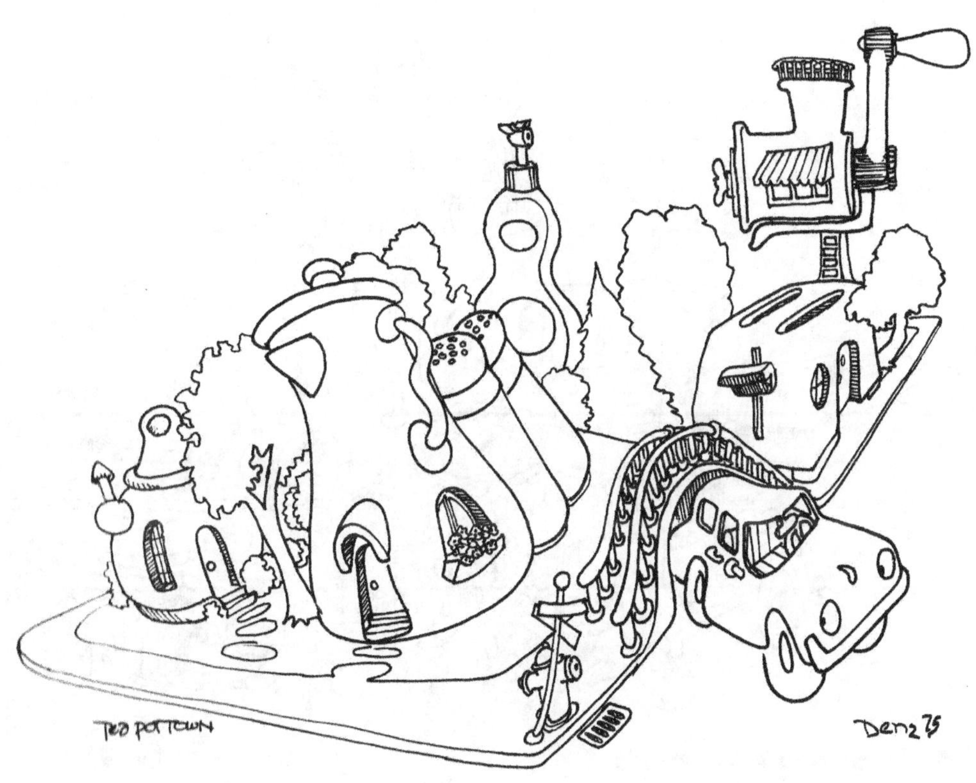
TED POTTOWN
Denz 75

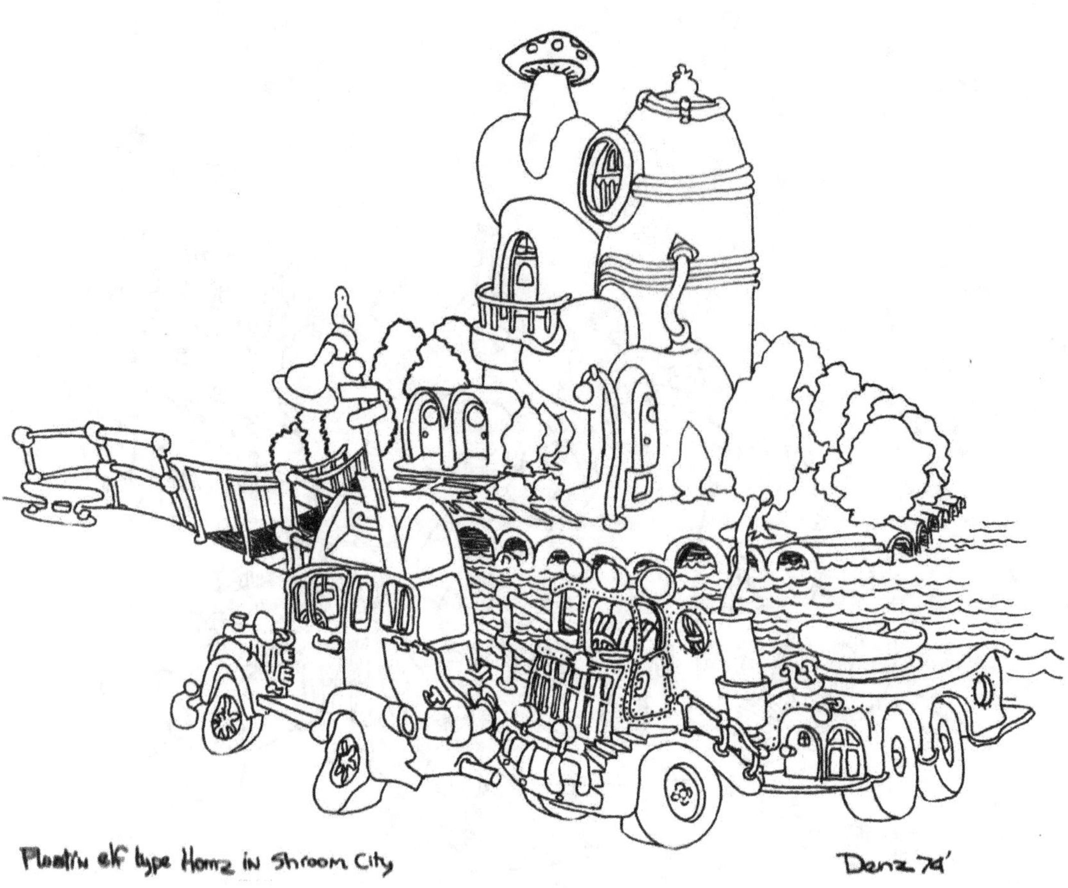

Plastic elf type Homz in Shroom City

Denz 79'

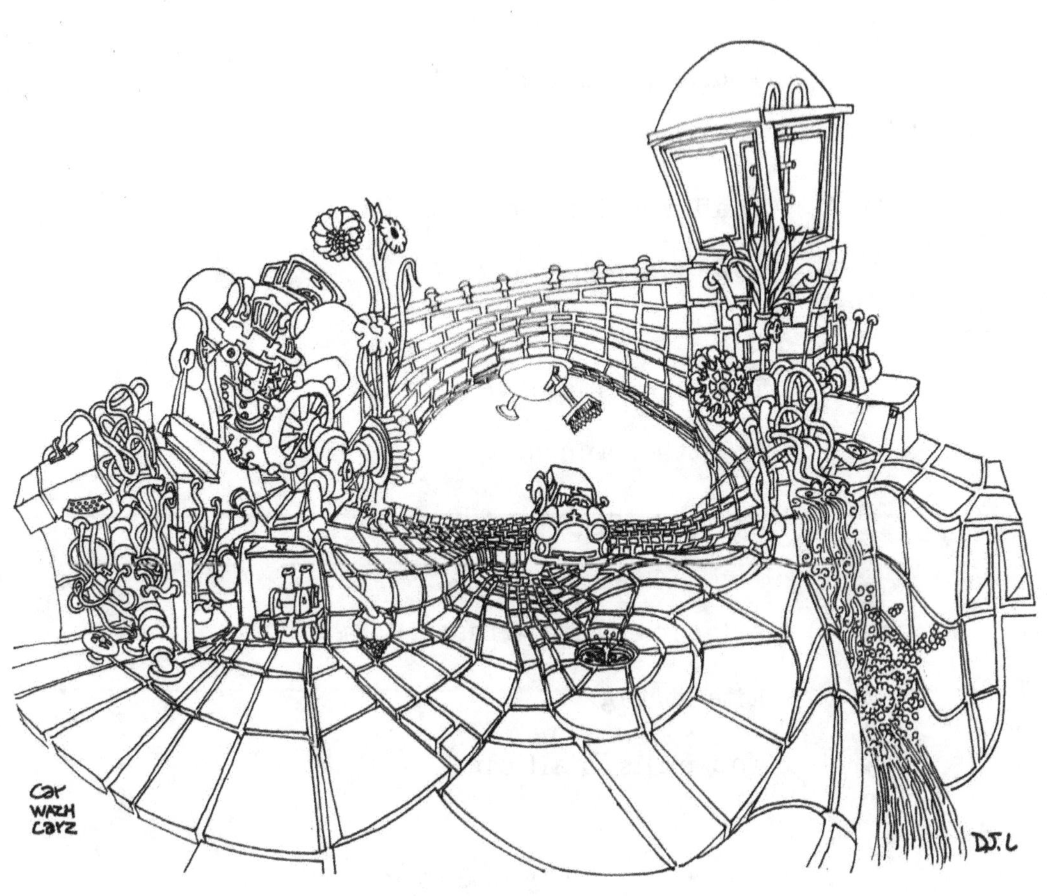

Car
wazh
carz
D.J.L

Today's a lazy planet

sunlight

shadows stroll with trees

over the horizon

The wind plays with dust

in little dances

as birds do bellyflops.

A fading train whistle is a

kite string

and pulls it all up.

Clyde Sanborn

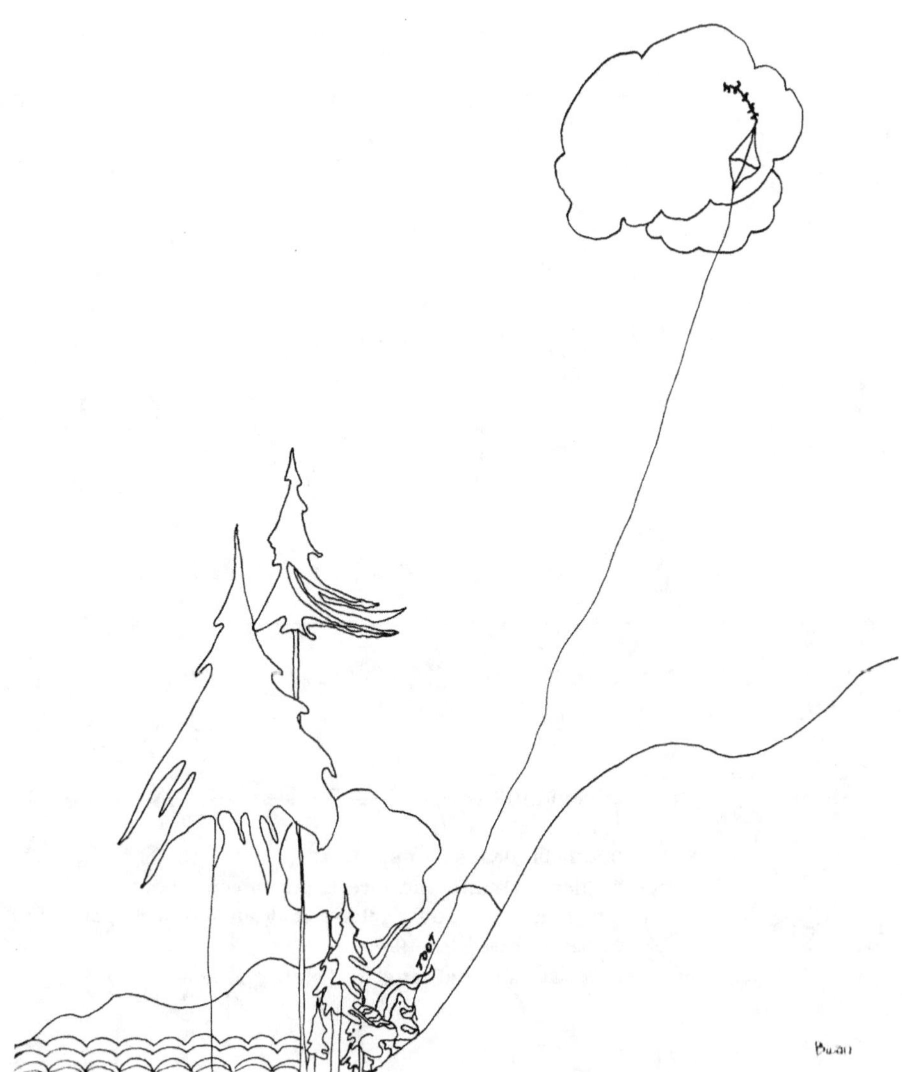

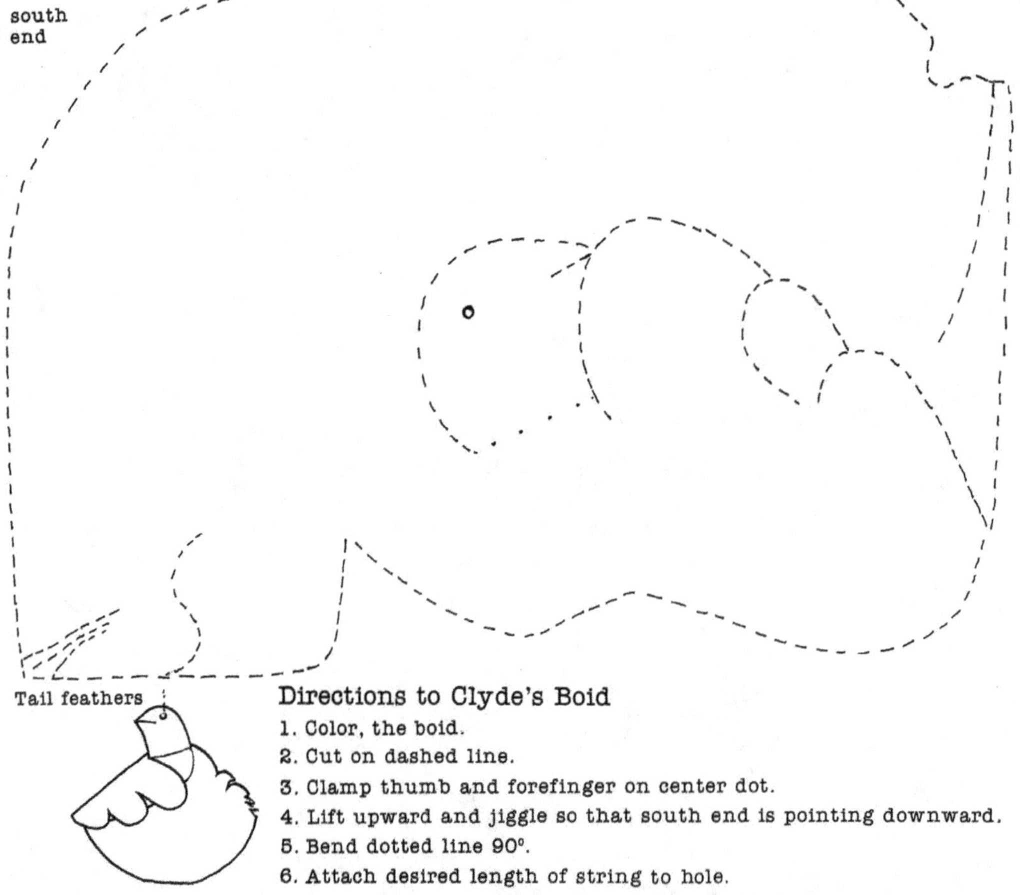

Directions to Clyde's Boid

1. Color, the boid.
2. Cut on dashed line.
3. Clamp thumb and forefinger on center dot.
4. Lift upward and jiggle so that south end is pointing downward.
5. Bend dotted line 90°.
6. Attach desired length of string to hole.

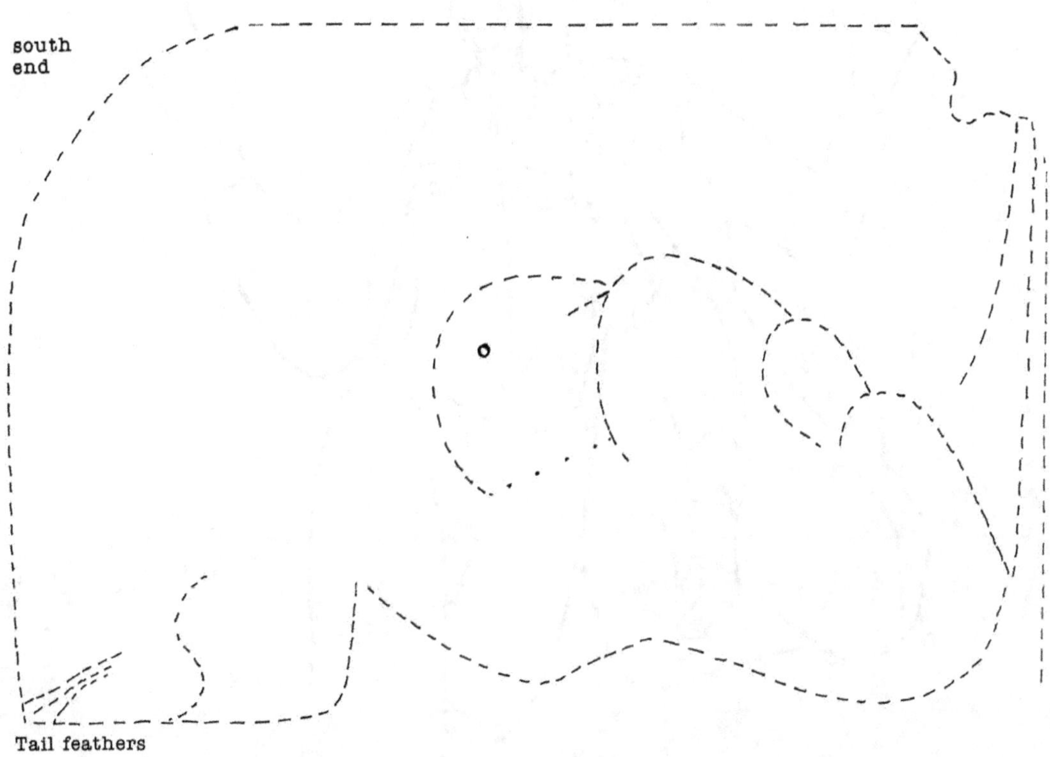

south
end
Tail feathers

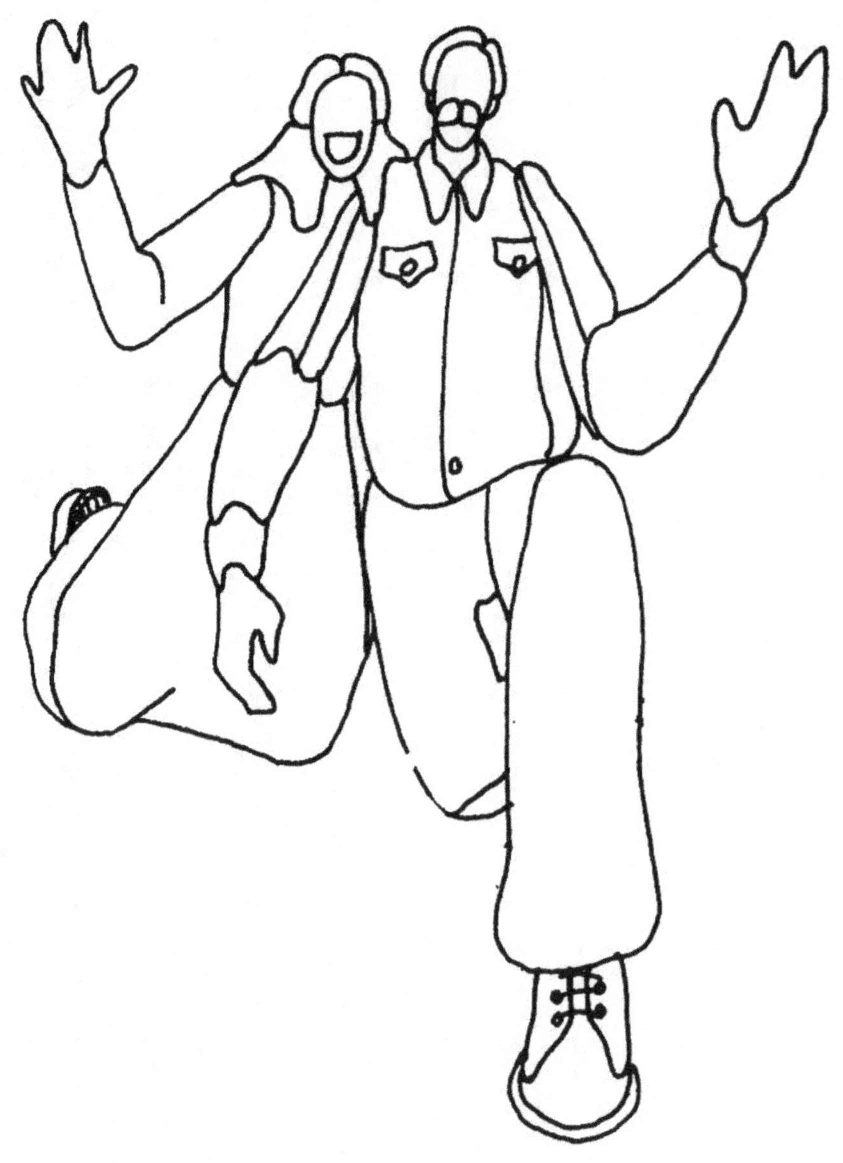

MICHAEL CLOUGH:

The next four years Clyde continued his life at The Deluxe. He became very good at pool. He wasn't a great player, but he knew every bump and wrinkle in that table and would leave a shark or hustler shaking his head. I was in and out over those years hitching around and spending time in Colorado then back to The Deluxe and sometimes crashing on Clyde's couch. Sometimes finding a place of my own. So I don't know the everyday of Clyde's life then. Mostly I think it became hanging out at The Deluxe.

In the Fall of 1975 after spending the summer in Denver and then picking apples in the Okanogan, I decided to move to Fishtown. I knew Charlie Krafft, had visited Robert Sund, and had been to La Conner several times. I decided that river life is the life for me. After picking apples, I stopped in Seattle. It was around Halloween. What, 41 years ago? A Halloween party at The Harvard Exit. Clyde and I got dressed up in some Mylar aluminum foil and velour and took some acid. I think they showed *The Illustrated Man*, maybe another movie, a big and mind blowing party.

The next morning I packed my gear, and friend Matt gave me a ride up to La Conner. Clyde shows later.

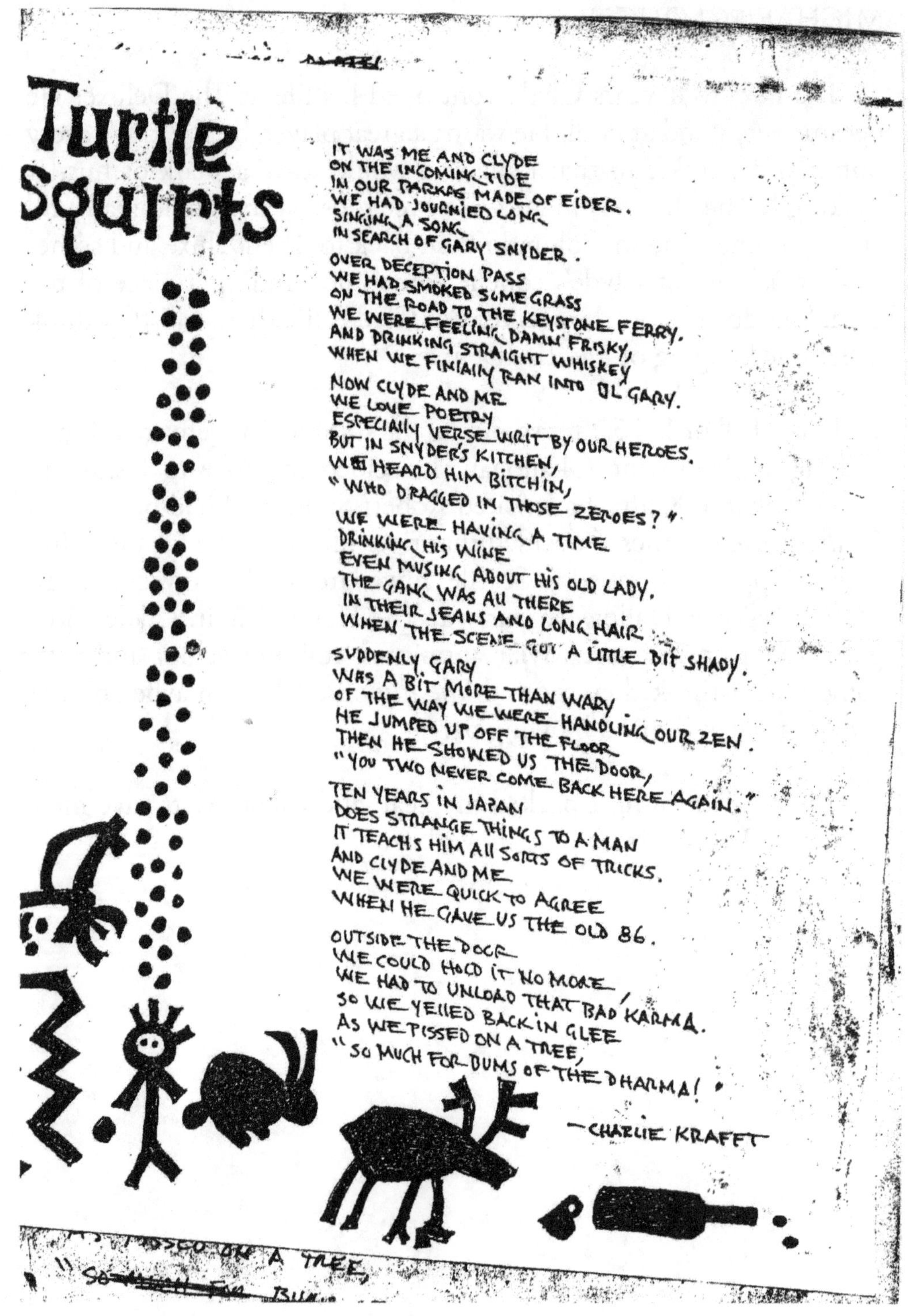

Original illustration by Charlie Krafft.

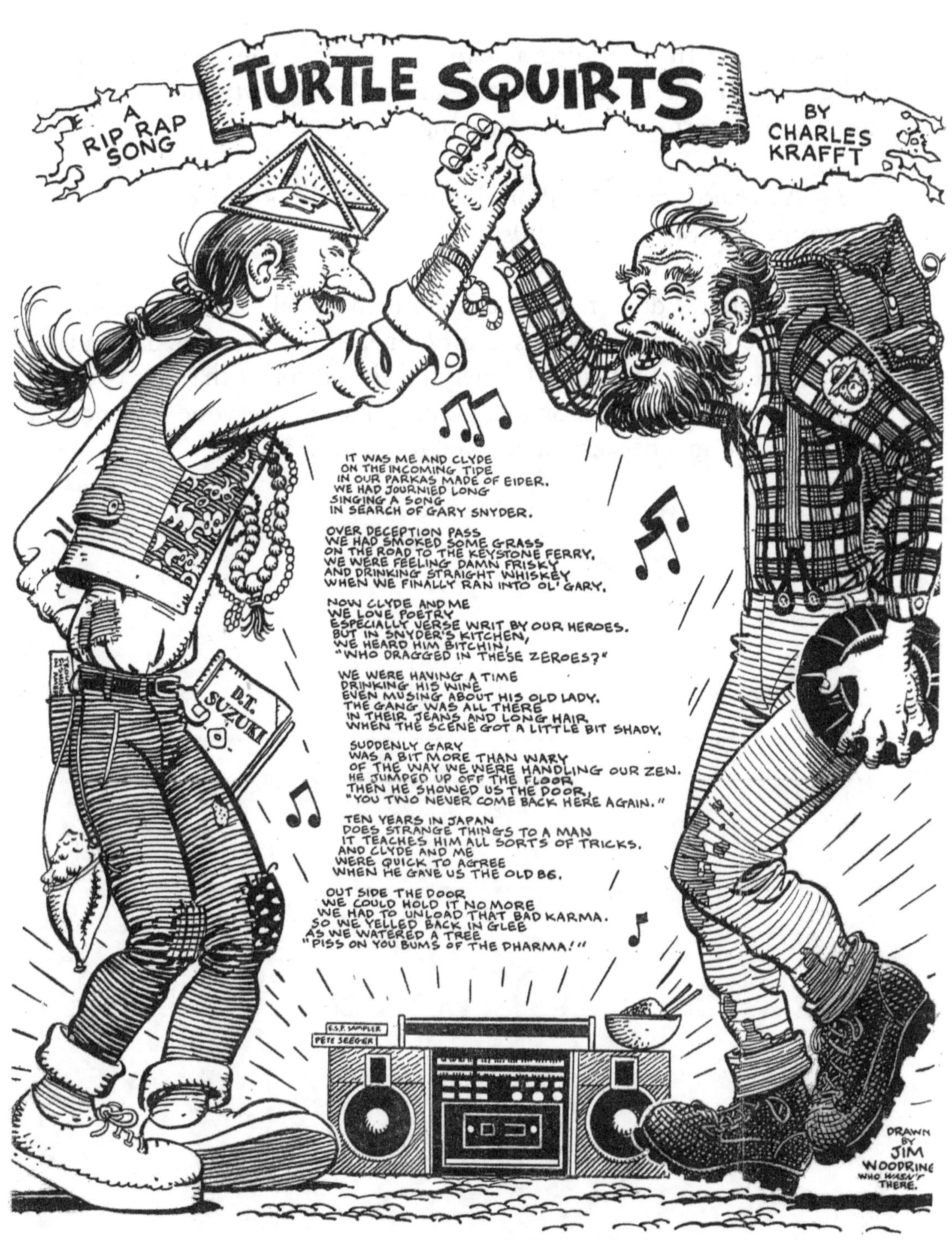

From *The Northwest Extra!* by Jim Woodring.

CHARLIE KRAFFT:

I believe the Turtle Squirts adventure was 1977. Gary Snyder read at the Centrum Foundation, Fort Warden, Port Townsend. Robert Sund was the warm up act that evening.

The Northwest Extra! collaboration with Jim Woodring came years later in the late '80s or early '90s.

To be honest, I don't remember too much else about that reading and the after-party in Snyder's cabin/apt. at Fort Warden. I recall Linn House, a San Francisco Digger and the editor of the first issue of *Planet Drum* was there. Snyder actually kicked everyone out, not just Clyde and me, because he wanted to go to sleep.

JOHN SCHAEFER:

One day I was driving to Olympia to pay my mother a visit and stopp'd in Seattle to say hello to Clyde, off Pine St. in the Capitol Hill neighborhood. Clyde was flat BROKE and wasn't making his rent. A couple months behind he was. I told him I knew of a shack on the sandspit a little way from La Conner, and if he wanted to go I would pick him up the next day. I think this was 1980. After Olympia, I picked Clyde up along with his cat, and we drove up to La Conner and the sandspit and Clyde moved into the shack. When the wind blew, it went right thru the cabin. But he survived it. Fishtown was just south of it, where he met Charlie Krafft. At that time I lived at Smuggler's Cove which was through the woods next to Clyde's new shack. Clyde soon discovered the "1890's Tavern" and had some credit for a short while, but then the ladies who owned the tavern cut him off. Beyond his wino orientation, Clyde was a fine poet. Very fine.

When I pick'd up Clyde in Seattle, I stopp'd at Traver Gallery on 4th Avenue and acquired a painting sale check which Clyde and I blew in La Conner. We went on a big four day benderous drunk—but created no problems towards us. Then I went back to Smuggler's, and Clyde met people on the sandspit—Allen Schermerhorn who lived there was a big help to Clyde. Allen was close to Clyde—one of six or seven people who lived on the spit in old ancient fisherman shacks.

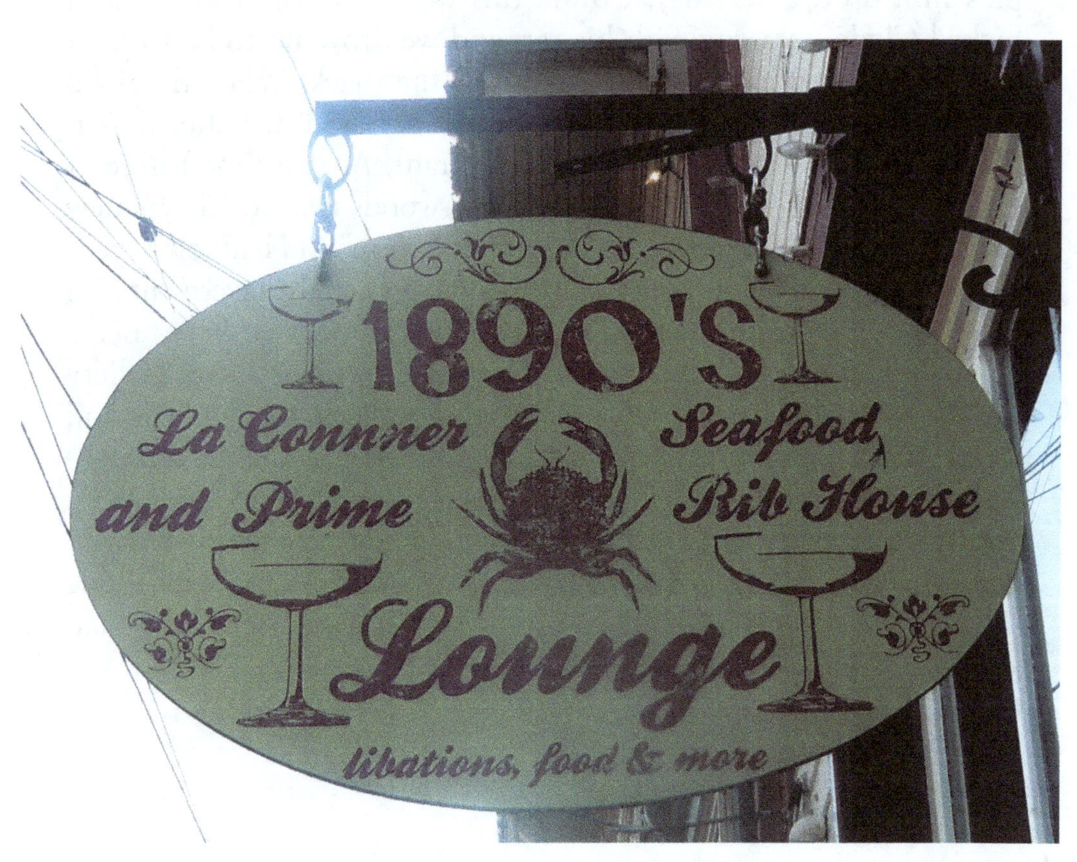

1890'S
La Connner
and Prime
Seafood
Rib House
Lounge
libations, food & more

CHARLIE KRAFFT:

Clyde named me "Checkbook Charlie" because sometimes I was the only one with money enough for another $2.50 pitcher of beer. I was famous for bouncing $2.50 checks at the 1890's and the La Conner Tavern buying them beers. The La Conner Rainier Bank would charge me $25 for every overdraft. Sometimes I'd get a $50 bill for $5.00 worth of beer at the end of the month. Clyde dropped the "Charlie" and just called me "Checkbook" after a while.

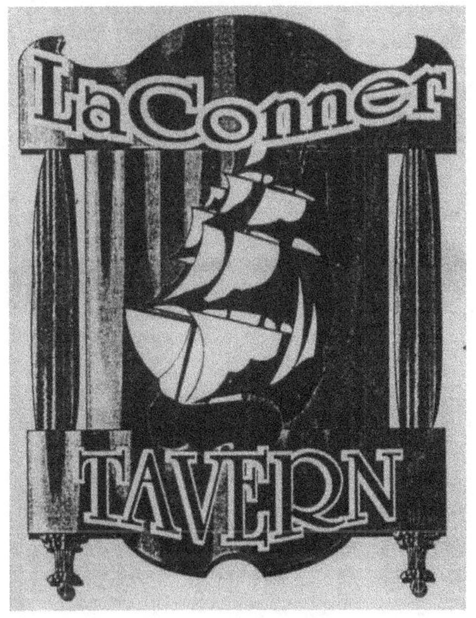

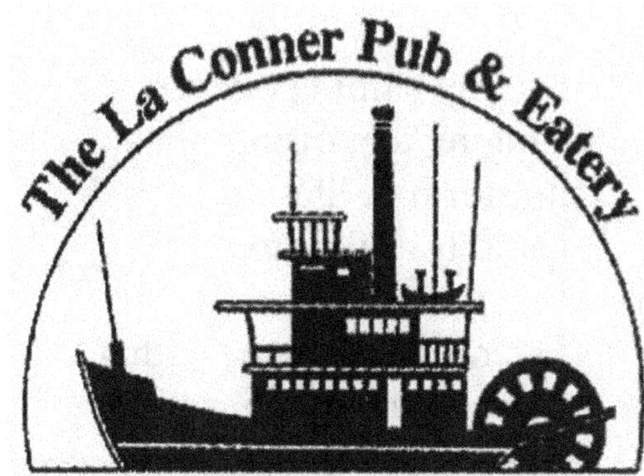

SHERRY THOSTENSON:

My husband and I both tended bar here in the early 1980s when Clyde was a regular visitor—along with several other of the "River Rats" who lived at Fishtown along the Skagit River. One favorite memory of Clyde is a watercolor painting he did for my husband on a piece of paper towel from the tavern's men's room. It is a sun (or perhaps a moon) over a landscape. Very impressionistic in style, and titled "For Matt on April Fool's Day." The little painting is framed and hanging on our living room wall.

Poem by DENNIS "BEX" BEXELL:

River Bhikku

In the bar, warm & light,
commotion of faces, smoky
intimations of a far gone dream.

He played the jukebox &
meandered the scene
through the waves of talk
& winds of minds,

his tiny flaming essence
clinging to a castoff buoy
no storm of illusion
could tear him from.

Later, threading the path
through the moon shining
field of newborn peas
to the high dike where

the succulent void
refilled the pockets of his soul
from what he left behind.
There, as he stood gazing

back on the lights of town,
knowing there was nothing
left to do but row on home
& take a nap.

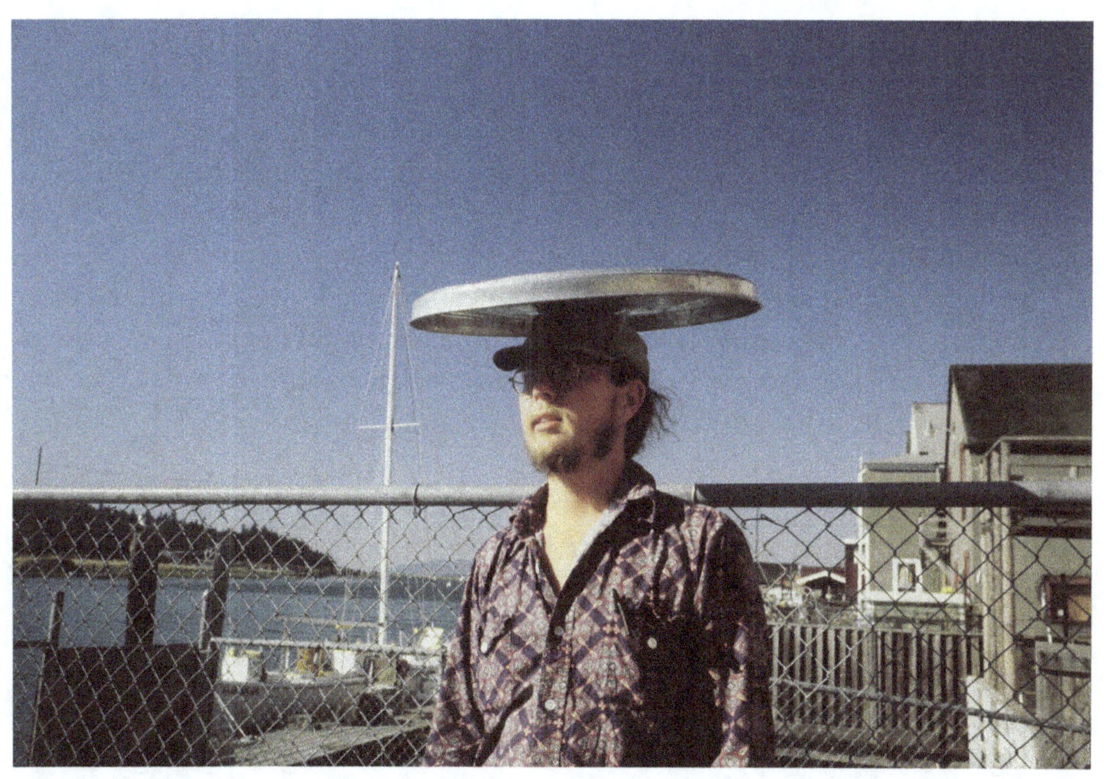

ERIK AMBJOR:

This is one of the few pics I have of Clyde, taken on the deck of the 1890's in La Conner, circa 1979 or so. It was on the occasion of Skylab falling back to Earth—no one knew precisely where it was to hit.

In the background, Robert Sund was reading an ad in the local paper for the hardware store: "Be the first on your block to see Skylab—Ladders on sale, 30% off!"

Clyde sprung into action with his response to the impending "disaster."

CHUCK EASTON:

I crossed paths with Clyde a few times back in the late 1970s, usually in the company of Robert Sund, either in La Conner or Seattle. Conversations with him were quite odd—he would make obscure comments tangentially related to the topic at hand, and then flash a mischievous smile. For a while I attributed this to the fact that he was generally drunk, but even when occasionally sober, he still seemed to make the same sort of strange pronouncements. He was an interesting fellow to be around, one of the unique characters from that part of the Ish River Country circumscribed by Bellingham, Seattle, Port Townsend and La Conner.

Looking back, Clyde and Robert remind me of two jazz players that are favorites of mine: bassist Jaco Pastorious and guitarist Mike Stern. Jaco and Mike played together for a number of years in New York and made some tours around the U.S. At the time they were both deep into God-knows-what-kind-of-drugs. My wife, Autumn, and I used to go see Mike Stern in a small bar in Boston—one time right in the middle of a tune Mike wandered off-stage laughing and incoherent, disappearing for a while. At some point Mike decided he was headed for trouble if he didn't do something, so he checked into treatment—he is still playing decades later as one of the top guitar players out there. Jaco never quit and was beaten to death by a nightclub bouncer a couple of years later.

I remember a night in Seattle when I was living at what Robert came to call Cloud House. A bunch of us had been just down the street for a long night of drinking and frivolity at The Blue Moon Tavern. Coming back at closing time, I headed down to my basement room, leaving Robert and Clyde to the front room. When I woke up the next day, I looked in the kitchen and discovered that between the two of them they had cleaned out every last bit of alcohol in the house: two bottles of wine and half a bottle of whiskey from the cupboard and a couple of beers from the refrigerator—all this after closing down The Blue Moon! They were both still sleeping off a night of heavy drinking. My housemates and I were amazed they had managed to consume all this and were apparently still alive to tell the tale.

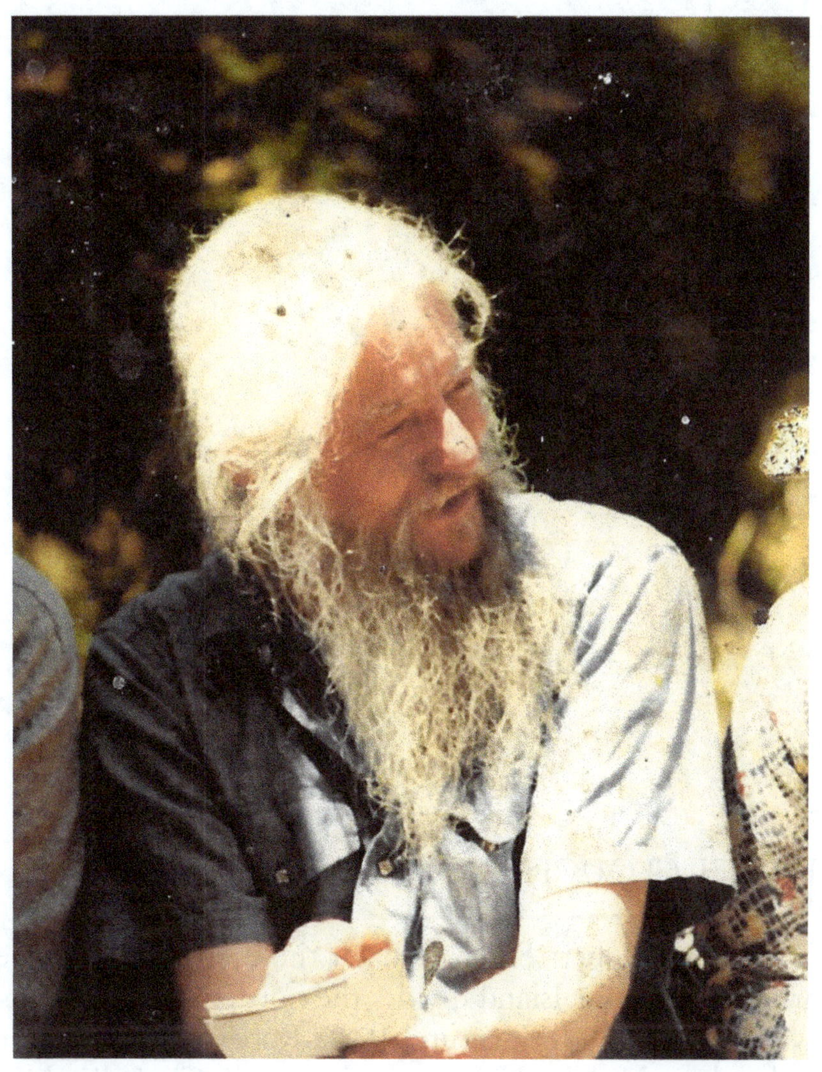

Robert Sund, photo courtesy Jimmy Zabik.

MICHAEL CLOUGH:

Robert and Clyde didn't get along, at least on Robert's part. They were miles apart in their approach to poetry, and Clyde could be annoying. He would show up at Robert's readings. And from the back of the room make comments and ask questions, interrupting Robert's performance and really pissing him off. I called Clyde, "Robert's Peanut Gallery."

CHARLIE KRAFFT:

Clyde and Robert were the town poets with a capital "P."

MICHAEL CLOUGH:

Clyde and Robert Sund lived on the North Fork of the Skagit near La Conner. Fir Island divides the north and south forks. Clyde moved to the north fork around 1978. Robert was living in town by then but kept his "shack" for poetic purpose. Clyde lived in various abandoned shacks tho living in is stretching it, more like sleeping, crashing, or hanging out. They were not homes. He had a tent one summer near Sullivan Slough. He wasn't on the River for Romantic reasons, it was free and he was homeless. Clyde usually went to Stockton to his mom's for a while in the winter. Get some real rest, new glasses, dentist, real meals, dry out. He was a fixture in La Conner. The La Conner that no longer exists. He would not fit in the cute clean tourist town that it's become although he never really fit In, but was accepted and loved by many, though he could piss one off and get sloppy. Robert certainly was not a fan of Clyde. I'm trying to give you a picture of Clyde but there was only one Clyde. He was unique and never unClyde.

2 poems by ROBERT SUND:

JULY 19, 1979

To Clyde

After a quick trip to the city
        to hear a poetry reading
I come home past midnight
        rowing downriver in the half-moon,
                        stars above
                    in the clear sky.

I tie my boat up,
        light one candle
        & sit long in the silence

A screech owl flies over the marsh.
Across the dike
        the bullfrogs strike their deep
                single-note song.
What a treat to listen to them.
They are not trying to teach me
                    anything.
They don't want to enlighten me
        or persuade me to their way
                    of thinking.
They are only singing,
                clear & strong.

I come home to hear
        the song I was waiting for
        right outside my shack.

SEPTEMBER 13, 1981

My neighbor Clyde
comes rowing up the creek.
The tide is very low today.
Beside my shack the dock is
    stranded;
    my boat rests on the mud.
I am afraid he will have to
walk the last few feet
        in deep mud.

"I've been praying for
    more water and less mud,
Clyde, but we'll have to
    wait for the
        evening high tide.
I'm out of beer,
but there's some wine left
from friends who visited
        just the other day."

Clyde steps out of the boat
twenty feet from the dock.
His leg sinks in mud
            up to his knee.
He drives one oar
    into the mud,
ties his boat to it and
comes sloshing ashore.
I pour him a glass of wine,
and we lift our glasses
        to make a toast.

Clyde says,
    "Here's mud in your eye!"

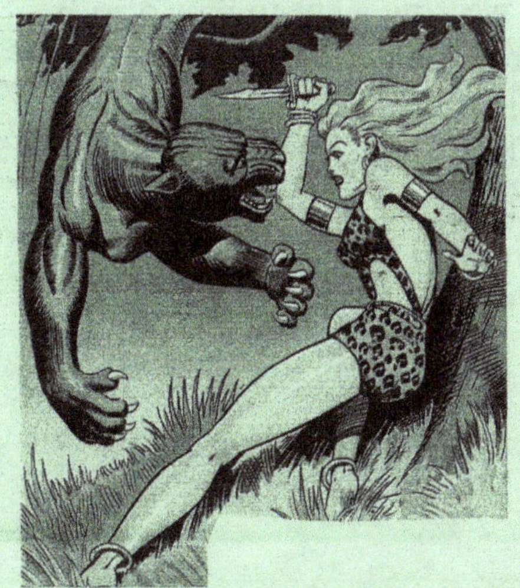

Villa de Jungle Girl
P.O. Box 338
La Conner, WA 98257

5 August 2016

Dear Allen:

   Sorry about the delay of my response: I've been much on the move
this summer.

   The truth is, I did not know Clyde Sanborn particularly well. He seemed
always present at each and every kind of gathering hereabouts, and when
our paths crossed he seemed to take special glee in bugging me about my
"literary success" -- although his mockery was never mean-spirited.

   In Zen, "jug monk" (I don't know how the Japanese say it) is a term
bestowed upon those spiritual aesthetes, who, while certainly holy,
are given to linger overly long at the sake keg. The master Ikkyu was
the most well known of these enlightened alcoholics (though those who
knew Alan Watts say he also could be listed in that category).

   I coined the phrase "mud monk" to refer to those who, like Clyde,
choose to live and write in natural, primitive conditions. There always
seemed to be an ample sampling of Skagit River mud traveling along on
Clyde's boots.

   Wish I could be more helpful. Good luck with the project. The reference
to Li Po is probably not misplaced.

Tom Robbins

MICHAEL CLOUGH:

Clyde would always be seen in town wearing a cheap pair of rubber boots. He had to slog through a lot of mud to get to and from town and river. There was a Summer Solstice party atop Bald Island. Clyde and I got to it with our sleeping bags, and a fine evening was had by all. The following morn when the sun made it too hot to stay any longer in our bags, we crawled out with our hangovers and I couldn't help but notice Clyde had his rubber boots on. I've always wondered if he always slept in his boots.

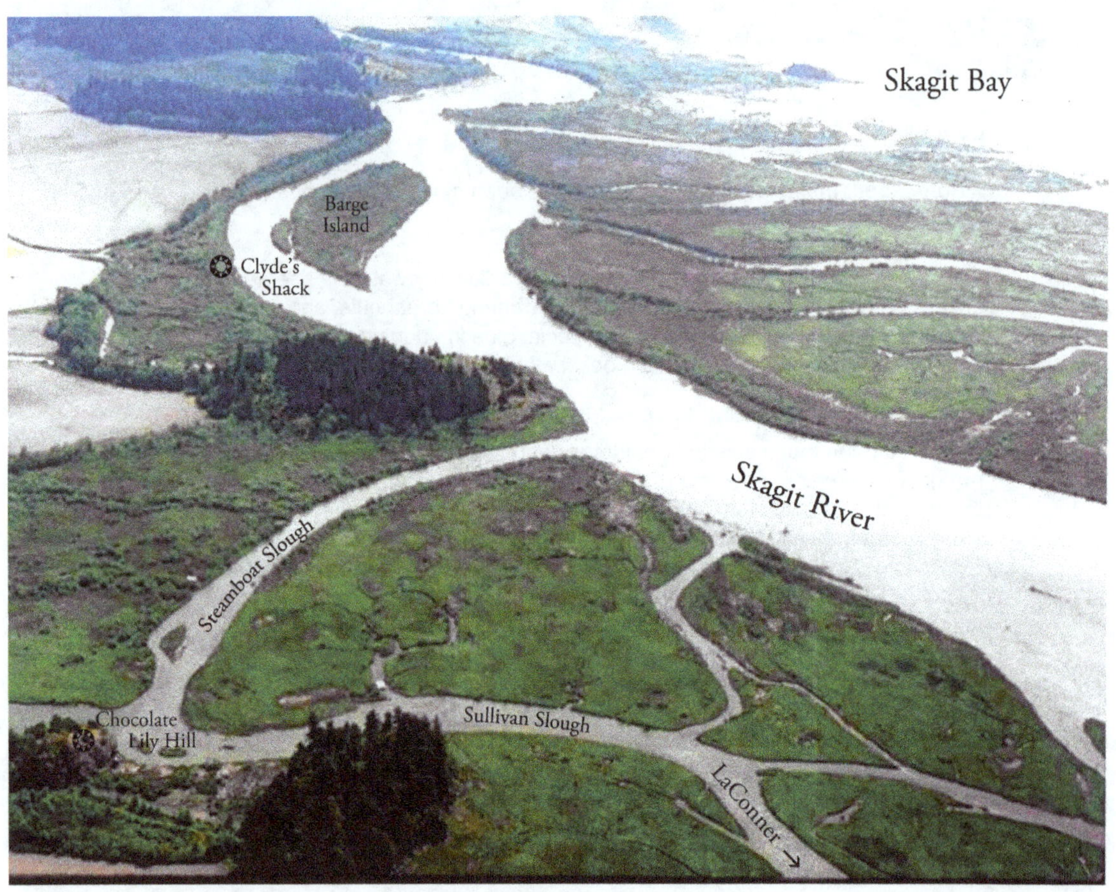

Aerial Map courtesy of Jimmy Zabik.

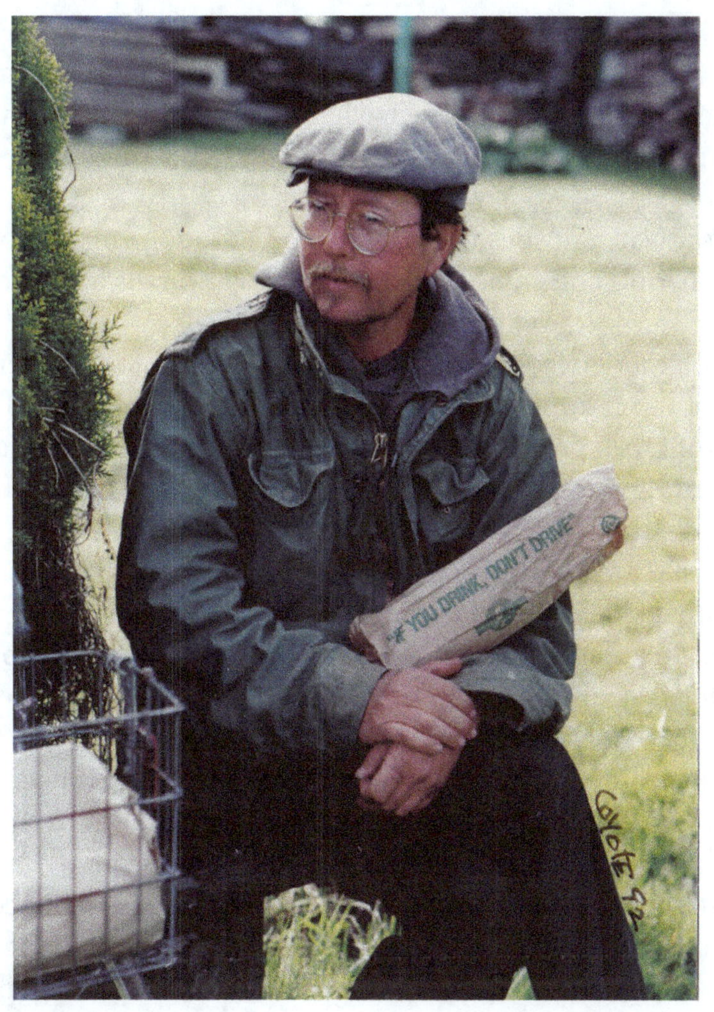

Photo by Don Coyote.

FRED OWENS' story, "Clyde's Bicycle" is published in its entirety on his online site, *Frog Hospital*. That name, Fred explains, comes from Clyde: "There was once a grocery store in a Quonset hut, run by Mr. Grobschmidt. Clyde thought that Mr. Grobschmidt looked like a frog, so he took to calling the store the Frog Hospital." Fred's story takes place in La Conner, "a small town on Swinomish Channel, where the tide flowed into Skagit Bay, and from Skagit Bay through Deception Pass to Puget Sound and then to the wide Pacific Ocean." What follows is an excerpt edited from Fred's longer work…

Frank had been living in LaConner, Washington for quite a few years. LaConner had been a quiet fishing village with shuttered stores and dogs sleeping in the street when he first found it in the 1970s. The scenery was beautiful and the rent was cheap.

The saltwater sloshes through twice a day, coming in, coming out, coming in, and coming out. The tide rises and falls and rises and falls again.

Only experienced fishermen and tugboat pilots understood the pattern of the channel's movement—how it was influenced by changes in barometric pressure, the phase of the moon, and the amount of water coming out of the Skagit River at any given time.

Seagulls flew overhead. Pleasure boats moved up and down the channel in a steady procession. The Indians kept their fishing boats on the other side of the channel. LaConner was on the east side of the channel, a regular American town. Swinomish village was on the west side, since time immemorial, a sovereign nation.

Frank and his old hippy and artist pals were relegated to a hangout on a side street, off the main tourist street and out of sight, a place called Café Culture, which Gretchen ran on an under-the-table cash basis. Gretchen mainly kept the place going because she could meet her buddies there at five o'clock and begin the real work of the day—getting drunk. But in the morning, Frank enjoyed the coffee crowd, reading the newspaper and talking with his pals. "What a bunch of nobodies we are," he said, more than once.

Frank struggled to make sense of things. Things needed to be explained. Things needed to happen for a reason.

But he wouldn't say too much about that at the cafe. That would invite a boring political argument. No politics. "I practice remaining calm while reading the newspaper," he proclaimed to his pals. "I read about violence, war, and the horrible cruelty of criminals. I read about the self-serving dishonesty of politicians. But if I feel my gorge rising, I pause and take a deep breath. I go to the Buddha, and I say this happened and that happened, and now I know this happened and that happened. I only observe. That's the way Clyde would have done it."

Clyde was the town drunk. Every village has an idiot, and every small town has a town drunk. Clyde died in 1996 and more than 300 people came to his funeral. They had a party in his honor at the picnic shelter in Pioneer Park. Frank didn't go. He appreciated Clyde, but in truth he couldn't tolerate him. Clyde used to sit on the front porch at Jim and Janet Saunders' house—their old house when they lived in town. He would sit there half the day, with his backpack and his jug of cheap wine, blowing smoke through his alcoholic wine-darkened cheeks, uttering Buddhist koans, speaking of profoundly inconsequential matters, a living legend, as legends go in a small town.

Clyde got his wine money from sweeping the parking lot at the grocery store or raking leaves or people just gave it to him. He wrote poems on scraps of paper and gave them to people, like this one:

Springs

There are many Springs today –

One is a new bird, another a warm stone.

One is a marsh hawk flying upside down,

And the last is the last fall

leaf that lived way up. Just landed.

Gretchen kept a copy of Clyde's poems at the Café Culture piled in with all the other books and magazines. "It's a good poem," Frank knew. "But I'm only half a Buddhist. This drunk monk, Buddhist monk, mindless wandering mind. This Gary Snyder, Jack Kerouac, Allen Ginsberg summit of the beginning of all things, and how it all comes back around, so you don't need to leave, you can just sit there, and save yourself all that trouble—I know all that."

Clyde wrote another poem that Frank really liked, about Paul Hansen's dog, Nero, a huge black Newfoundland. Hansen was a misanthrope, a poet, and a Chinese scholar. Nero always rode in the front of the Hansen's small pickup when Hansen came to town—those rare visits to Café Culture, because he couldn't stand people anymore. But when Hansen came to town, Frank always liked hearing him laugh. Hansen laughed like a very loud donkey, you could hear him all over town. This was the poem that Clyde wrote about Olsen's dog, Nero.

Nero Woof

Me ride in car with Paul.

Me smell and watch.

 Me listen well and sit in car.

Me be good dog and wait.

Me good big dog.

Me wait and rest.

"That one is good. I know a good poem when I see one," Frank said. "It's entirely accurate. That's what Nero is like. And if you understand the dog, then you can understand everything, and the universe begins to make sense.

Jim Smith, who enabled Clyde in a big way because he admired losers, kept a portrait of Clyde in his studio, a wood cut print, and he kept all the clippings of Clyde's life in a box—kind of a shrine. This one had been in the newspaper:

Cars, vans and bicycles crowded into every available parking spot in and around Pioneer Park on Wednesday, March 20, for a memorial potluck for the late Clyde Sanborn. Sanborn, 47, was found dead Saturday morning, March 15, on a sand spit near the south end of the Swinomish Channel. He was the victim of an apparent drowning accident. Tears filled the eyes of many of the hundreds of mourners, others laughed and talked about pleasant memories of Clyde. Artwork and poems, written by what locals believe was the last "River Rat" in La Conner, were on

"I'm just petty and selfish," Frank thought. "There aren't going to be 300 people coming to my funeral. Everybody liked Clyde, that was all. Being drunk all day didn't have much to do with it."

But Frank was tired of the bum life, the deadbeat poets, and the stoned fish. He used to hang out with Clyde a lot in the early '80s, when Clyde had his cabin out by the Sandspit. Clyde and Nearly Normal Jimmy had adjacent cabins—shacks, really. Jimmy had a yellow dog named Amigo, and Jimmy and Clyde lived the life from Cannery Row, going into town to get enough beer, the cheapest, and coming back out to the Sandspit, a wonderful place to get drunk. It didn't matter where you fell down, there were no rocks, or if there was a rock, it would be covered with soft velvet moss, you could lie down and see the stars—and be drunk enough to see the stars, because the clouds hid them from sober people.

But that was back in the '80s. More people were hanging out on the River back then, before all the yuppies came, when LaConner was quieter. Nearly Normal Jimmy had moved off the Sandspit after the time he got so drunk that he climbed a utility pole and sat on the raised platform next to the transformer and somehow touched something that electrocuted him and put him in the hospital.

Nearly Normal Jimmy got his picture in the paper for that escapade, and he was deeply ashamed and never came back to LaConner for many years. He quit drinking altogether, although he made up for that by smoking pot all the time. He didn't really go away. He just found a cheap old farmhouse that some old farmer would let him live in for a little work. That was out on Fir Island, only ten miles from LaConner, but Jimmy never once came to town after that.

One by one, the River Rats disappeared and Clyde was the last one, officially, that is—the last one to be a poet about it, and he drowned, fittingly, it seemed. Clyde could handle a row boat drunk or sober, as good as anybody, and it was a mystery to his friends—a good end to his life, but still a mystery that he just fell out of his boat and drowned.

And they never found his bicycle either.

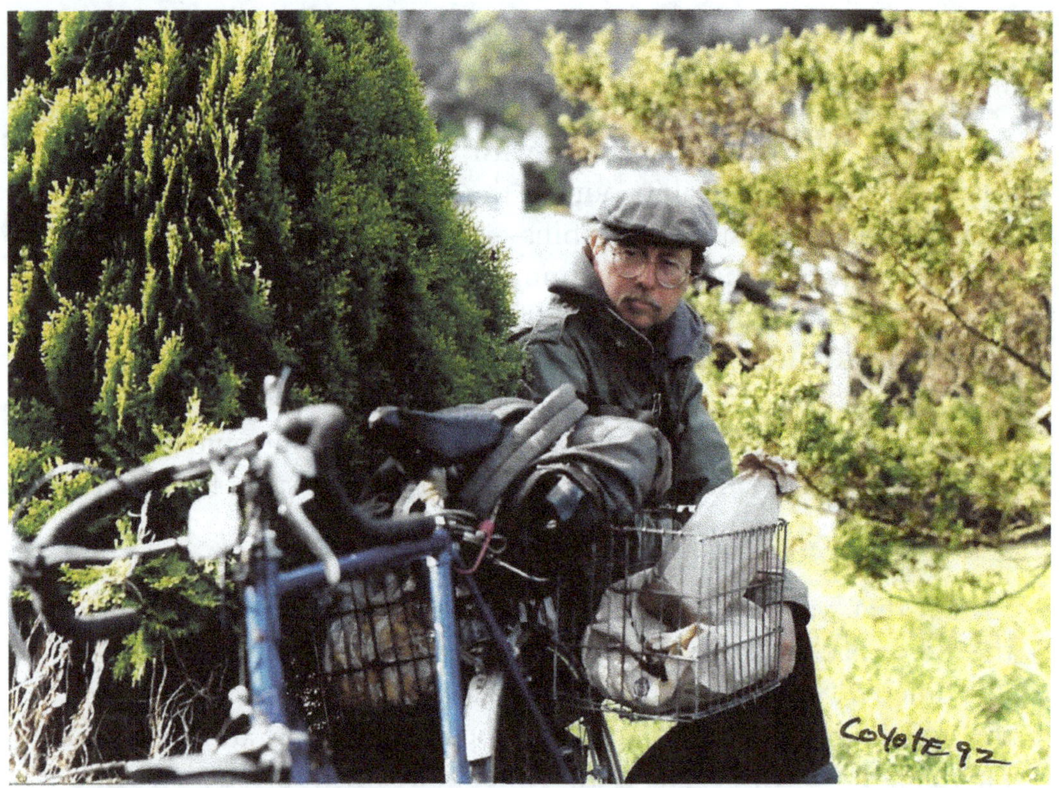

Photo by Don Coyote

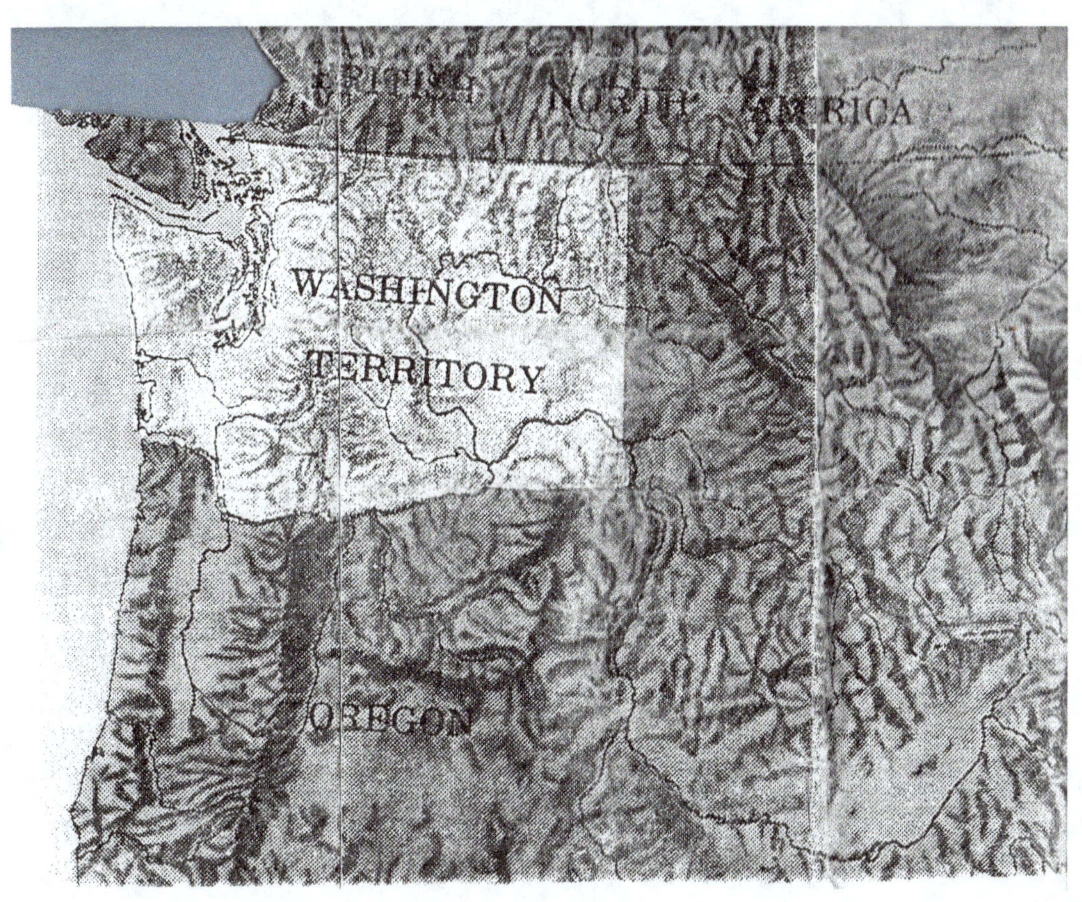

A scrap of map Clyde kept folded among his belongings.
The following pages are a collection of his handwritten poems:

there is a single
cloud, that
happens

over and
over.

Talent Feline

This, your poem, purr pure
rub against the leg.
Now we're outside, with

Spring, II.
____

Spring can be tedious
when one has
    not been sprung. /L.

for Rosie Cat / 5.13.95ish
____

ure purr purr purr cat, and

. morning birds.   /c.

143

N.F.S.   for la-la land

This poem is not for sale.
And if it was, i wouldn't
sell it, much.

                          lc.

Wages

War   for S. Brown

War is a bird
that forgot
how to land.

                              c.

Feb/2/91

Sailing

Jumping up and down on
the toy boat,
    Les and Sandy sometimes
inhale
to create
        fair winds.

("the situation is hopeless,
    but not serious").

When her keel was laid,
    the hurricanes and waves
    kissed her gently.

                        L.

                for Sylvia

... it's just one of those lives. —

the pretty girls live here, Hmm...?
and the plants, hmm...?
And life lives here with
Sylvia cat, hmm...

Well...

                        C.

Poem to a flower
—

with earth
   and air
around you,
   tyfoons and
such —
   and people
stomping around —
   and animals, bugs,
insects and birds
   eating you —
   you're
      still
         standing!

   A gift
      for someone.

Spring   for L.

The earth belched
and flowers were.

                          /L.

Spring II

Oh, to be in love,
when the skunk
cabbage is in bloom. o/c

for Gary   spring)

Revision

When i began revising
  this poem,
there were more words.
Now, as i think of it,
  there aren't so many.
Soon, there won't be
  any left.   ⌐c.

Poem to a Stone   : 1-11-92

—

It's odd, sitting here.
Wind and water on me;
life is funny.   ⌐c.

old silent dragon tongue
and well flowered mama —
i don't know about
their lives,
but conversation leads
to common thoughts.
They must move
and the moon moves
too.
The trees send them
old true thoughts.

Clyde poem courtesy of Sheila Farr.

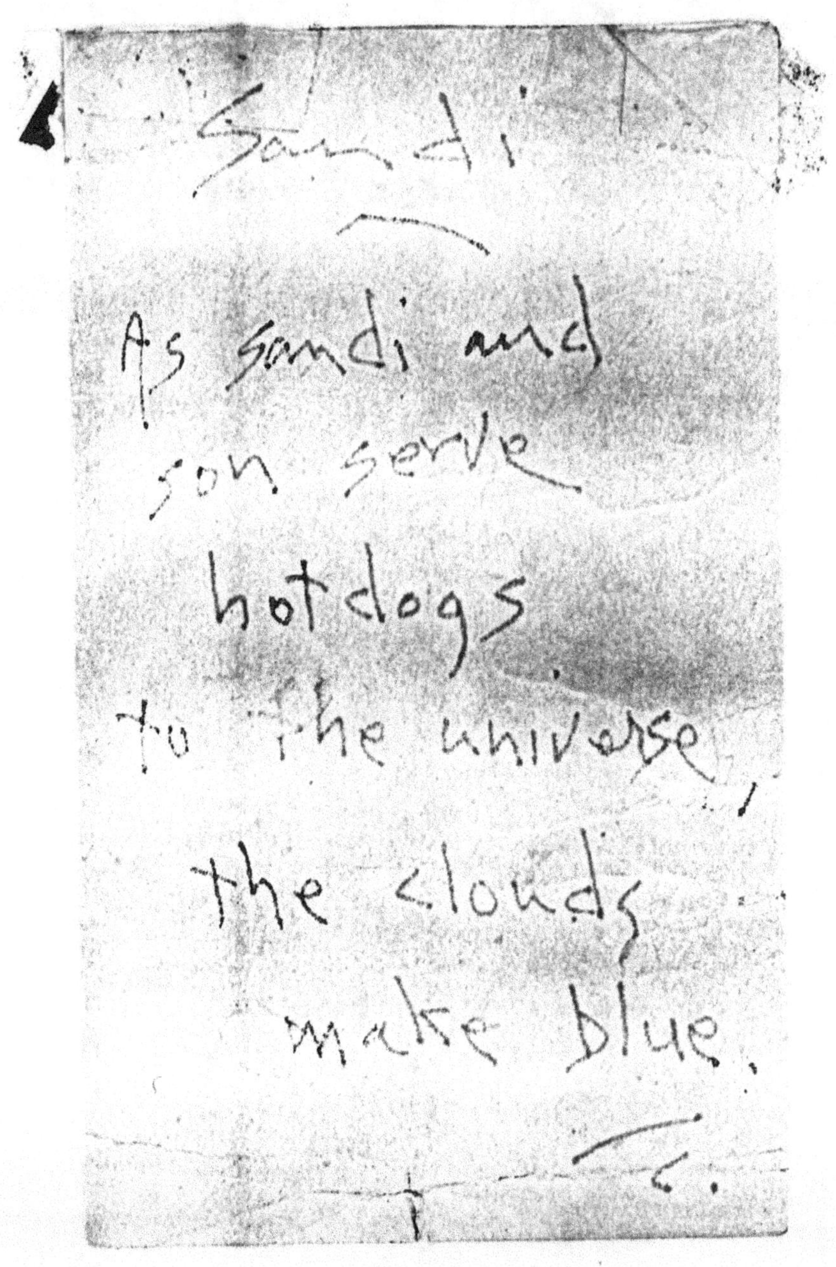

A Clyde original from owner of Sandi's Yogurt Shack, "Jo" Koles.

Clyde poems courtesy of Jim Smith & Janet Saunders.

Lori & Gary
:
are gently
with their hairy,
when they hold
hands it's
electric. The
little birds
smile up. /c.

Clyde poem courtesy of Gary Clay & Lori Kyle.

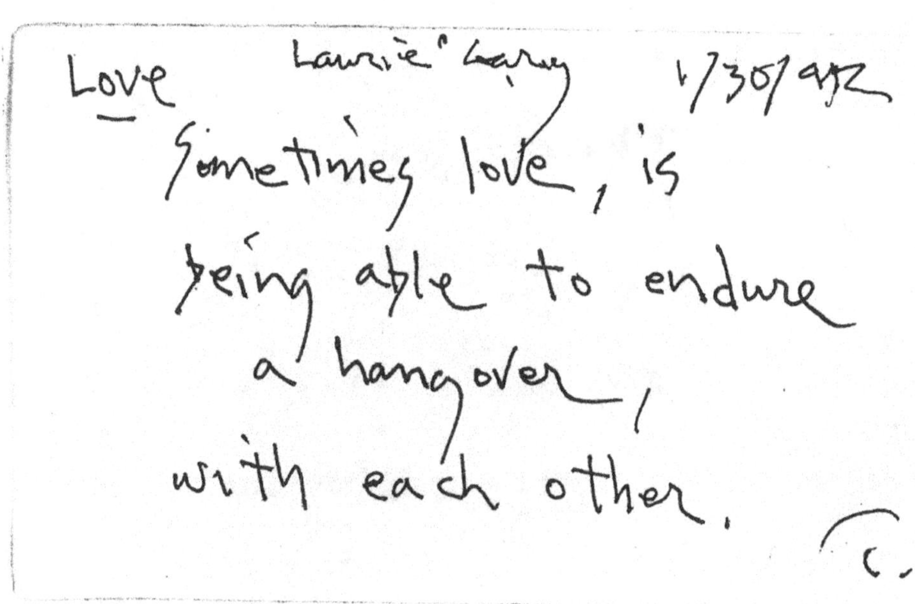

LORI KYLE: Clyde gave me this one [below] after he found out I'd been giving him non-alcohol beer at our house:

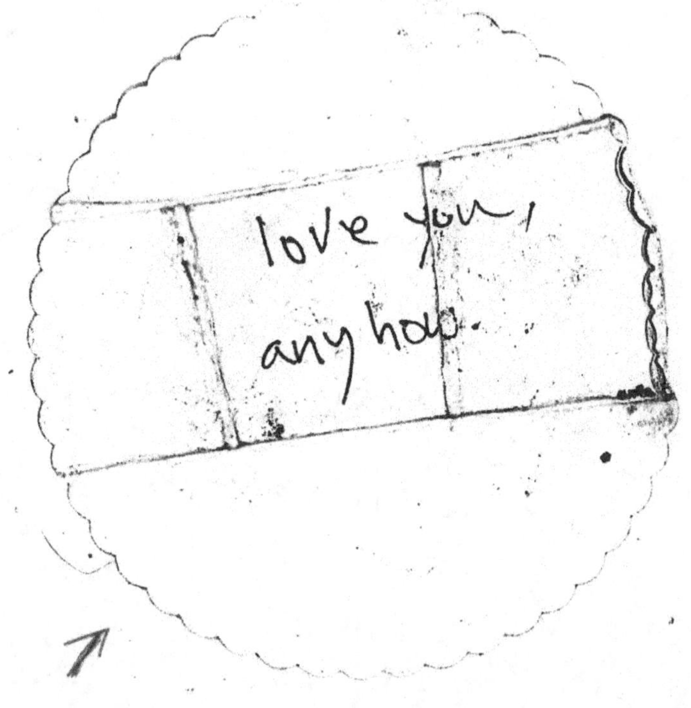

They are
are worried
about me
dancing —

for L.

Standing on her feet.
The universe smells her socks.
The sky goes by with it's eye.
Looking, looking for mirror.

Choice joyce voids,
with gentle violet/blue —
as her tender heart
explores.

for Joyce

As the ink,
due to strength and gravity,
pours out, and the clouds
drift among our legs and minds —
the

Autumn
—
In late fall
if confused,
remember that in the
opposite hemisphere
people are falling in love.. /c.

Clyde's "Autumn" courtesy of Jeff Langlow.

Autumn

The prince of leaves
    turn over, towards
    the princess.

And kisses
    are a
better fate
than wisdom my lady —
    i swear by all the flowers —

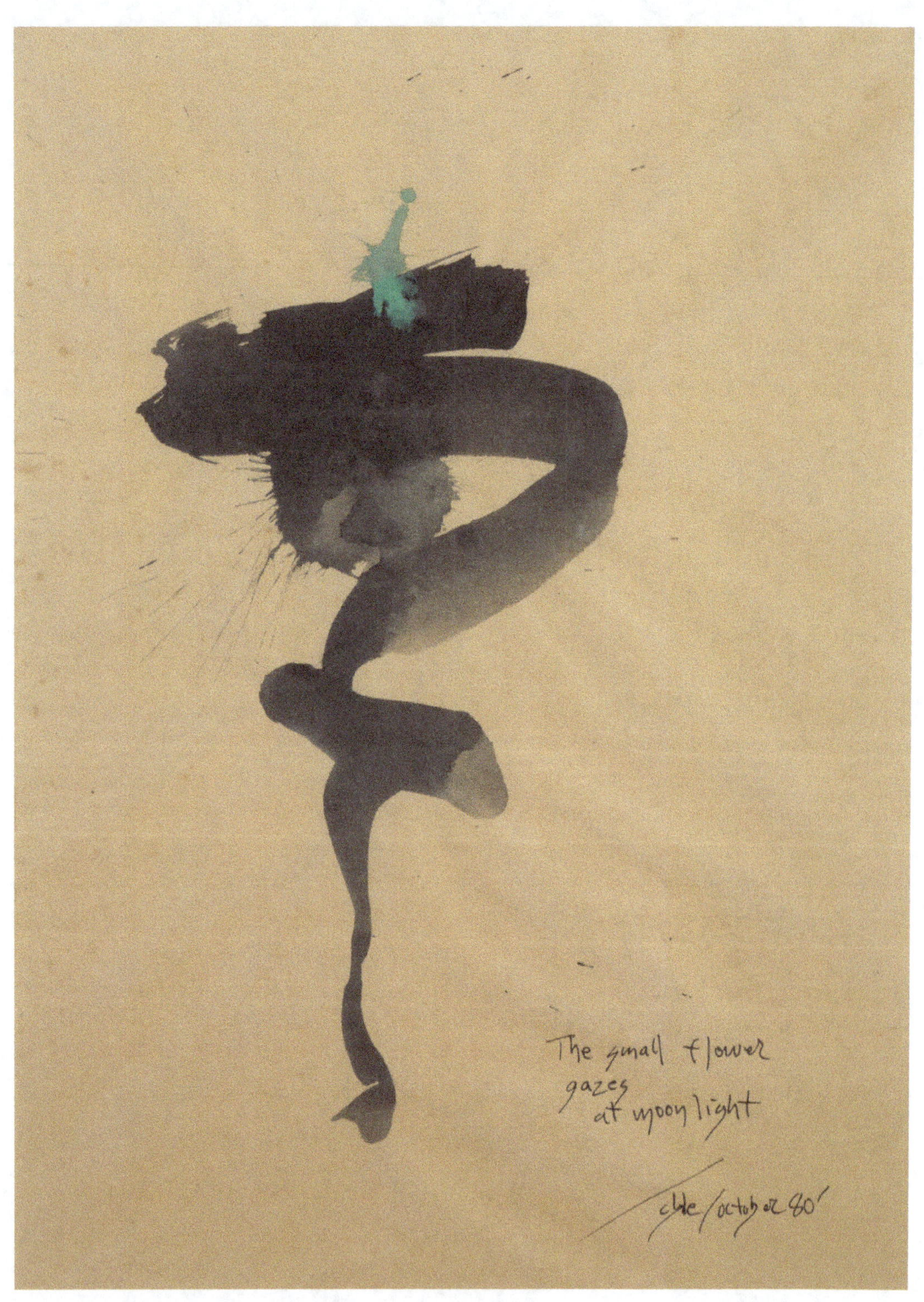
The small flower
gazes
at moonlight

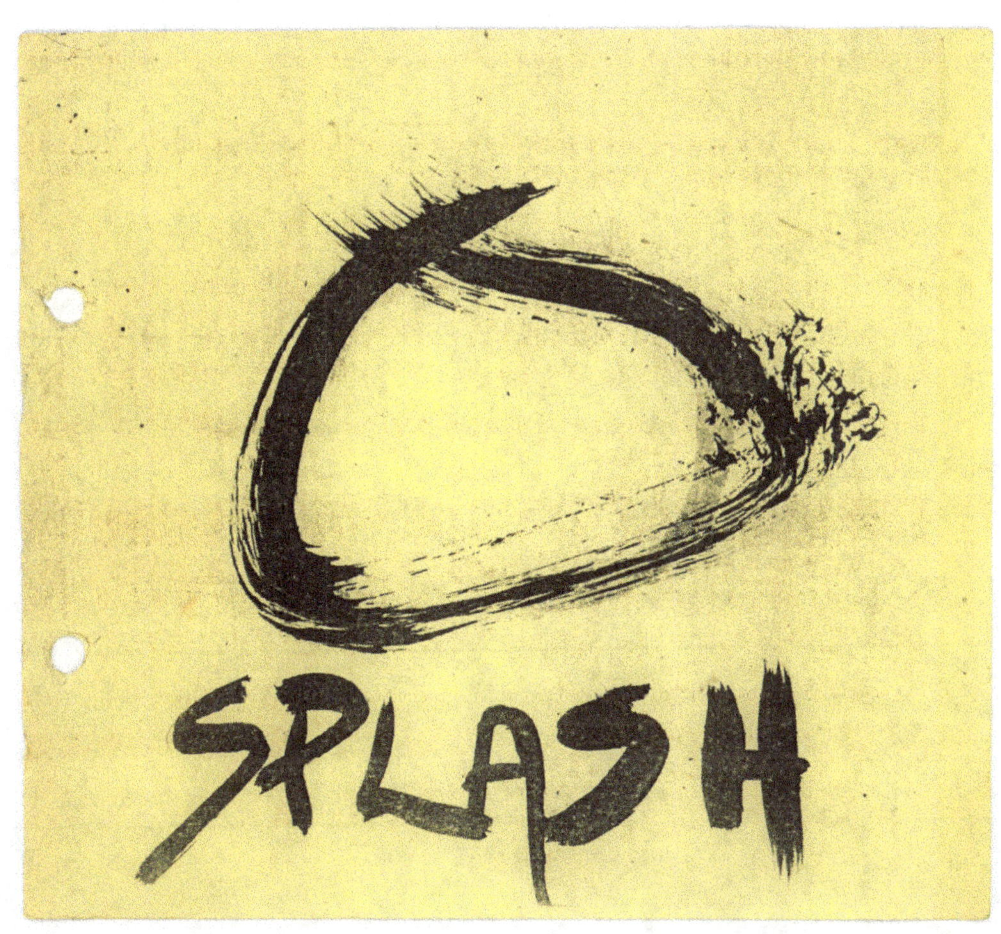

Splash is a little holepunched book that Clyde made in California.
He gave this copy to Janet Saunders:

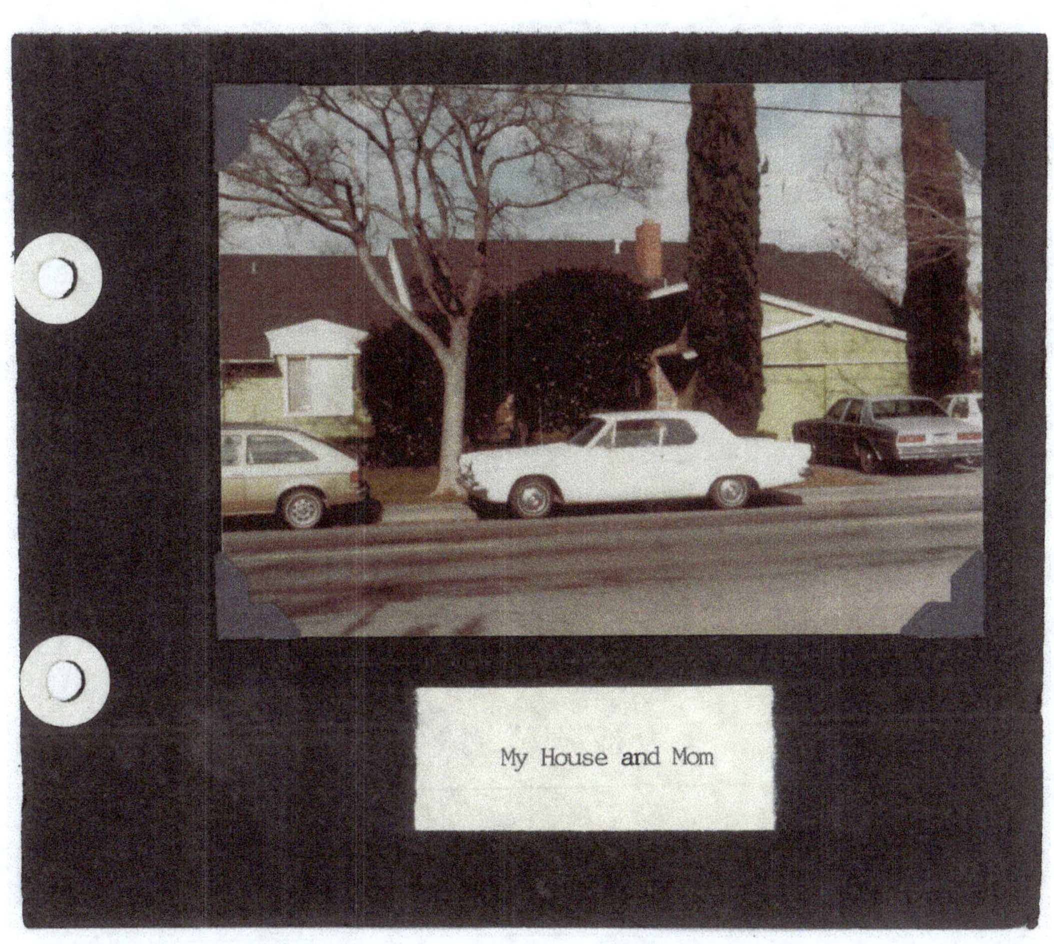

My House and Mom

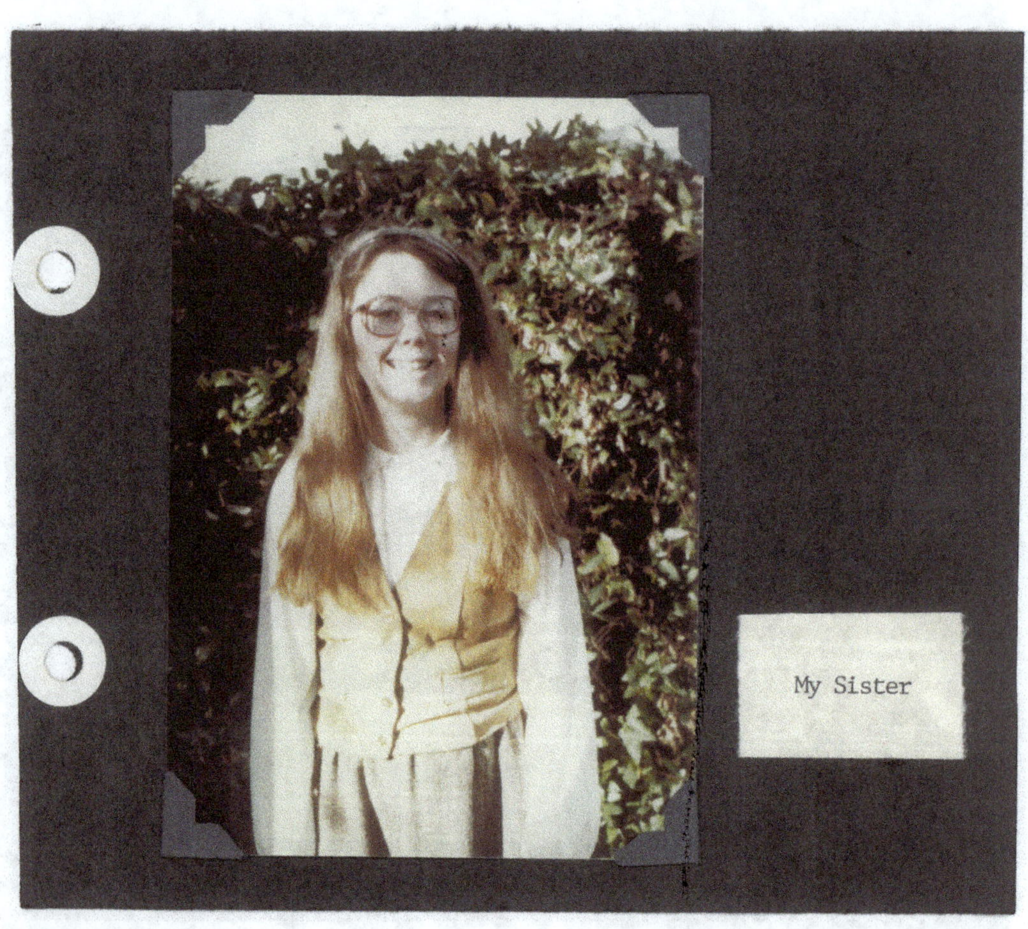

My Sister

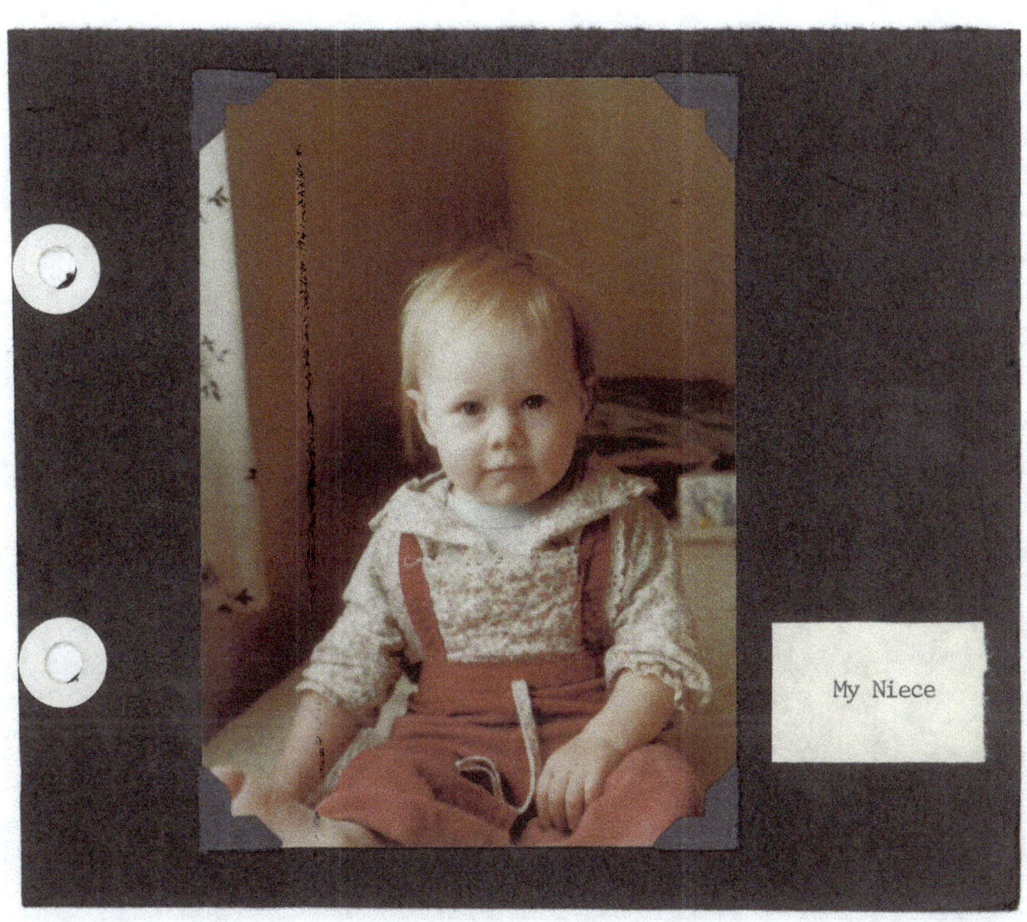

My Niece

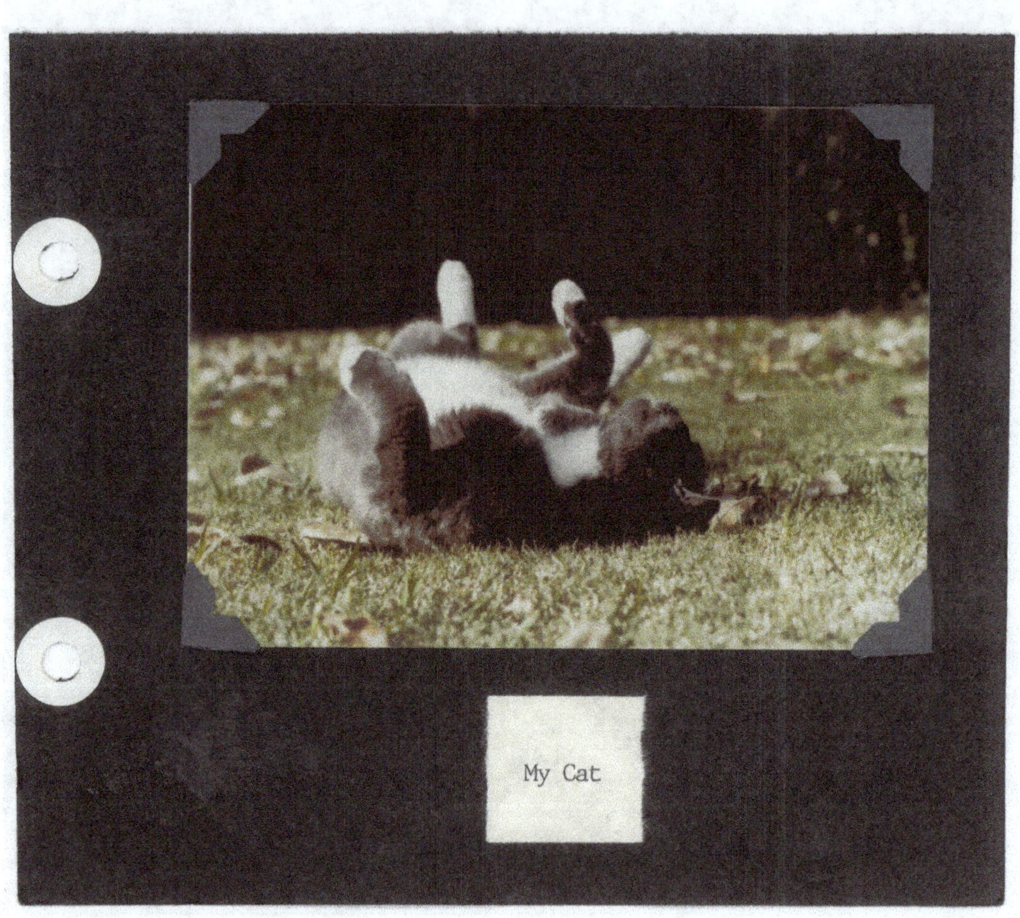

My Cat

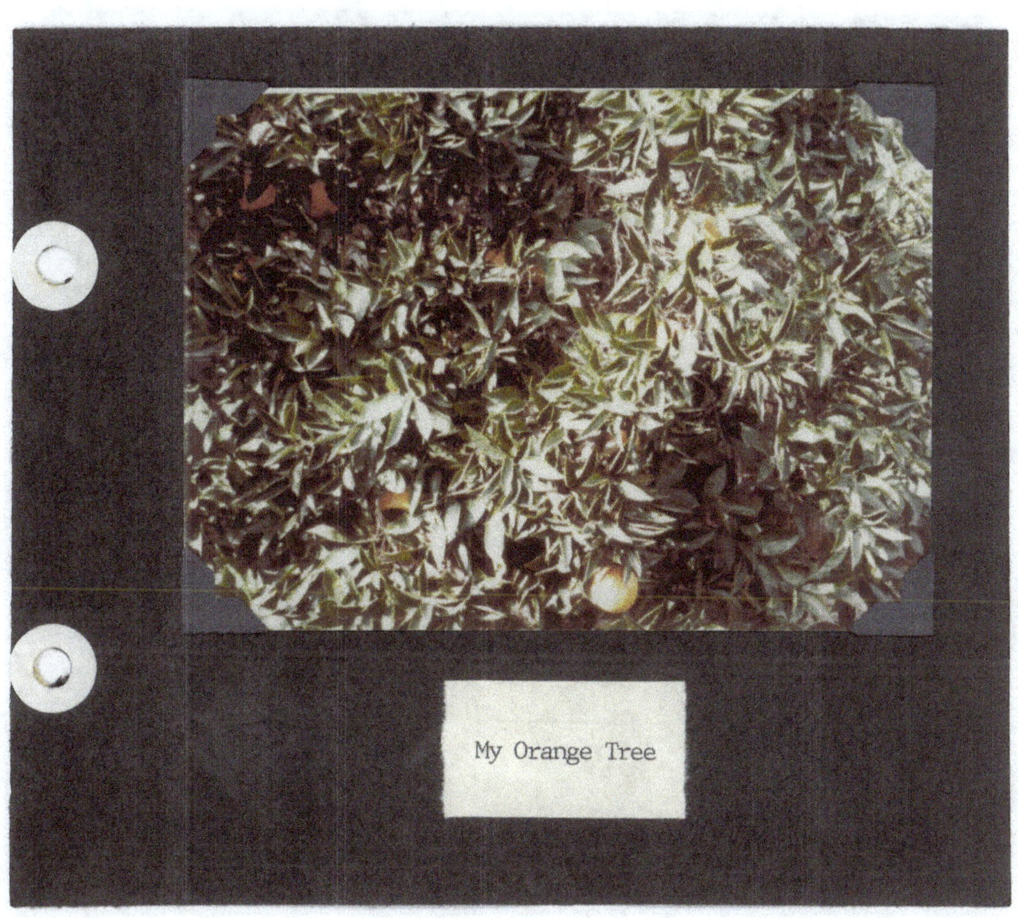

My Orange Tree

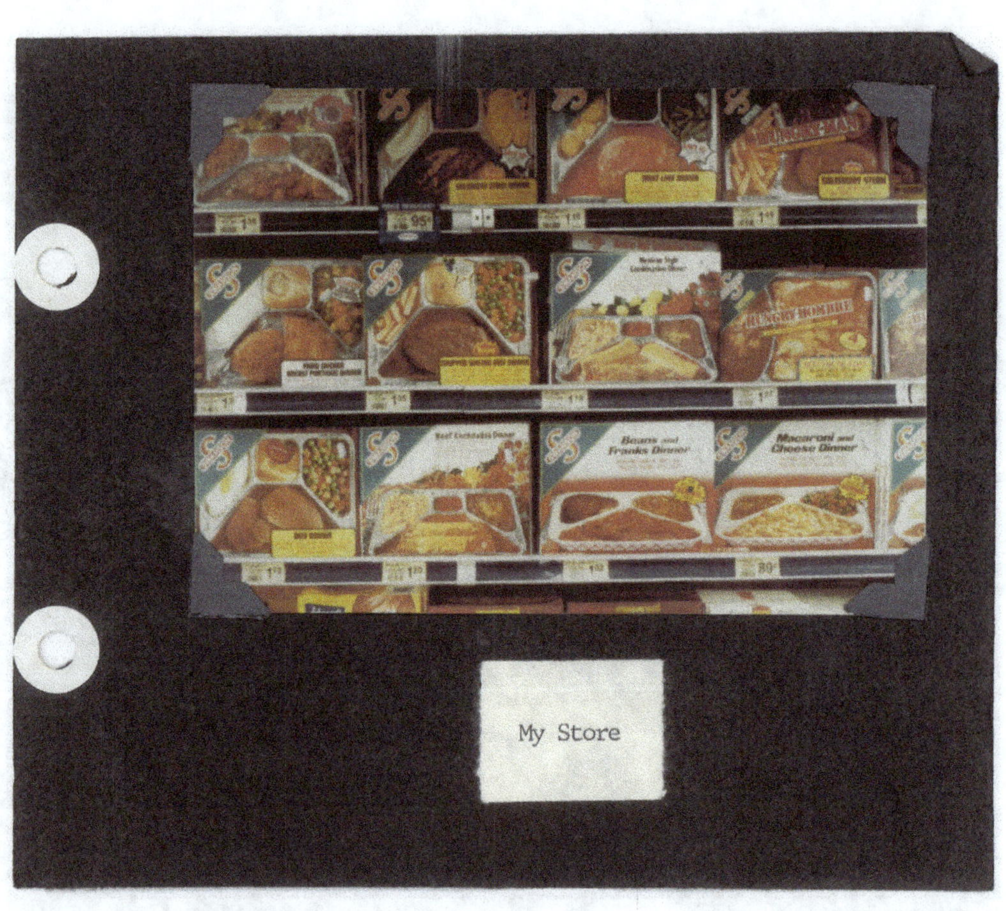

My Store

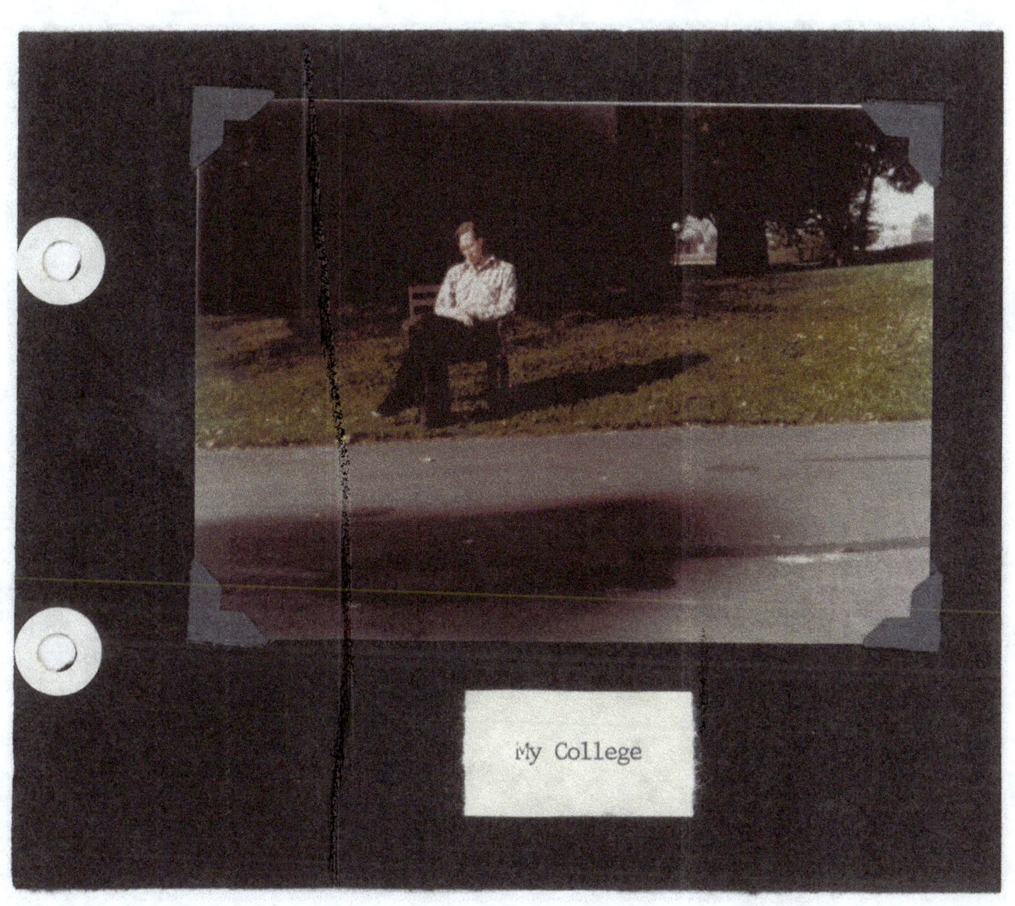
My College

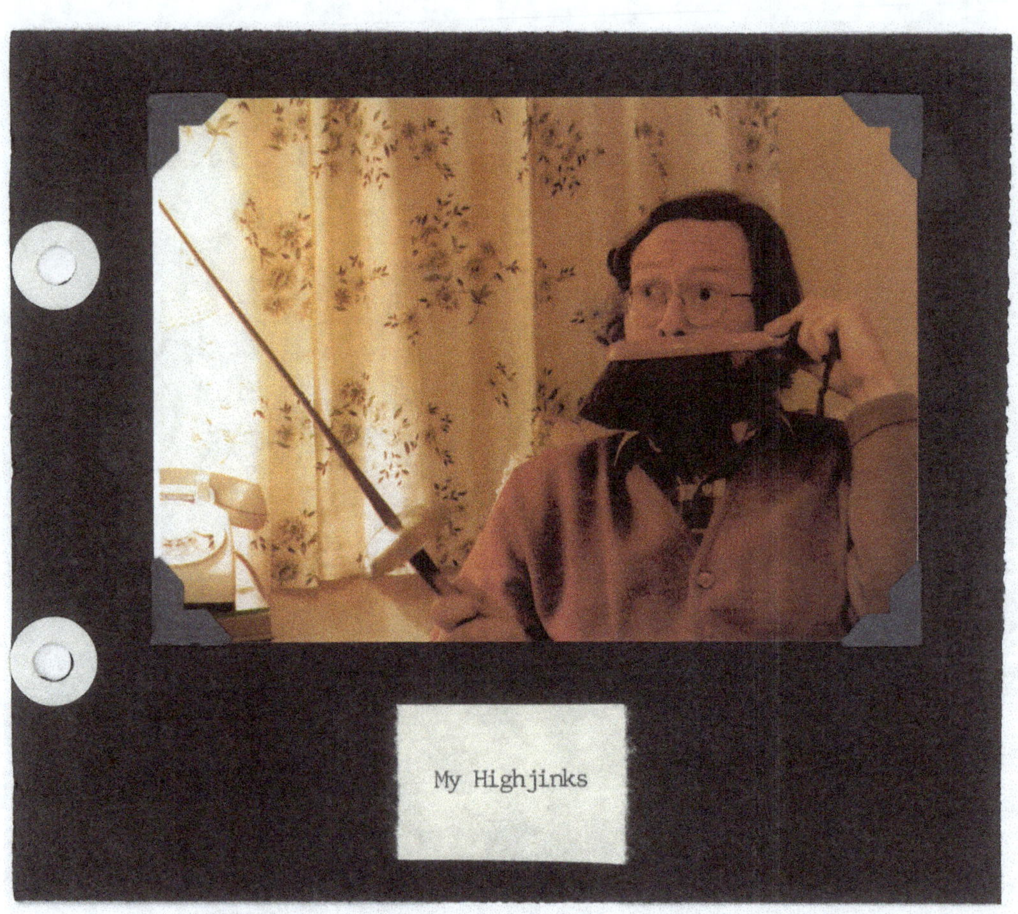

My Highjinks

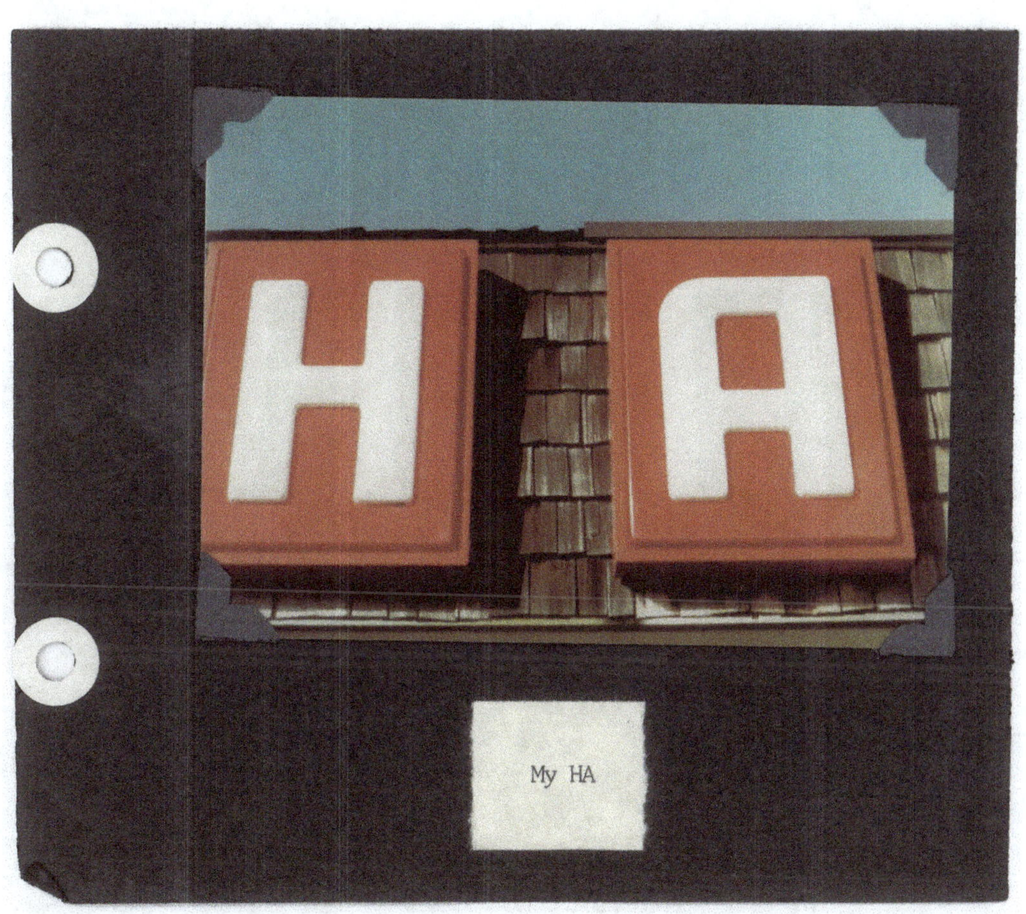

My HA

1981

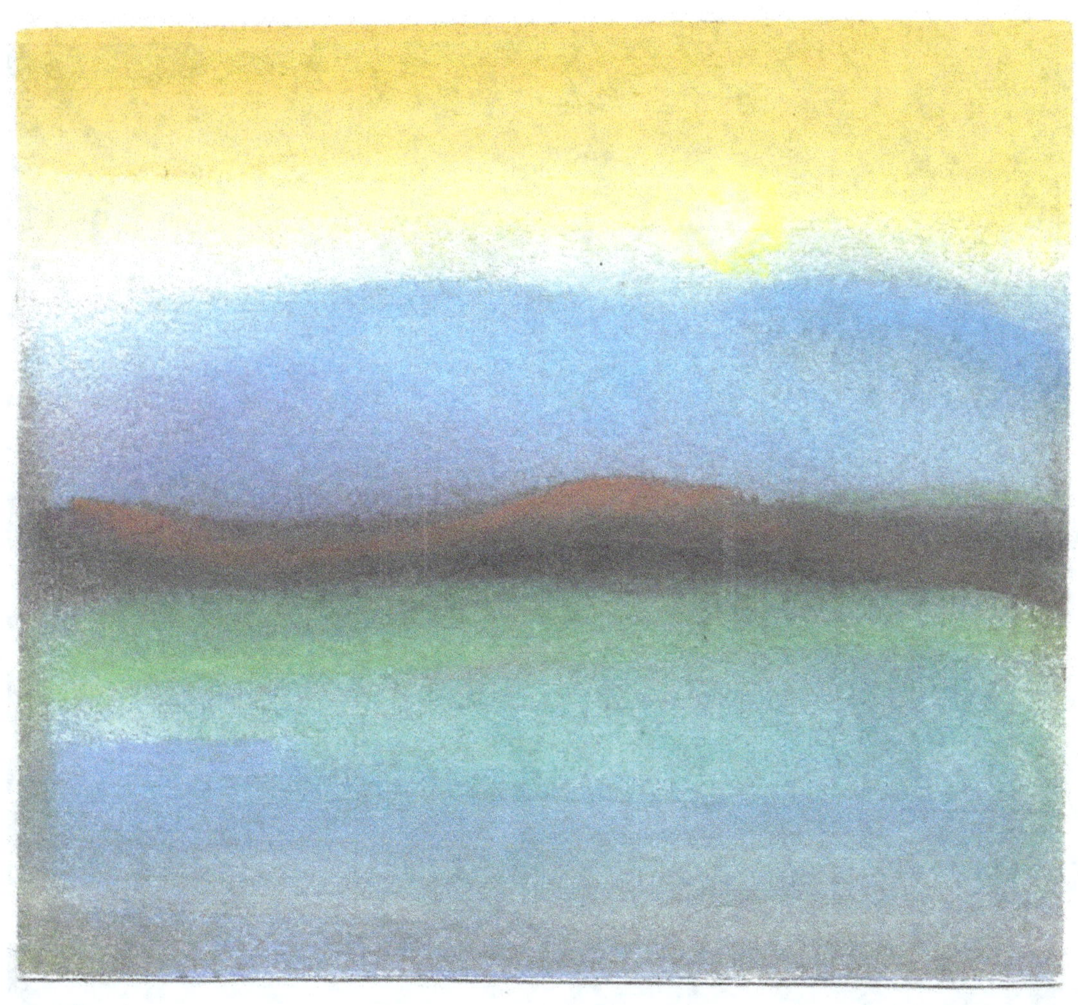

Clyde Sanborn painting, 1981.

JOHN SCHAEFER:

Here is a painting Clyde did while visiting me on the river, while we went through ½ of a 5 gallon plastic container of sake. Clyde has a marvelous time sense—he always appeared when my rose petal wine and blackberry wine were ready for consumption.

for James

I was sitting at Jimmy's
    learning humility,
watching
the fly in mid-air swimming
in the sunshine . . . .
and noticed an
indefinable something about the place.
        what was it ?
the
This place lacks the woman's
touch —
        no curtains,
        on the east window.

for James . . . . . on April Fool's Day
                                        clyde

Poem by CLYDE SANBORN:

For James

I was sitting at Jimmy's
    learning humility,
watching
the fly in mid-air, swimming
in the sunshine…
and noticed an
indefinable something about the place.
    What was it?
Ah!
This place lacks the woman's
touch—
    no curtains,
    on the east window.

For James…one April Fool's Day
82   Clyde

Opposite Page:
Clyde's fading poem framed on the wall in Jimmy Zabik's work shed:
"He was talking about my house on the sandspit, which used to be
his house. That's where it came from."

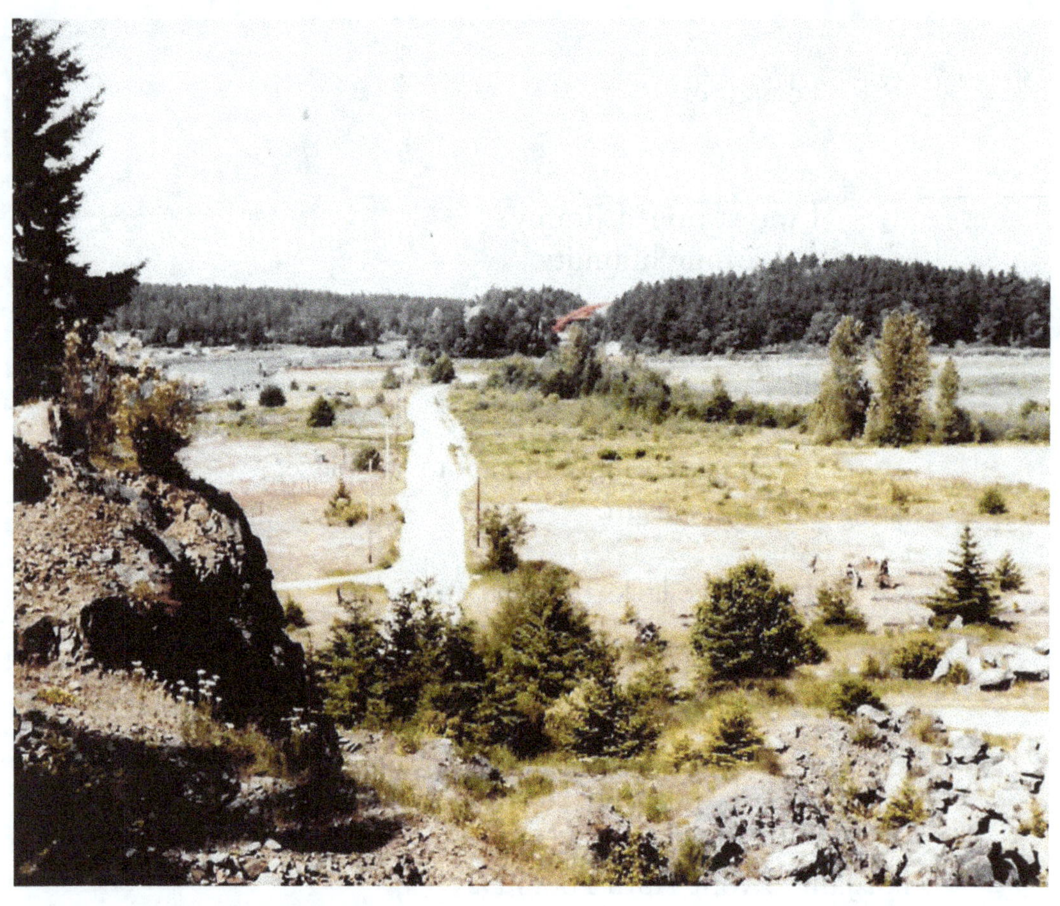

The sandspit, La Conner, Washington. The red Rainbow Bridge is visible at top of photo.

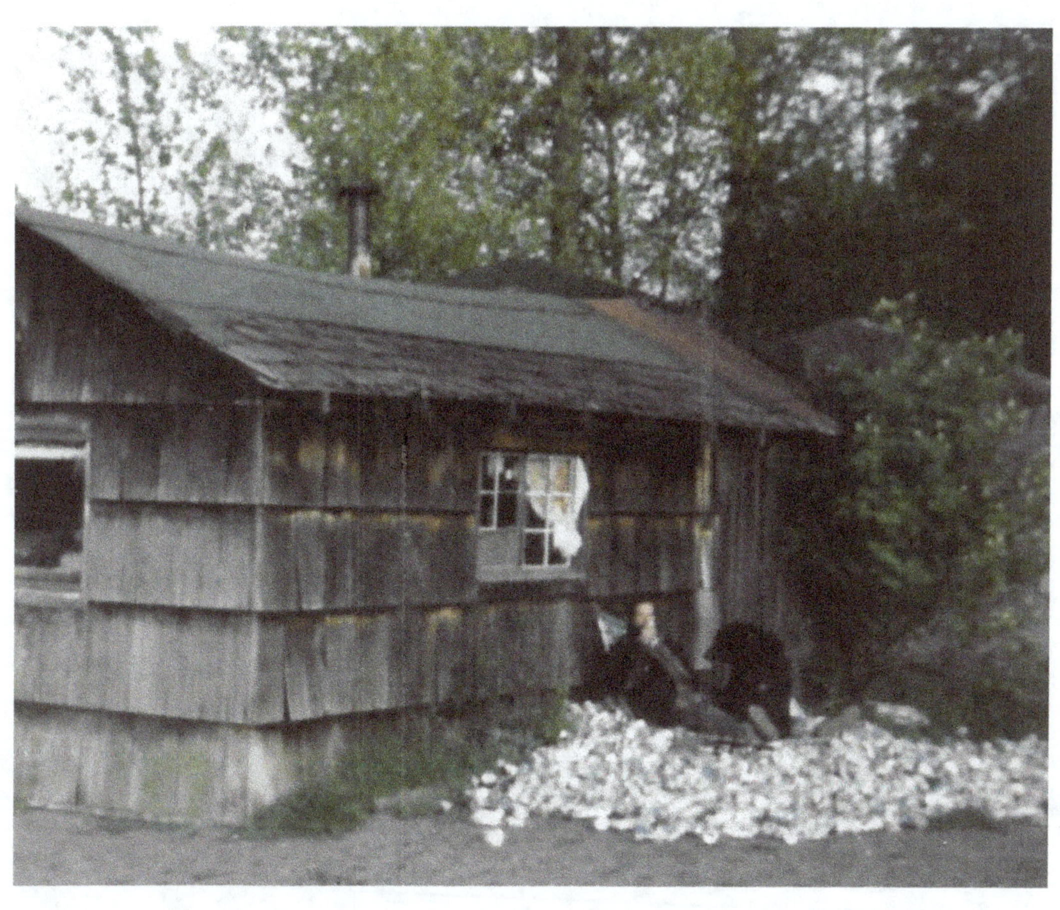

Clyde's shack on the sandspit, with Jimmy Zabik and Zeke and a pile of empty cans.

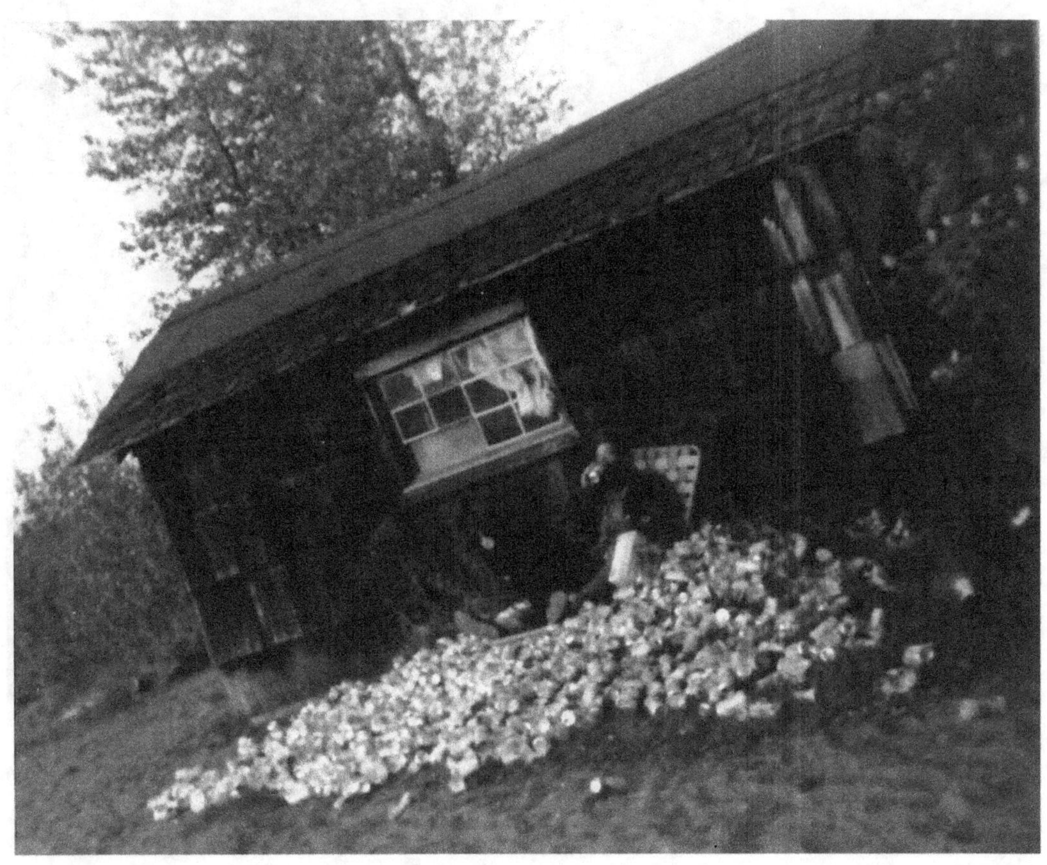

JOANNE ZABIK: One time there was a party and I ran into Bex. Nobody was there so we wandered over to the sandspit to see if the party was at Jimmy's house. And I said, "Where?" and Bex said, "Well, right there." And I said, "Nobody could live there!"

JIMMY ZABIK: I had a pile of beer cans outside my window.

JOANNE ZABIK: So whenever anyone had a beer they'd throw it out the window. All I could see was this mountain of beer cans.

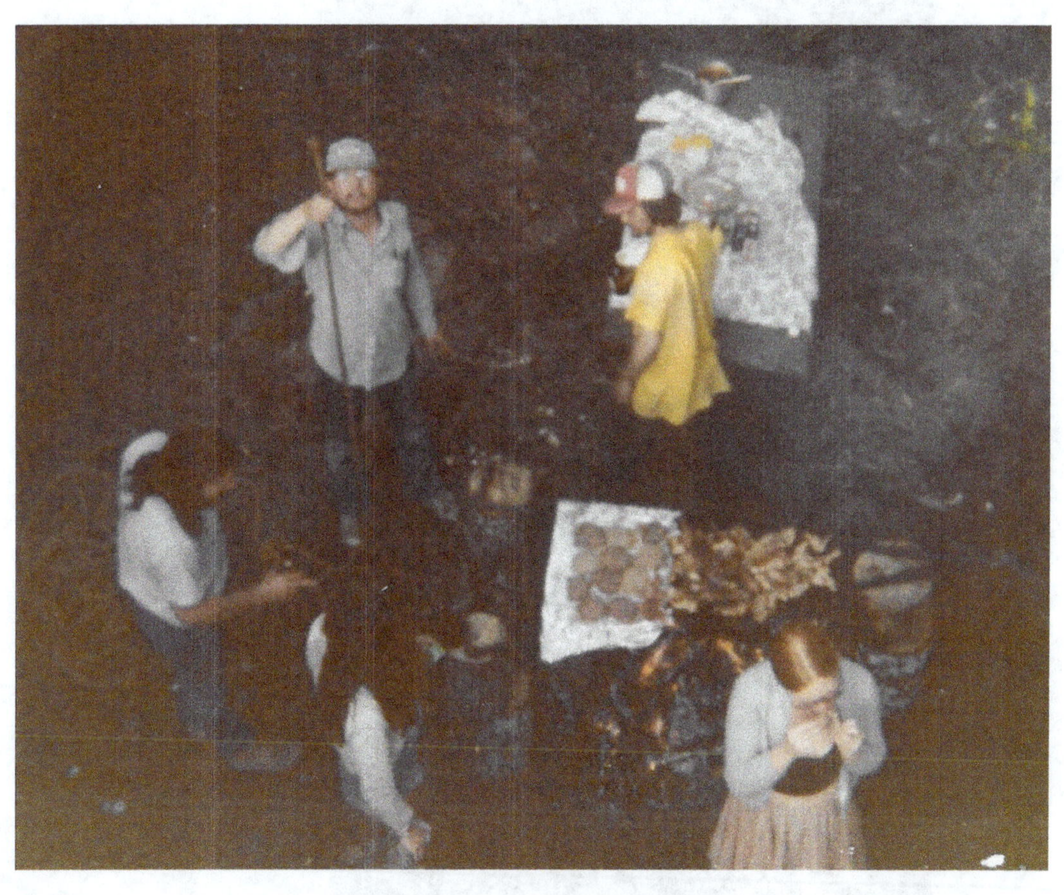

Clyde at cookout, with Jimmy Zabik and friends.

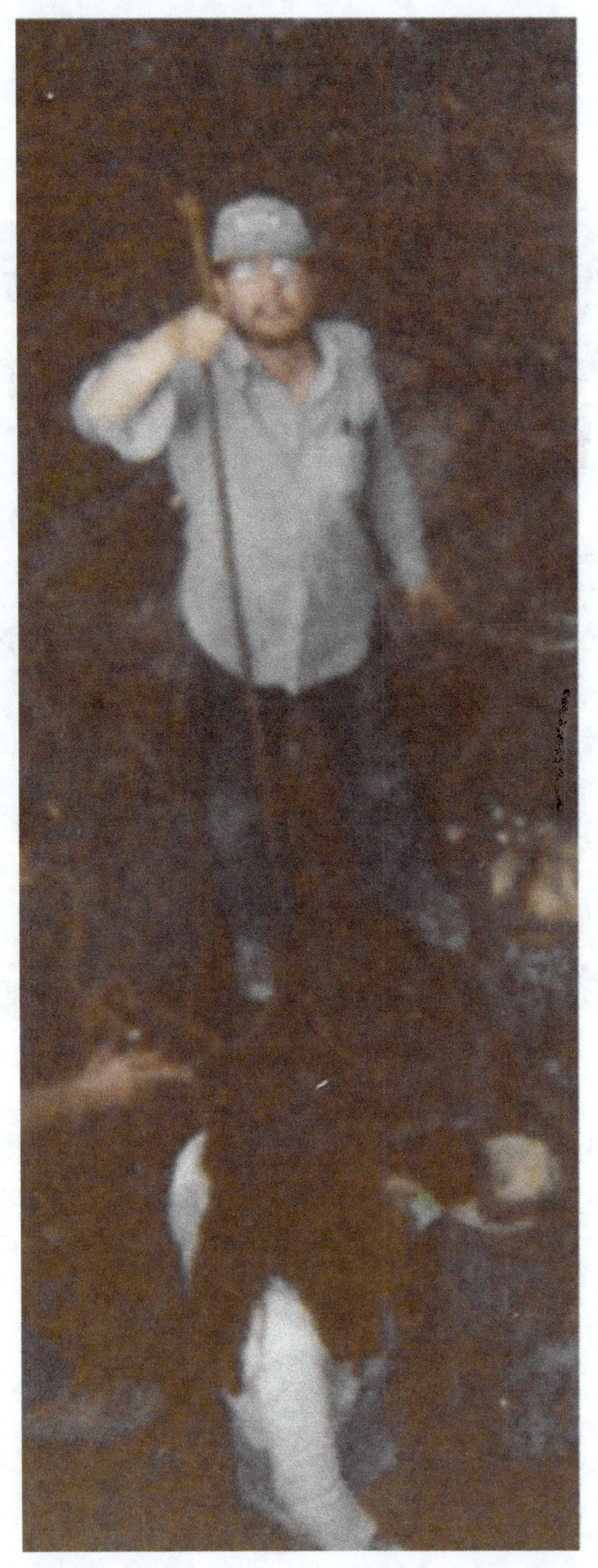

MICHAEL CLOUGH:

Shack: I never ventured out to his Digs, and it's not like he entertained at home. However when living on the Sandspit he did have several relationships with women i.e. girlfriends. At those times I'm sure there were some signs of domesticity.

Otherwise imagine his shacks as pretty spare. Not out of a sense of some Zen minimal code. But how much can you carry around or really need? I think he mostly crashed. On one occasion he moved to Mount Vernon with one of the gals. Got a job at the Unemployment Office, he could be quite domestic. The first thing to do—buy a TV set. I caught him at it.

I think he had occasional urges of "normalcy" usually spurred by having a "relationship." "Normalcy": a home, partner, regular sex, cat, dog, vehicle, a television, a comfortable spot inside a comfortable place. The Clyde side won out.

Back to the shack. I think he always had a guitar and one of those things that go around the neck that hold a harmonica in front of your mouth for his Bob Dylan act.

In the early '70s in Seattle we were also roommates next door neighbors, and sometimes would crash at his places between my travels. Rents were cheap at that time even on a dishwasher's salary. Slightly furnished. Livable basic. He always had the prescribed Bohemian basics. Books, writing materials, a few favored objects, maybe a sketch pad. At times he had some stuff of some smallish monetary value. Always ended up in the pawn shops.

SARAH SANBORN:

I remember him telling me that he did not believe in ambition. Clyde was a Buddhist, and so, no, he did not believe in achieving ambition, and accruing stuff. He would say that if you own too much stuff, then the stuff begins to own you...So true.

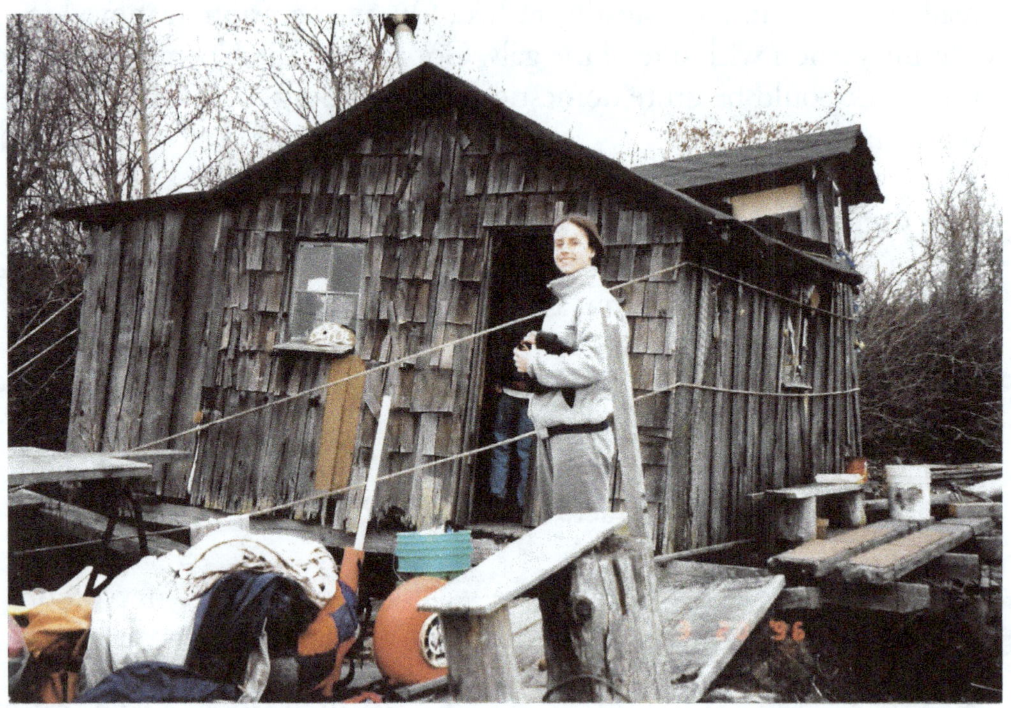

EDITOR: The day after Clyde's memorial, niece Sarah Sanborn traveled by canoe to Clyde's shack where she recovered three of his prized paperbacks, poetry by Theodore Roethke, Alan Watts' study of Zen, and *The Bhagavad Gita*. Clyde's original copies appear on the following pages:

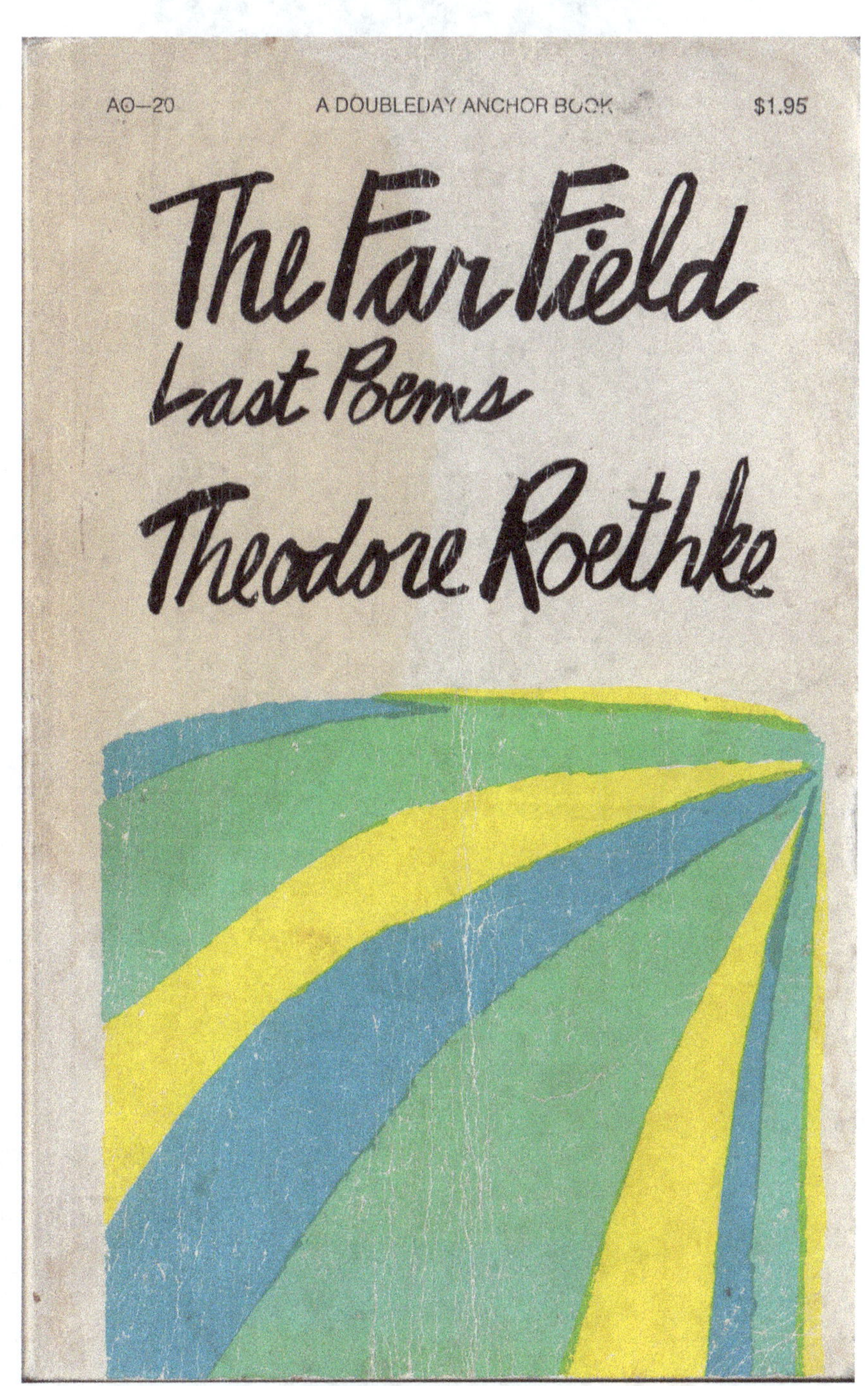

AO—20
A DOUBLEDAY ANCHOR BOOK
$1.95
The Far Field
Last Poems
Theodore Roethke

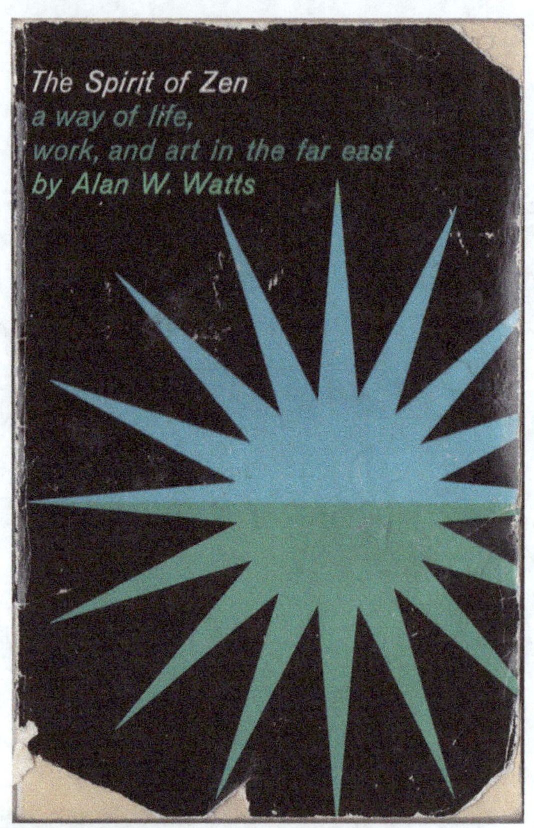

The Spirit of Zen
a way of life,
work, and art in the far east
by Alan W. Watts

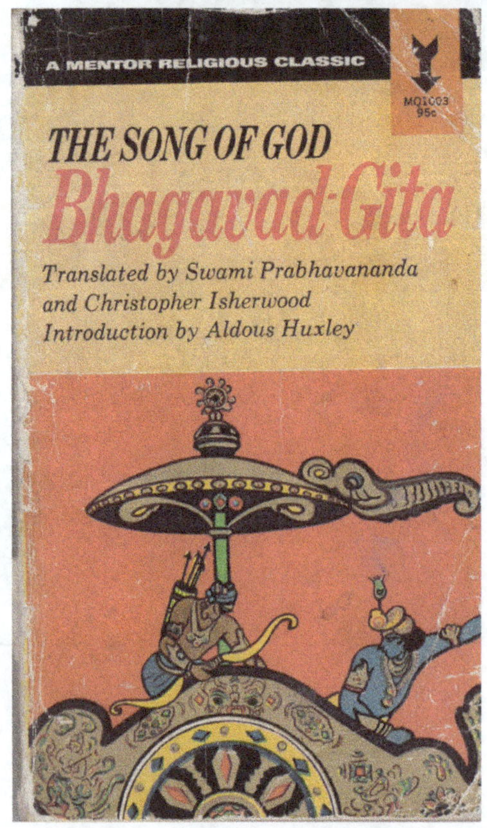

A MENTOR RELIGIOUS CLASSIC
MQ1003
95¢
THE SONG OF GOD
Bhagavad-Gita
Translated by Swami Prabhavananda
and Christopher Isherwood
Introduction by Aldous Huxley

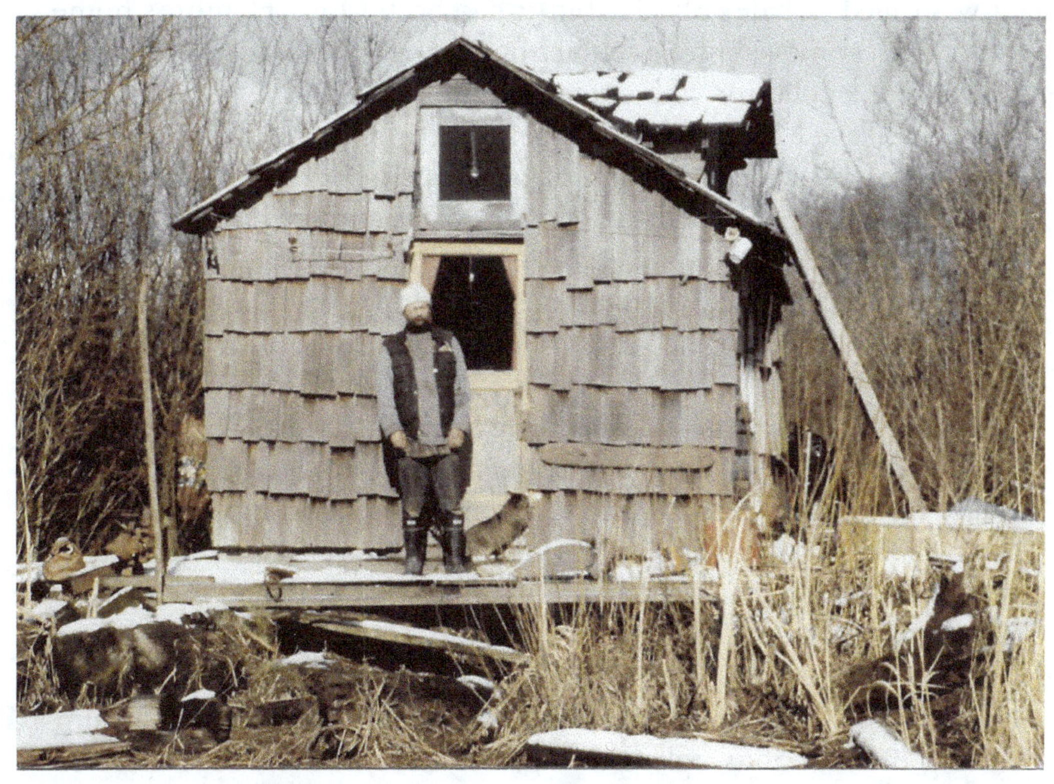

JOANNE ZABIK:

I found a picture of Clyde's house. Ivan Peterson moved in after Clyde left. This is Ivan with his swimming cat, Pushka. Jimmy can't remember a thing about the inside, although he was in there many times. I was in it once when Ivan lived there. It had two rooms, one behind the other.

CHARLIE KRAFFT:

I spent only one night with Clyde in his shack at the Sandspit. It was called "Clyde's Shack," but it had been Oscar Hambre's home before Oscar moved into a rental house in town. He was an old Norwegian junk collector who operated a junk store in the lower level of the Pike Place Market in Seattle before retiring to La Conner where he was forever collecting parts of old boats he planned to assemble someday into one shipworthy enough to get him to Alaska.

After Oscar passed away at age 75, a hippy named Lyle moved into Oscar's shack on the sandspit. I don't remember Lyle's last name today. He was a peripheral in my life there. Clyde moved into what had become "Lyle's Shack" after Lyle moved to Sedro Wooley. John Schaefer brought Clyde to La Conner from Seattle with his cat because he'd lost his Capitol Hill apartment after missing a couple of month's rent. He was jobless and couldn't afford another. John told Clyde about the shack outside La Conner that Lyle had vacated, so Clyde moved in.

The only thing I remember about that night with Clyde was him telling me to, "Shut up!" The sugar content in the beer I liked to drink jacked me up so much I could never sleep. When I was on a bender, something I could usually count on Clyde to accompany me on, I'd just keep nattering away to anyone who was around, and that night it upset Clyde so much he told me to get along home when dawn broke. We'd been drinking all day and late into the night. He wanted to sleep and I wouldn't let him.

His shack was a fairly basic uninsulated 2 x 4 shingled clapboard affair with a flat tarpaper roof. Unlike Robert Sund and Guy Anderson who always turned their mean hovels into idiosyncratic museum-like collections of interesting art and found objects, the inside of Clyde's shack was fairly raw. There were a couple of paned windows, a cooking woodstove, a bed, a table and a kerosene lantern or two. Quite possibly he had an unframed poem, or a drawing pinned to the wall, but the place was no "shackteau" like some of the refurbished gillnetter's cabins up river.

I never spent the night at Clyde's again though we spent many other days sitting in the town's taverns, or outside in the summer on one of two public wooden staircases in La Conner drinking wine and watching the world go by.

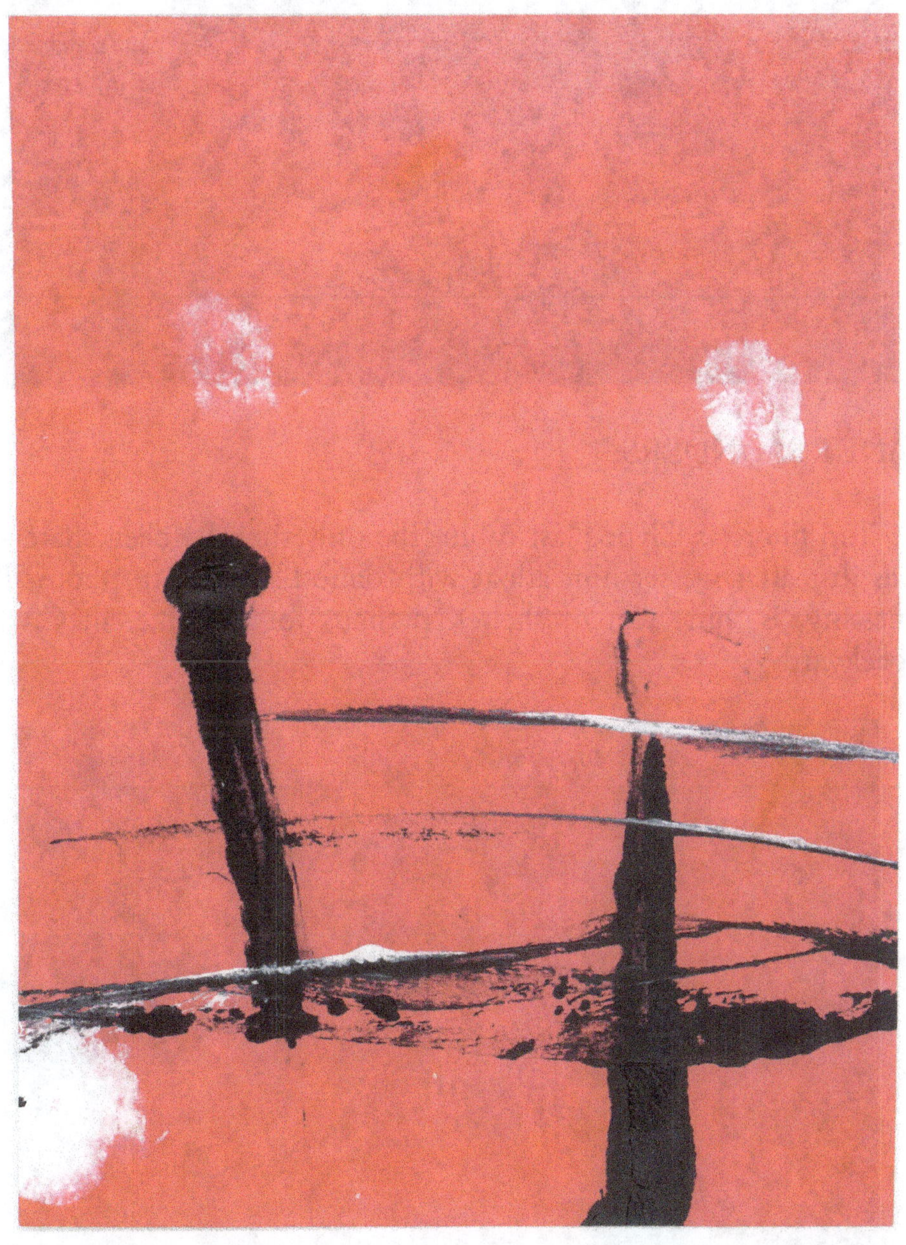

Clyde painting.

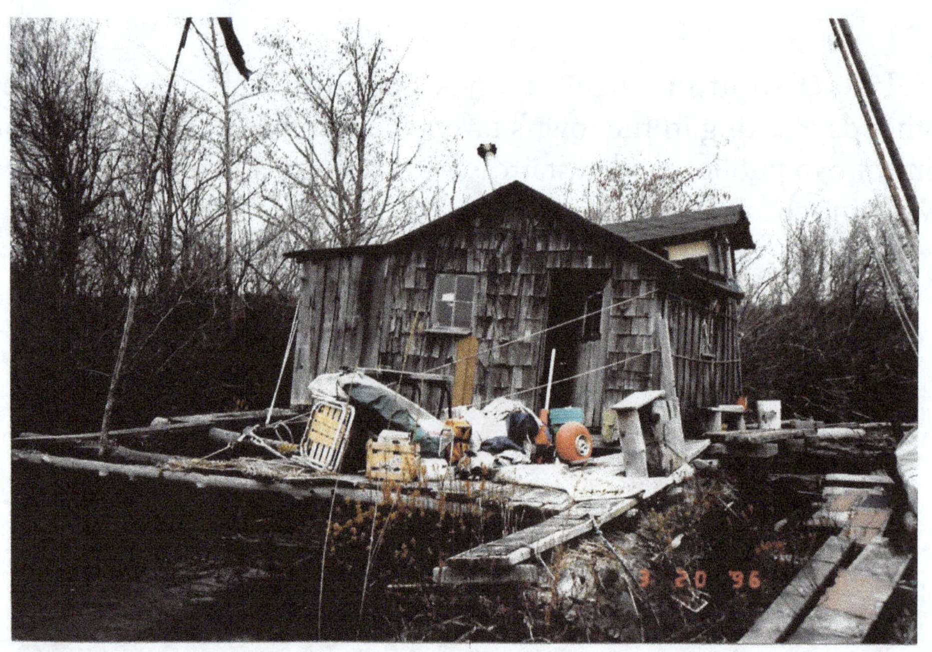

JANET SAUNDERS:

Top photo is Clyde's last cabin, the only time I'd been there—it was just after we set him afloat with daffodils. Bottom photo, I'm guessing, is some sort of shelter, perhaps for his bike, in Clyde's "backyard."

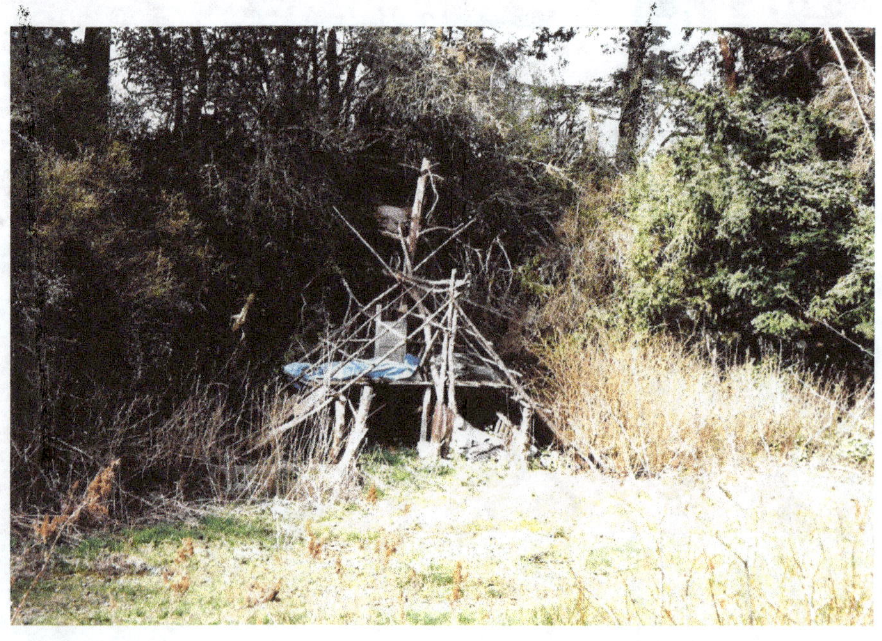

MICHAEL CLOUGH:

Clyde was not one for small talk, like talking about the weather. I do remember him mentioning the weather once. He said, "Hell isn't Hot. Hell is Cold! Cold, Cold!" I think he may have had some experience with that.

Want Ad: For Rent

Nice, newer, new or modern 2 bedroom mobile home. All electric. New near malls. Near busline. Far from fear. In court. 485./monthly. References required. Note from mom. All cement, no sun, stars or wind. Floral carport. Drinking pets, smoking children only. No people need apply.

P.S. First 3mos. cleaning deposit. 2 mos dirty deposit. Deposit on the deposit! 35.00. Dep. on the dep. dep, no extra charge ~~deposit dep~~. Teflon bib for rude volcanoes.

Clyde's "Want Ad: For Rent" courtesy of Jan Sanborn.

CHRISTINE WARDENBURG-SKINNER:

My first memory of Clyde was in 1983, sitting in the back seat of my VW van and staring at me in the rear view mirror. New to the Skagit Valley, I was being shown around by his good friend John Schaefer, painter, dweller then on the South Fork of the Skagit River, and Clyde's good friend. A new woman in the Valley was of great interest to Clyde, especially if a friend of John. John and Clyde reminded me of the *Cold Mountain* poets, Han-Shan and Shih-te. Clyde's take on the world, like the fabled Han-Shan, was of the transience nature of life; his was a true Buddhist-nature.

Over the following twenty-some years, Clyde was usually at whatever event was happening. I participated in a writer's group in La Conner in the 80's, held in the evenings in a room under the old Black Swan Restaurant on 1st Street. Of course, Clyde was a poet, and an excellent one, so he was always there. A woman participant was a burgeoning travel writer and frequently contributed. Clyde was not fond of her writing and constantly criticized her efforts, baiting her might be a better term. One evening she got so angry at him that she stormed out of the room and slammed the plate glass front door so hard we all feared it would shatter. He did not harbor fools, and when writing was concerned, she unfortunately fell into the Clyde bin of dismissives. My memory is that he too was 86'd after that display.

Clyde could be very funny with his owl-like wisdom and observances of life around him, wry and quick. Of course he was well-known as the town drunk, arriving wherever on his bike or getting a ride with a friend. My husband and I, for years, have hosted a Winter Solstice gathering. It became a kind of "go-to" holiday event, and Clyde, of course, was a regular. One night when the party was surging, counters heavy with wine, table laden with potluck dishes, conversation going a mile-a-minute, Clyde climbed up on a chair and with a silver knife banged his glass calling for attention. Slowly, the room settled into complete silence, at which point Clyde got down and went about his business. He was still there in the morning, draining half-filled glasses.

In addition to John, Clyde had three very good friends, Jim Smith, Michael Clough, and Ruth. Jim was a kind of laid-back saint who embraced the outlier, always and without question. Michael knew Clyde in the Navy and it was he who brought him to the Skagit Valley. Ruth is an artist, scholar, and wanderer who lived in La Conner for many years and became Clyde's "girlfriend," despite being many years his senior. They were a fabled couple.

My time with and knowledge of Clyde was intermittent and very partial. But we shared moments; holding hands, sitting on the floor at one of the early "Dada-like" events at the Edison Eye, the Skagit Valley's early and marvelous art gallery, listening to poets read and music play; wrapped in Clyde's old army jacket as the late night grew chill on a summer solstice gathering on Bald Island, laughing, comfortable in our company. In hindsight, true, small gifts of time and being.

These lines from a Red Pine translation of one of the *Cold Mountain* poems fit Clyde perfectly:

> Relax in the village square
> before the sky, everything's empty.
> No direction is better or worse,
> East just as good as West.
> Those who know the meaning of this
> are free to go where they want.

dear Jan   April 22, 1981

i can see now the Christ spirit coming into
the world. I guess i get hung up on the words
too much. It's just that Lord Jesus has been
so (his name) misused and abused. Jesus got
plugged into the "christ consciousness." But other
folks have too. I think i can feel the manifestation
of the Christ. It' sorta like comin' in to balance
out all the "bad" stuff. A little love can do
wonders for a lot of hate.

I got a big chunk off my ego, for my birthday. Linda
and i just went through a hard place. It looks
as though we'll be going our own seperate paths, soon.
And it was really hard cutting that attachment to
her loose. But we both came out the better for it.
For now it's for us walk around seperately, in
the body, but together in the Spirit. Comprande
sisterino? Si. I guess i'll just stay in my truck
(camper in the back) for now, an' see what
manifests.
Keep centered, walk in light, be here now, stay open,
let yer light shine and keep your sense of humor.
That photo of Bethany made me feel - wow!. Looks
like a sharp kid to me.
                    love to you and Bethany
                         and the world — clyde

P.S. If you want to know anything
about airbore carburetors, let me know.

P.P.S Jan, what's your last name?

JAN SANBORN: A letter from Clyde in 1981: We often discussed,
religion, spirituality, metaphysics, and philosophy. They were always
the 'topics du jour.'

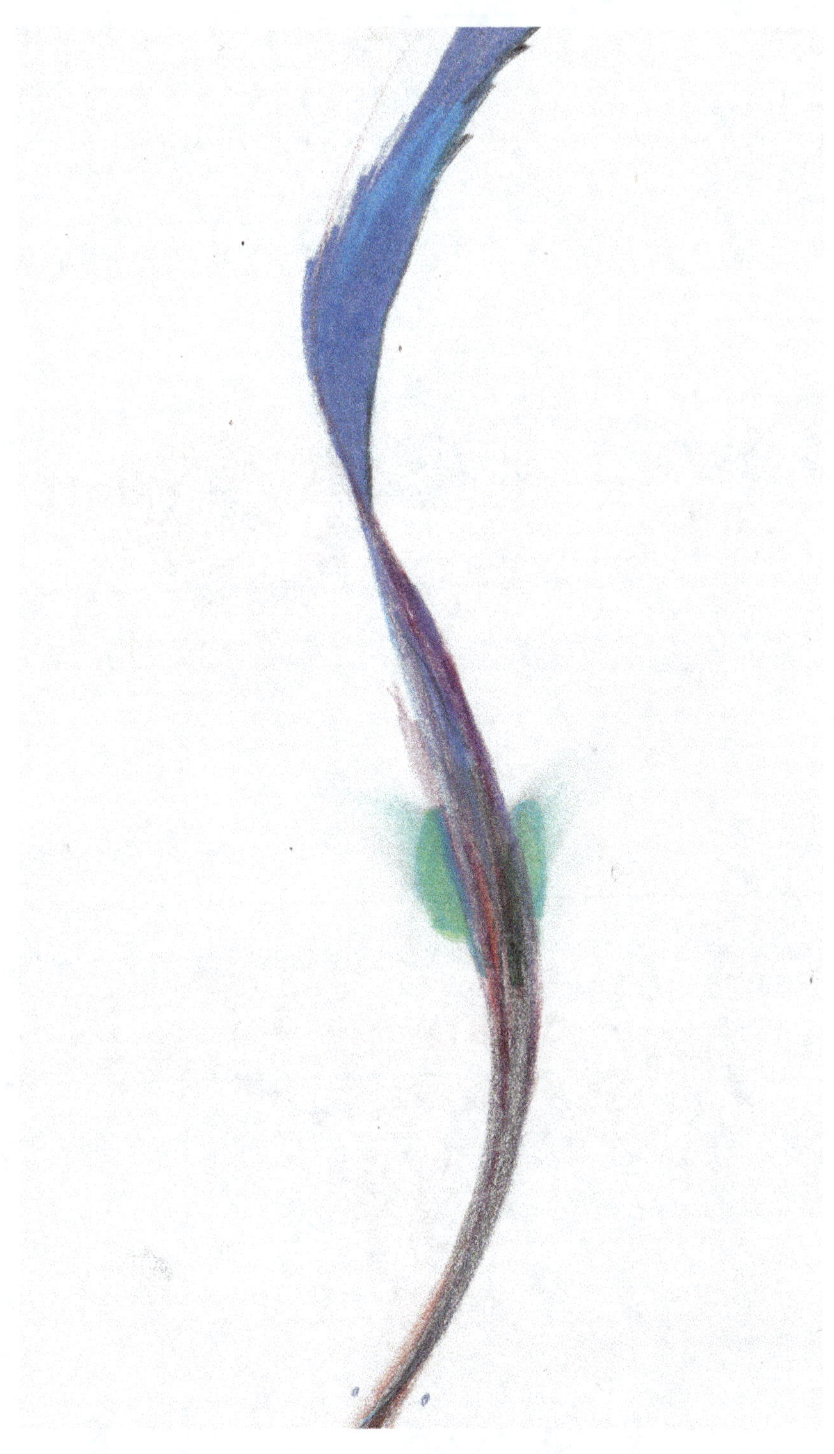

Card [cover] from Clyde to Sarah Sanborn--turn for inside:

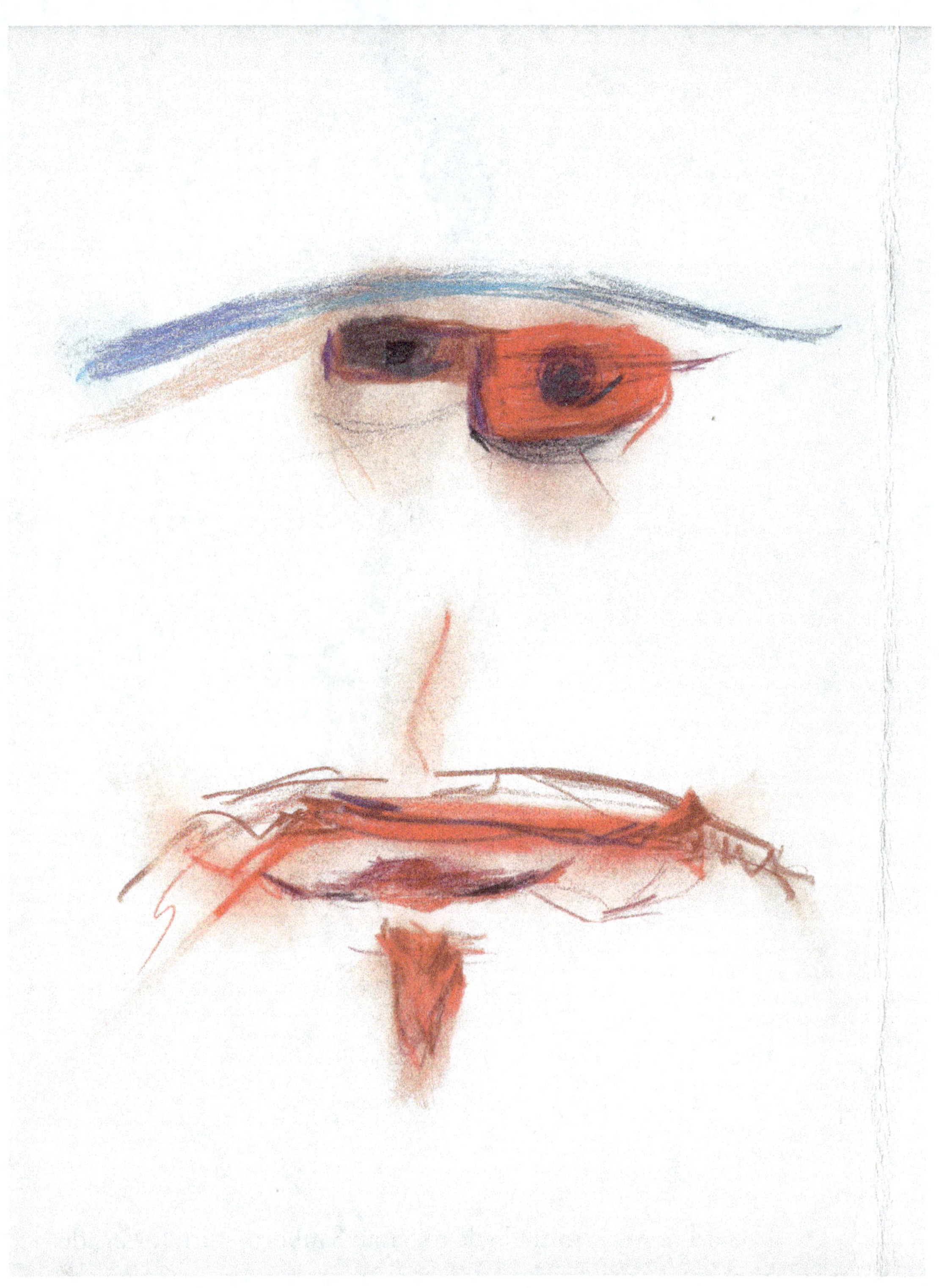

MICHAEL CLOUGH:
(Written to Editor during Skagit tropical storm, October 14-16, 2016)

Finally ready. Got firewood in. Last two days getting boat and motor in shape just in time. The wind and tide blew in close this afternoon so got stuff off the floor. The last two years got water. Winds tide barometer. Never this early Climate Change? Got very wet floor. Not that time of year should not have that. Don't think I will. But I want to thank you. Gives me something to do. I am 83.4 percent or so alone, have been for years. And writing this Clyde stuff maybe because I'm with myself so much I've told stories to myself so I remember and is good to share. Storm's exciting. Don't have to worry about losing power so I'll remember stuff and tap and always paintings to work on and I hope my floor doesn't get wet. Later
Sent from my iPhone

High tide going out. Big wind yet to come. Life on the river. High tide in morning if conditions met makes problems. Not life changing but about a foot of grace which seems to be shifting with climate changing. I should and might jack up again. But probably won't get wet on this one. So I'm awaiting the wind. So enough about me.

So return to Clyde.

So another possible title

SO! a word that Clyde was fond of.

SO go with the Flow or just So or just go with the flow or whatever SO!

Where was I?

I left Seattle to La Conner.

Fishtown didn't work, so La Conner. John Schaefer came. La Conner was a really exceptional place made so by pioneering artists Morris Graves, Guy Anderson, Charlie Krafft, Tom Robbins, Robert Sund, a bunch of hippies and Rock and Roll at the 1890's tavern. So. It's a quarter to 9 I can hear the big wind, but it's around the bends not shaking the cabin. So I will continue later after the storm.

Later M
Sent from my iPhone

The big wind missed.

So. I don't mean to say Clyde said So a lot. It was more a poem. SO. Nothing more. Not as a question So? Not as an addition. Not as a pronoun. Maybe a verb. Maybe all. Only So. Then silence.

A one word poem.

Sarah Dancer

—

... so she decided to dance.
  she would sit by trees
    for hours watching the
  wind move the leaves — and
cats, when they pranced, and birds
    as turned in the air.
  yes: to move, to move all around.

SARAH SANBORN:

He wrote "Sarah Dancer" for me in 1991 during a visit when he was housesitting Gwen and Oz's place—I think in June or July. He drove up to Kenwood (grudgingly—he hated traffic and freeways!) and stayed for a few days. He sat at the kitchen counter for about 3 hours and ripped this one out as well as the poem "To Roger (from Deanna)" [page 36] He was so sentimental…

MICHAEL CLOUGH:

One of Clyde's claim to fame and high point of his life was he got to sit in the driver's seat of Further, the driver's seat where the madman Neal Cassady drove the Merry Pranksters on their epic trip. It was retired on some property of a Navy buddy of his.

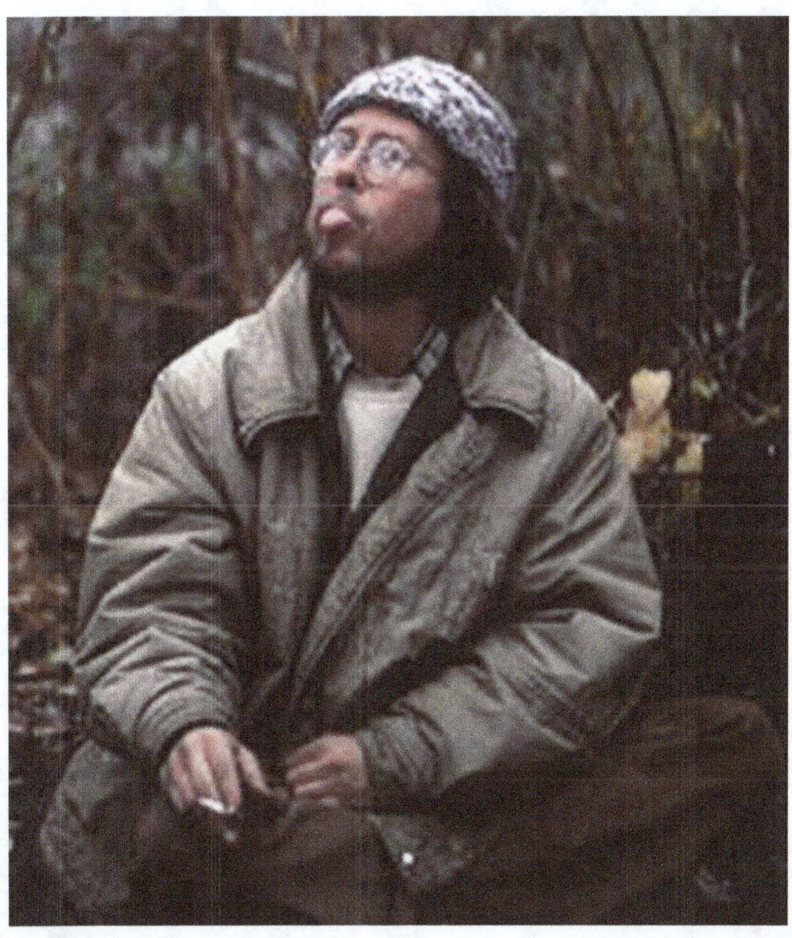

Monk: Why did the Bodhidarma,
go to China?

Master: Ask that post over there.

Monk: I don't understand you.

Master: Niether do i, anymore
than you.

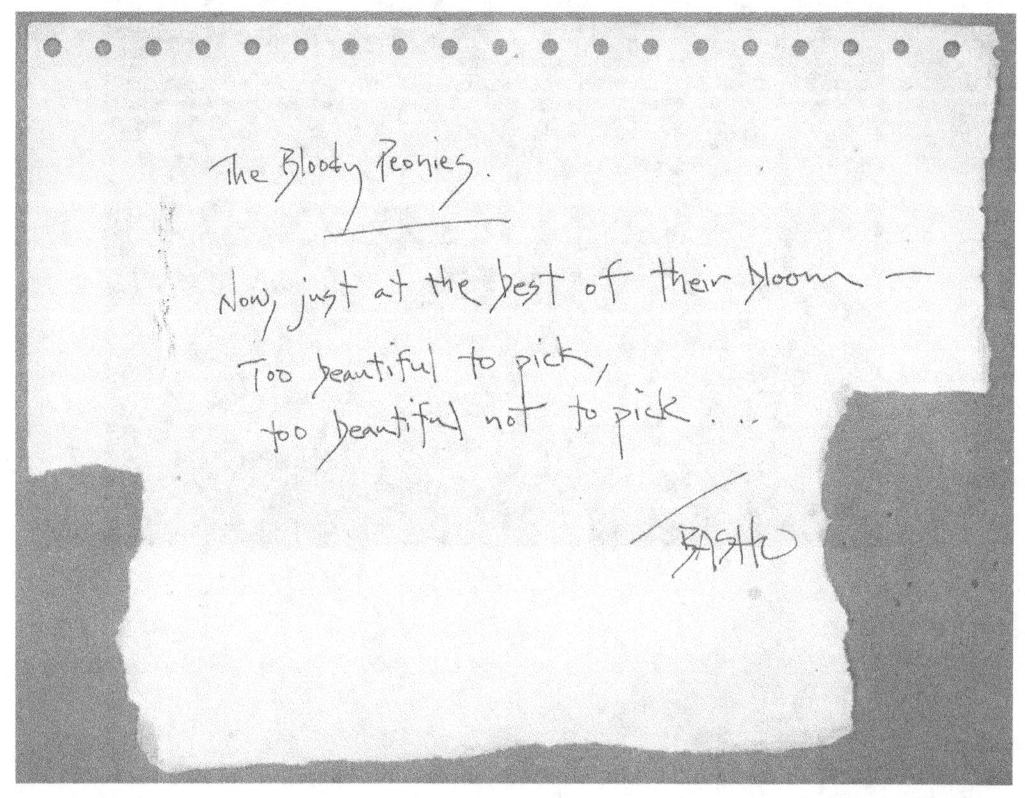

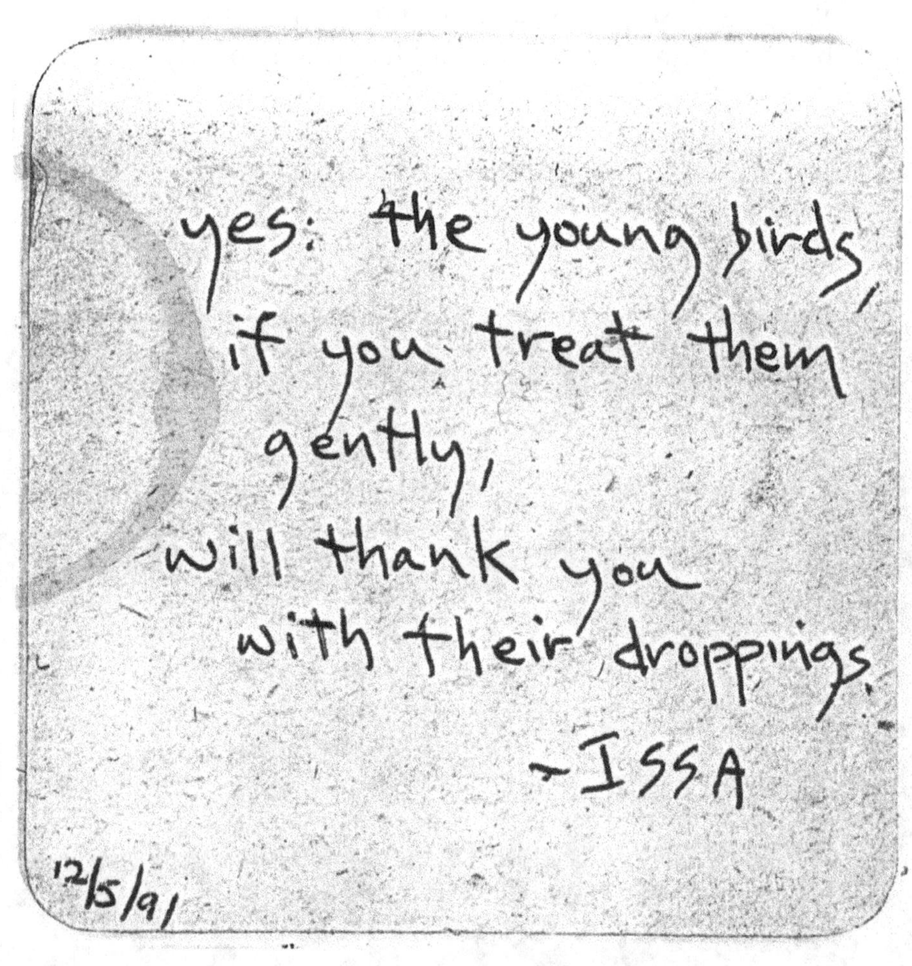

Clyde's bar coaster, courtesy of Gary Clay & Lori Kyle.

MICHAEL CLOUGH:

I think Clyde's ship may have been in a harbor in Japan for a short
while, but I think his interest in Buddhism was mostly street Zen.

202

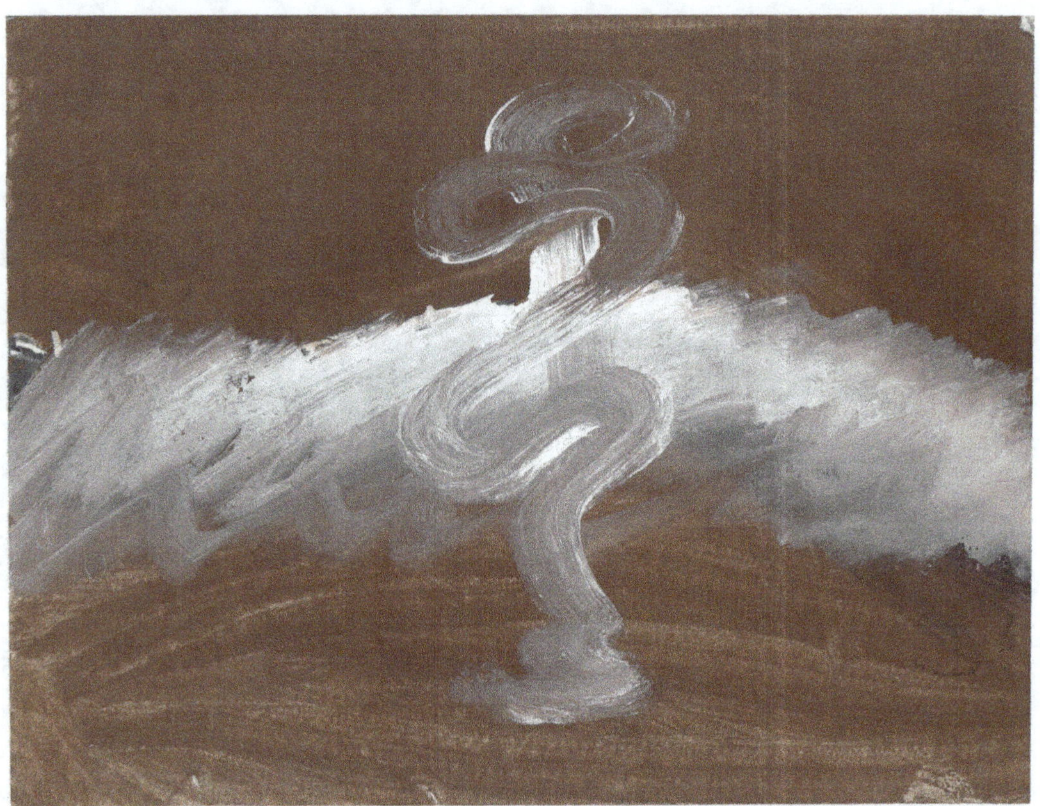

Clyde painting, courtesy of Bo Miller.

JOANNE ZABIK:

He did yoga. I've seen him do headstands.

JIMMY ZABIK:

In the 1890's, he drank a beer standing on his head.

Written on back of Clyde's envelope to Sarah Sanborn:

DON'T POUT; JUST ZEN IT OUT

O

D

A

YES

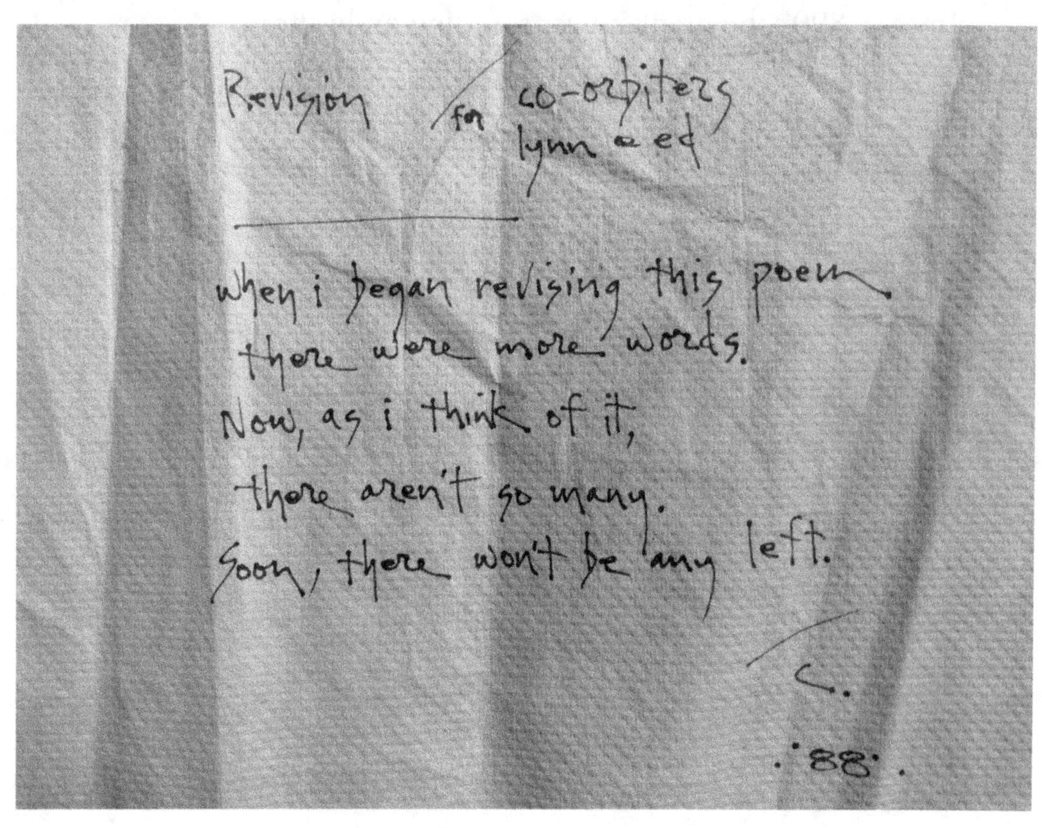

Clyde's "Revision" 1988, courtesy of Lynn Hays & Ed Nordin.

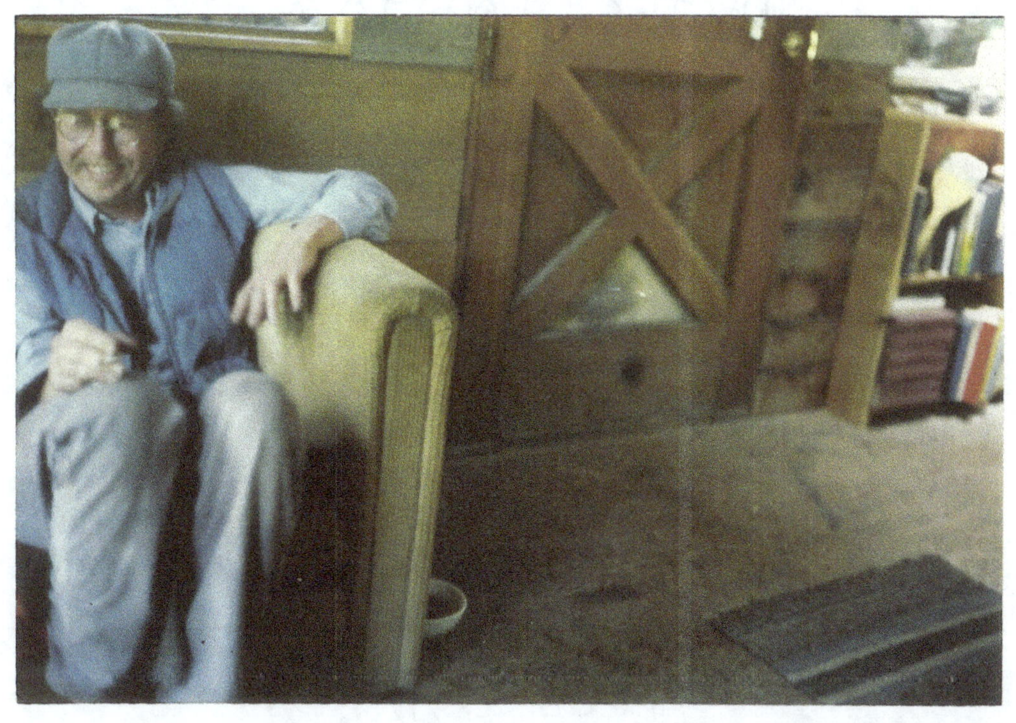

Photo of Clyde in John Schaefer's cabin near Conway, Washington, 1988.

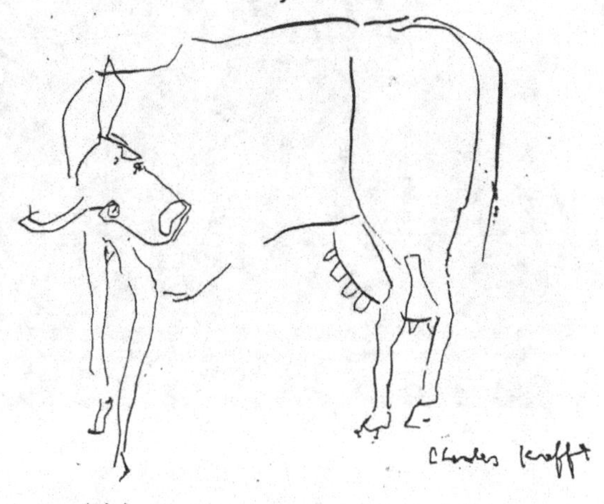

Poster/Invite from the "Fishtown Is a State of Mind" gathering
in protest of the clear-cut logging of the Fishtown woods in 1989.
Illustration by Charlie Krafft.

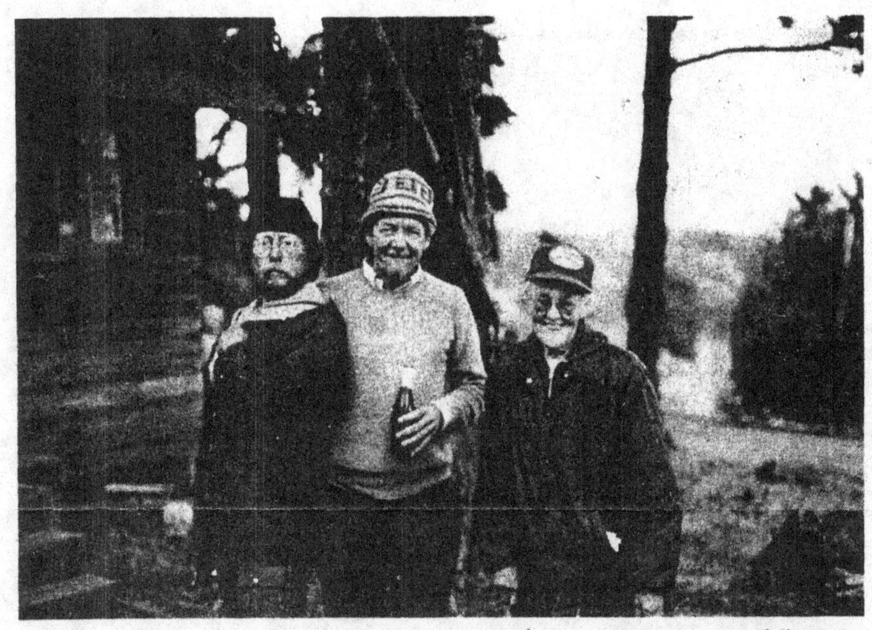

FISHTOWN IS A STATE OF MIND. Clyde Sandborn on the left, Paul Hansen center, and Margaret Lee on the right. Margaret hosted a wonderful party on her farm at Gage's Point, next to Fishtown. She has lived there all her life, spending her days outdoors looking after her small herd of Jersey milk cows. The Fishtown Woods were logged right up to her property line, and she got pretty angry at the loggers for cutting down some trees that her fence was nailed too. Not all of the Fishtown cabins were destroyed, because some of them are on her property

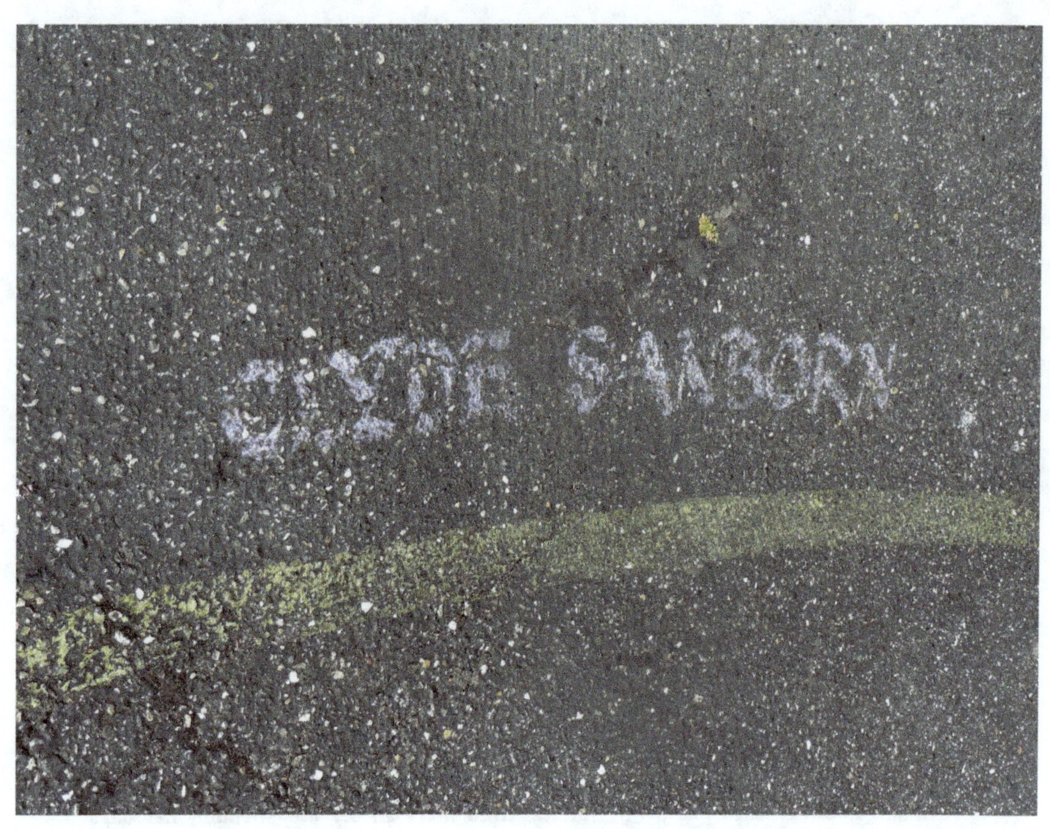

The Vacant Lot, La Conner, site of the fading labyrinth.

MICHAEL CLOUGH:

There's some history there. That area used to be what used to be called a "vacant lot." All the way from behind the post office to the corner. No shops, dental office, museum, no buildings. There was a line of old poplar trees and some gravel parking where the parking lot and Joan's building are now. When Ron Wolfe, a local ambulance chaser, had it bulldozed for development, Robert Sund wrote in the *The Puget Sound Mail* that the loss of those trees was like La Conner having its teeth knocked out. One of Clyde's poems was painted in a walking maze on the asphalt.

EDITOR: On the pavement of the parking lot behind the Museum of Northwest Art, Joan Cross commissioned an artwork by Maggie Wilder: a large labyrinth with Clyde's poems calligraphed along the edges: *The silence of snail sleep* and *Frog jumps, earth moves.* The plaque on the wall of the building explains: "A labyrinth is a path for walk-ing meditation…Walking a labyrinth is a gift of time that we give ourselves to be mindful of the present—a reflection more about the journey than the destination; about *being* rather than *doing*." The paint on the asphalt has faded, the green lines of the labyrinth and the poems that once circled it are nearly worn away.

JOAN CROSS:

He wrote one liners on napkins often at the bar (1890's on First Street) and sometimes he would stop by my house on 4th and Cale-donia which was on his way home to his shack on the river. He called me his black-eyed Susan.

CLYDE SANBORN FAMILY PHOTOS, with comments courtesy of JAN SANBORN.

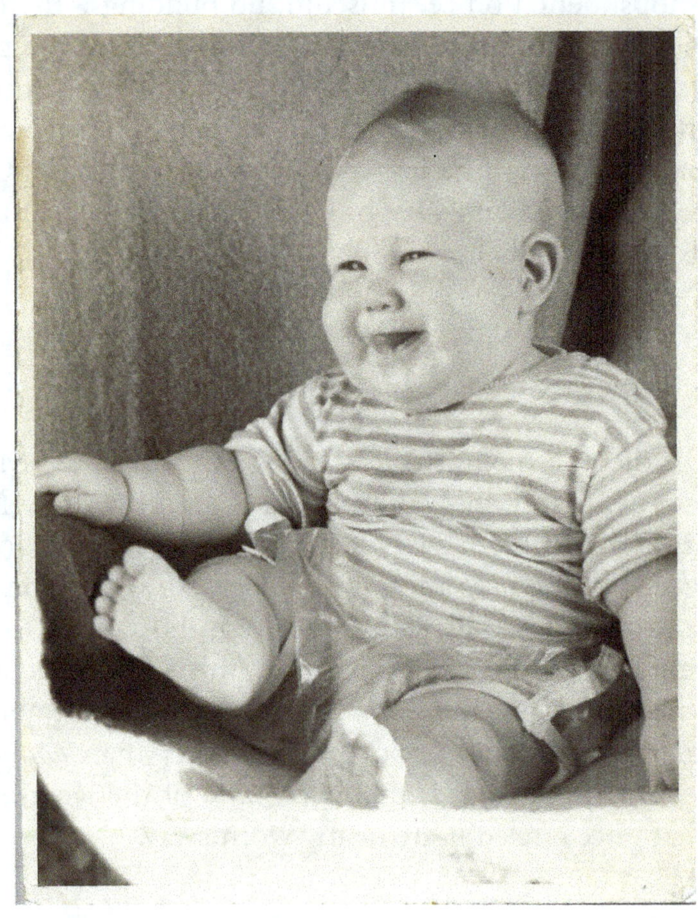

A Clyde baby photo, around... 9 months maybe? (Is that him I hear, from the other side? "Jan. Really? My baby picture???")

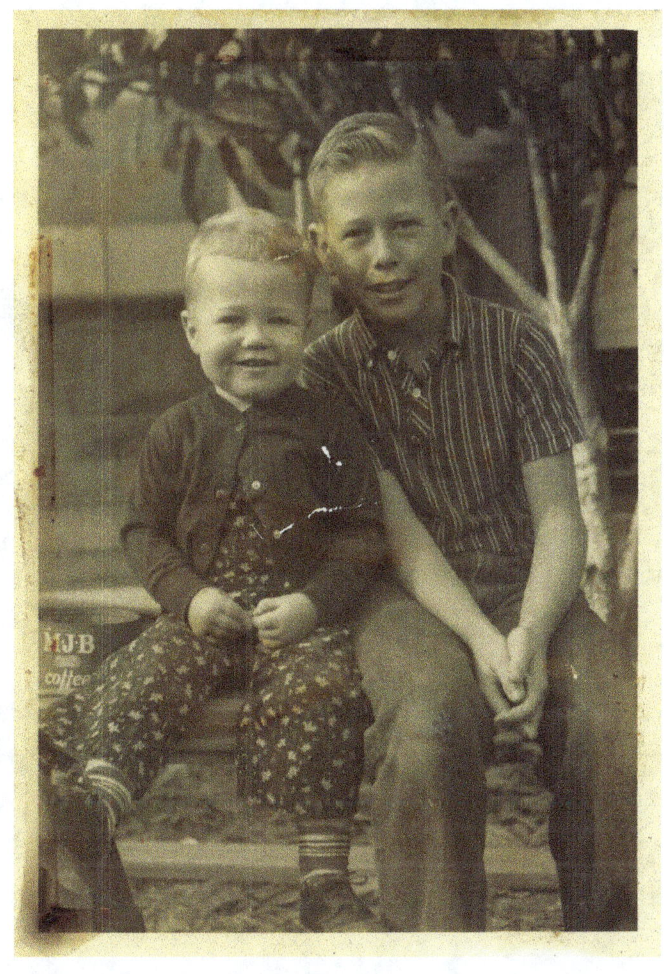

Chris and Clyde: Chris is our brother, and two years my senior. I believe this was taken before my family moved to Stockton, still at our house in San Leandro, a few months before I was born. The move took place shortly after I was born. That would make Chris almost two years old and Clyde, almost 11.

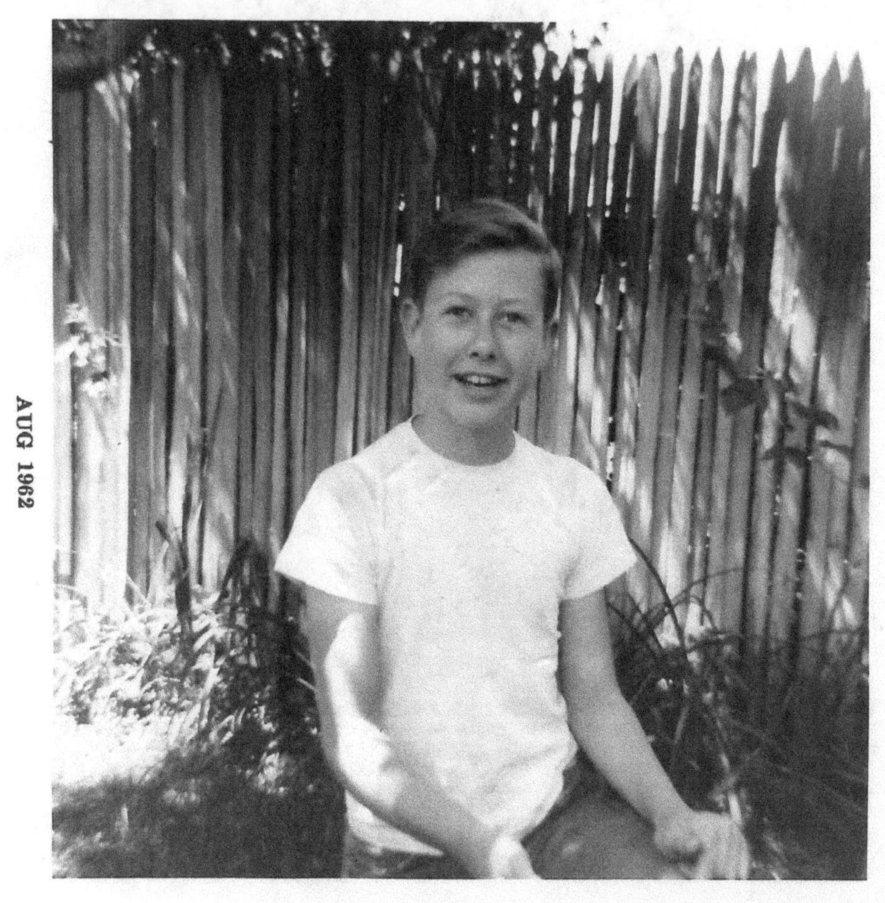

Our backyard in Stockton, California. Clyde was 14.

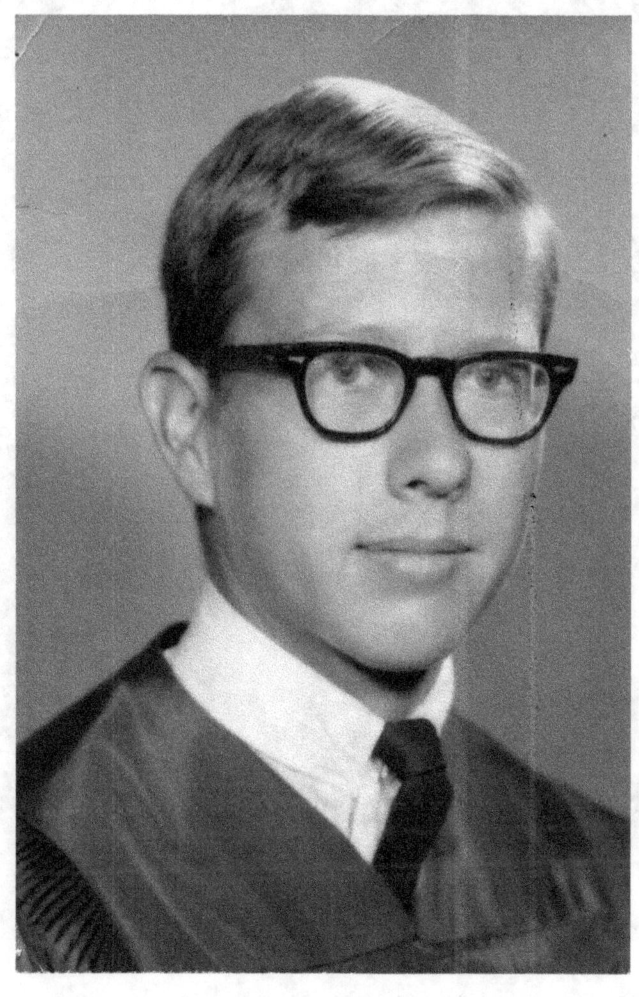

Clyde's high school graduation photo from Amos Alonzo Stagg High in Stockton.

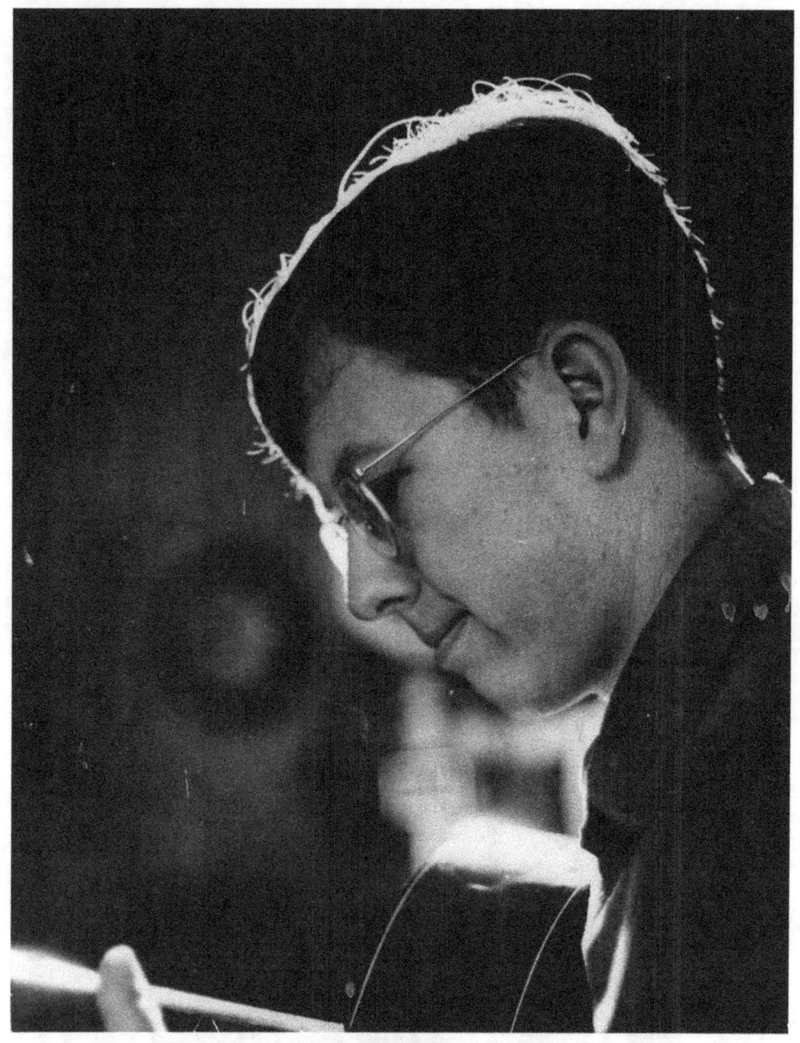

Clyde's self-portrait: He does look very young there, doesn't he? He always rued his baby-faced appearance (which actually worked to his benefit as he got older). The glasses are the clue, for timeline, because he didn't get the wire frames until he was in the Navy. I know he took some classes for a while at the local community college (San Joaquin Delta College), one of which was a photography class. I'm quite sure it was at that time he took the photo as a class project.

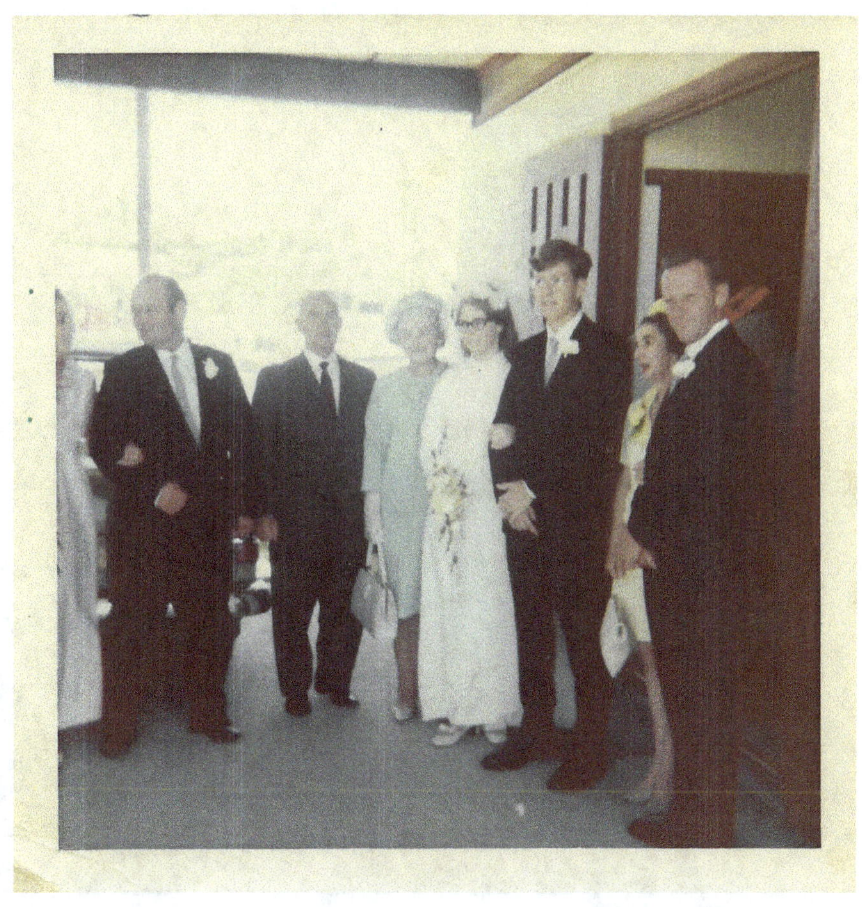

Yes, I knew Kathryn. I still have a letter from her somewhere, in one of my keepsake boxes. I also have this (not very good) photo of their wedding day in Christchurch, New Zealand, 1969 or 1970. We emailed one another after Clyde died. She remembered him fondly, despite their difficulties. Their marriage didn't last long, sadly, about a year. I don't know if Clyde ever quite got over her.

After San Diego, they came to live at our family house for...nearly a year, I think? The breakup occurred during that time. I was young therefore not privy to details, but she left and Clyde moved up to Seattle.

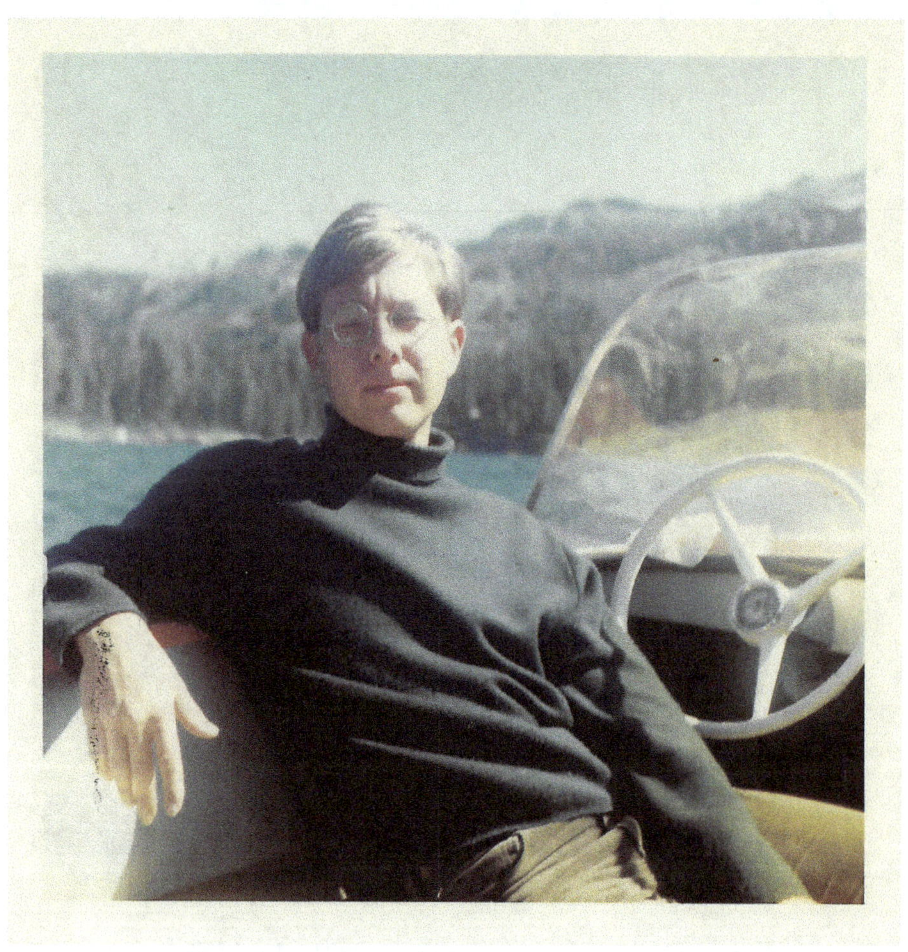

Clyde on our boat during one of the rare times he vacationed with us up at Silver Lake in California, 1971 or 1972. (Silver Lake Family Camp was our regular summertime destination, but I believe this was the only year we took the boat). I was on the boat that day. I think the whole family was. As far as timeline, I'd place him at about 22 or 23.

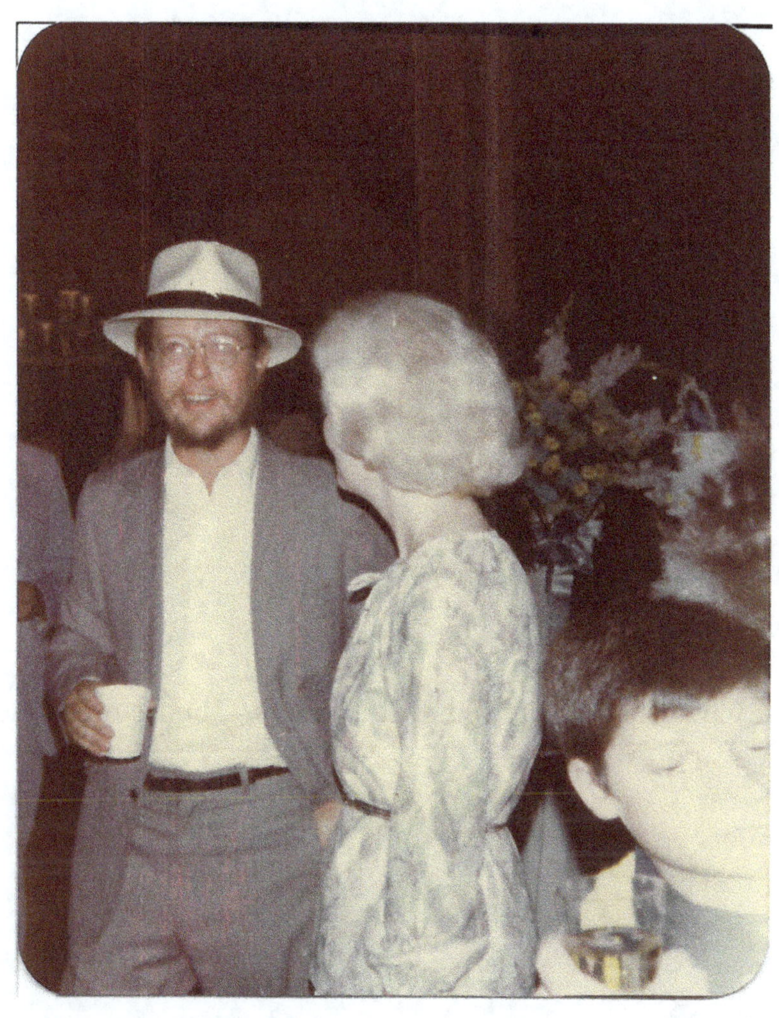

Clyde at his brother Chris' wedding, c. 1981.

MICHAEL CLOUGH:

Clyde always referred to the past as "The Before Times."

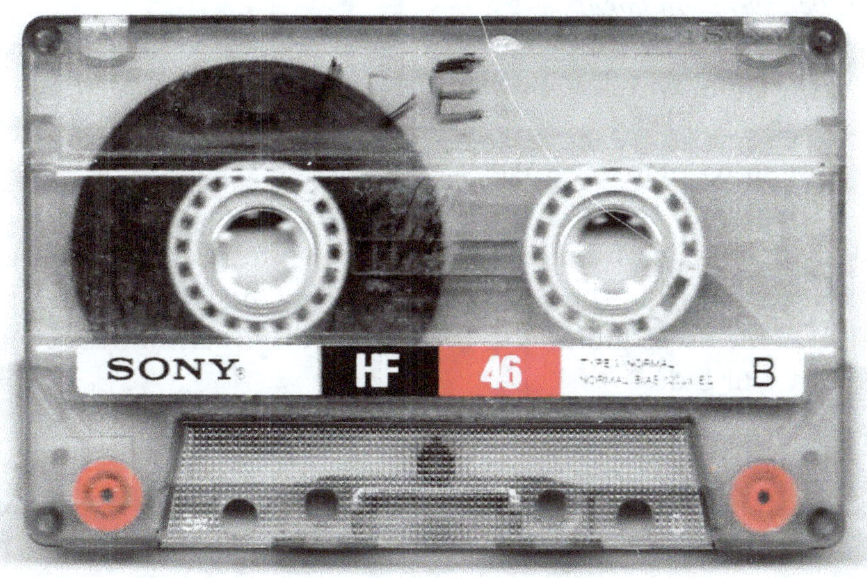

CLYDE SANBORN INTERVIEW CASSETTE:

EDITOR: Janet Saunders found this cassette tape, simply labeled 'Clyde.' The specifics of it appear lost in time, although Michael Clough and Jan Sanborn deduce that it took place in La Conner. Jan told me, "I'm quite sure he was at Lori's house, and at least one of the girls was her daughter. I was only there once, but it was quite an old white two-story house, on a bit of land (1/2 acre maybe), that she rented. I think it was on the east side of the river, of the main road a few blocks." Michael added, "Clyde was imbedded in La Conner and never missed a party unless they wouldn't let him in. So remains a mystery…Maybe a school project? Interview an old hippy? Sorry I missed that party. Was great to hear it, I laughed a lot, totally Clyde." Although the year is unclear, it took place on May 7, at a quarter to 4. There's a slow building raucous party going on in the background and several times the tape is stopped, to little avail of quieting the room. Clyde is interviewed by two girls in 8th grade, Roxie and Missy/Misty? and presided over by Lori, who chimes in at certain points.

When were you born?

"How about why?"

[Tape stops. Starts again]

[Clyde blows harmonica] "We got heavy into Bob Dylan and he did this song called 'The Time's They Are A Changing.' And he sort of turned me on to guitar and the harp." [Plays harmonica of 'With God On Our Side.']

Are you ready, Clyde? What's your name?

"I don't have a name, but when I came out of the womb, my parents named me a name. I don't know why people do that to one another actually. They say your name's Clyde. Alright, fine. I'll accept that. My name's Clyde."

What do people call you?
Lori: River Clyde.

"Nope. They call me Clyde."

Lori: River Clyde is descriptive. We know which Clyde we're talking about. We know you don't like to be called Crazy Clyde. You get real bent over that one.

"That's true. Next question."

When were you born?

"April 21st. In this incarnation on this physical planet in this meat body.

What year?

"April 21, 1948."

Where were you born at?

"Now, see, I'm an English instructor. You don't say where were you born at? You just say where were you born? Cause you're using a past participle there."

Okay, where were you born?

"Oakland, California."

What were your parents' names?

"Clyde and Gwen."

Okay.

"This is heavy interviewing. I'm real nervous. I have to tell the truth to these girls. Next question."

Where did you live most of the 60s?

"Well I spent my first 11 years in the San Francisco Bay area. Then when I was 11 we moved to Stockton, California which is in the central valley of California about 100 miles directly east of San Francisco."

Did you ever live in Haight-Ashbury?

"I took drugs in Haight-Ashbury and ate hamburgers in Haight-Ashbury and played with the cool, cool folks."

Lori: I told you to interview Clyde!
Where did you go to school at?

"No, see you did that 'at' again. You say where did you go to school?" [blows harmonica]

Where did you go to school?

"I went to school in several places. I started out in elementary school in Castro Valley, in kindergarten on up to 5th grade. Then they moved us to Stockton and then I went to Junior High School for a few years there. And they sent me to high school. I just barely made it through high school because I never liked being in school, I hated school. All the way, all the way, I hated it."

Did you ever go to any college or university?

"Yes. I tried junior college five times, but each time I got bored. I wanted to be an astrophysicist, I wanted to be a veterinarian, I wanted to be a photographer, I wanted to be an artist…I went so far into school that the teachers were boring. So when I found out, I didn't go to school anymore because I can do more."

Were you ever a hippie?

"I am a hippie. I am one of the hard core original hippies. I had bells, beads, I took LSD on Haight Street, meditated, do yoga, do music." [blows harmonica]

Were you ever in the Navy, the Army?

"In the Navy."

Were you in any wars?

"Now you must learn, Roxie, one thing. You really need to sit."

I don't sit. I'm not a sitting person.

"Okay, fair enough. Now, I was in the Navy for 3 years and nine months."

Were you in any civil rights movements?

"Yes. Do you work for the FBI?"

No, we don't work for the FBI.

"Yes, could you rephrase your question?"

Were you in any civil rights movements?

"Yes."

Any you would like to share with us?

"Peace on earth. When I was in the Navy, about my second year out, there was a peace march about 1968, because we didn't like fighting, so yes, I was in a peach march…A peach march [Southern drawl] I was down South a little later on…" [blows harmonica]

What kind of clothes did you wear?

"About like right now…Well, I wore beads and I had some bells hanging off of my belt, temple bells from Nepal, and the reason you have the temple bells hanging off of your belt is when you're high on LSD or some higher psychedelic drug, it reminds you of reality, it keeps you centered. That's why we used to have the bells."

How was your family life when you were a kid?

"That's a good question. When you try to answer a question like that it's hard to answer because you can always compare. How can you define it? Because you're living with one family, you can't really compare it, so therefore I can't really define it. It was sort of okay. They gave me free reign. When I was 15, I started looking out the window a lot and I wouldn't do my homework anymore, I'd just stare out the window and talk to my dog Hector. And they thought there was something wrong with me and they said, 'Son, would you like to see a psychiatrist?' I said no. Because I wasn't interested in their scheme of things. I was not interested. I got along better with the cats and the dogs and the trees and the plants. Because the humans [whistles] they didn't have much of a clue what's going on. Does that answer your question?"

Yeah. What kind of music did you listen to?

"Well, we started out with Elvis Presley [harmonica blow] then… that's a good question. Swing music I like a lot, 40s…" [tape stops for noise in other room as the partiers sing 'Do Wah Diddy Diddy.' Then tape continues.]

We're back.

"Take two."

You were going to tell us about the music you listened to.

"I started out with Beethoven and Bach. They were good. Then I got into Elvis Presley, real early, 'Love Me Tender.' I got into Chopin, Chopin was pretty hot. I got into Dave Brubeck, and then I got into Bob Dylan." [Clyde sings end of 'My Back Pages'] "My guard stood hard as abstract threats, too noble to neglect, moved me into thinking, I had something to protect, good and bad I define these terms, quite clear no doubt somehow, ah but I was so much older then, I'm younger than that now."

What was life like?

"Exactly like this, only different."

Did you drive a car?

"I've driven several cars."

What kind of cars did you drive?

"Well, I had a 56 Chevy station wagon that was a nice bomber.

I had a Chevy truck about 73 with a camper on the back. That's about it. I'm a bicycle person. I drive bicycles. Because I gave up cars when our police chief says, 'Clyde, you got two weeks to get that thing out of there.' I couldn't afford it because of my lifestyle, to pay for gasoline, insurance. I couldn't afford operating a big clunky heavy duty metal vehicle."

We have two more questions.

"Alright."

How did the 60s affect your life?

"Well, I have friends like Lori for starters." [The girls laugh] "Basically it was an explosion of consciousness that centered around Haight-Ashbury at the time when there was a big focus in San Francisco, a getting together of souls, an explosion of consciousness to spread happiness around. We would have liked to always be there because it was such a happy time, but we had to spread out across the planet…"

What were the words that you used to describe your feelings? Like cool, groovy and peace.

"What it is. People would say that a lot. What it is. We would say right on, or cool. Cool is still a catch word. You don't want anything, everything's all right. That's what cool means."

What did you do for a living?

"Well, I was in the Navy from 67-71. Then I became a dishwasher. Then I did short-order cooking and waiting on tables in a restaurant. Then I sold some painting. I'm an artist too. And I'm a poet, I would sell poems. And play music. And paint houses—" [end of tape]

JANET SAUNDERS:

Clyde's odd jobs: lawn mowing / house sitting / hole digging / nail hammering / massaging the occasional back...

MICHAEL CLOUGH:

I hired him once to help me remove old carpet and sand the maple floor in a house while the owner was gone for the week. Clyde quickly discovered their Liquor cabinet and it was empty by the time I finished the job.

MICHAEL CLOUGH:

It was Halloween. I stopped at Jim Smith's. We got in costume for the evening. I was Calypso Joe, Jim a Canadian. We were sitting in the Lighthouse Bar when in walks Clyde: an onion sack of leaves over his shoulder, whistling "Autumn Leaves." He was stopping at tables. He would scatter some leaves and say, "Hi, I'm Autumn." The bar tender was not happy about the dead leaves being tossed about.

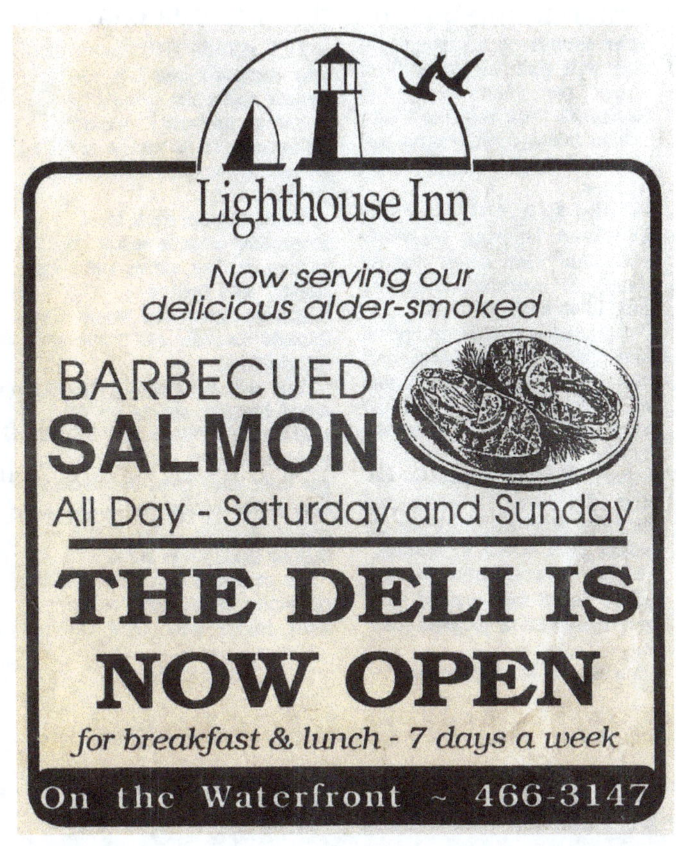

JIMMY ZABIK:

One time he was directing traffic in La Conner. Drunk as a skunk, right where the main road turns and makes a left, he was directing people to go on up the hill.

MICHAEL CLOUGH:

Clyde always loved drink. As long as I knew him it gave him a creative mood. It also happened that he became a Drunk. A harmless and a very entertaining one, but that persona comes with problems. Not an easy life. "Go with the flow."

JIMMY ZABIK:

Clyde and Bex were coming from Jim and Janet's house on Pull and Be Damned Road. They got pulled over for speeding and they were given a warning. And the next day they were pulled over for going too slow. So both of them ended up doing community service on the rez.

BEX:

We got a ticket. I went to court and did some community service, picking up trash. Clyde went to court and he got off. That was Clyde. I think the muses looked after him.

Muse —

any of a number of a number of
sister goddesses, originally given as:
Aoede (song), Melete (meditation), and
Mneme (memory) ——
but more commonly as
the nine daughters of Zeus and
Mnemosyne, who presided over
various arts. Calliope (epic poetry),
Clio (history), Erato (lyric poetry),
Euterpe (music), Melpomene (tragedy),
Polyhymnia (religious music), Terpsichore
(dance), Thalia (comedy), and Urania
(astronomy).

I'm glad to see Rose
in Spring
    because she is more beautiful
than ever. — This is easy to say
as easy, as it takes a butterfly
    to move one wing
    in Spring.

clide/75

ROSE GARNER:

    These two poems by Clyde on Lighthouse napkins I taped in my
journal:

Another moon in the
      locust branch.
Winter crawls down the fir trees
the goat cries wavering.

Someone could say it all
with a few pencil lines.

—standing at your door
the rose stuck in my thumb
      no one to answer.
        Choices
like two twined backs,
poles of a curious magnet
      —I walk between them
      Empty
      dropping my gift
         learning one of the
         lessons of love.

Poem by LI PO:

Overnight with a Friend

To bathe, to let float away the griefs of a
    thousand ages,
and then to drown
in a hundred jugs of wine.
A pretty night, perfect for talk, for philosophy
and a moon so bright. What sort of man could
    sleep?
Finally, finally really drunk, we slept
in the open, on the mountainside,
Heaven and Earth, our covers, our pillows.

JAN SANBORN:

Let's see if I can channel Clyde: "Yeah....(as he stands by the water with his backpack, waiting for lowtide, with a carton of cottage cheese and a bottle of cheap beer, maybe a loaf of bread in it, just bought at the store with the $10 made mowing someone's lawn in town, rolling a smoke)...it would be nice, wouldn't it? [Thoughtful pause] Some of us are lucky to find a piece of charred wood and a rock to scrawl on when a poem passes by, but we do what we can."

Not perfect Clyde, but reminiscent...

SARAH SANBORN:

Clyde was never afraid to be himself. He lived peacefully, studied Thoreau, and Buddhism, and lived like a monk.

I remember him telling me he was even a therapist to some friends, in La Conner, along with other odd jobs. His perspective on life was freeing, and I remember when he taught me to meditate, in the lotus pose, he could trace my thoughts, and knew when my mind was getting off track from following our breathing, I was amazed he could do that, he was telepathic, and an extremely sensitive intuitive empath.

```
The new bird sits on the old volcano.
    Mother earth rumbles.
    Tossing girdles over the edge
      the dawn arrives.
    Using a cane that is used by an angel friend,
    we think, and think about our thinking.
```

Clyde's "The New Bird" courtesy of Jan Sanborn.

MICHAEL CLOUGH:

Clyde liked to give advice. It was usually something like "Go with the flow; Everything is Everything; Don't sweat the small shit." He'd really piss the women off by starting out with, "You know what's wrong with you?" He did have some practical advice for me once and I follow it. If you drink a bunch, make sure you have a lot of water to drink when you go to bed. Healthful advice. Allen Schermerhorn was living next to Clyde on the sandspit. Late, late one night he heard some noises outside. When he looked out his window he could see Clyde in the moonlight wading out into the muck of the marsh; it was low tide and Clyde had a bucket a long rope tied to its handle which he was throwing out ahead of him; trying to scrape up enough water to quench his thirst.

MICHAEL CLOUGH:

He 'had' boats usually slow leakers. Borrowed, abandoned, gifted with a broken oar, maybe even two. He usually didn't have too far to go and for being an ex-sailor he wasn't great on boat lore. Usually not tying them well, or pulling them far enough up on the bank to prevent sinking with incoming tide. I don't know what boat he was in on his final sink. Someone said it was a kayak. I don't know how he came by it and heard it was never found.

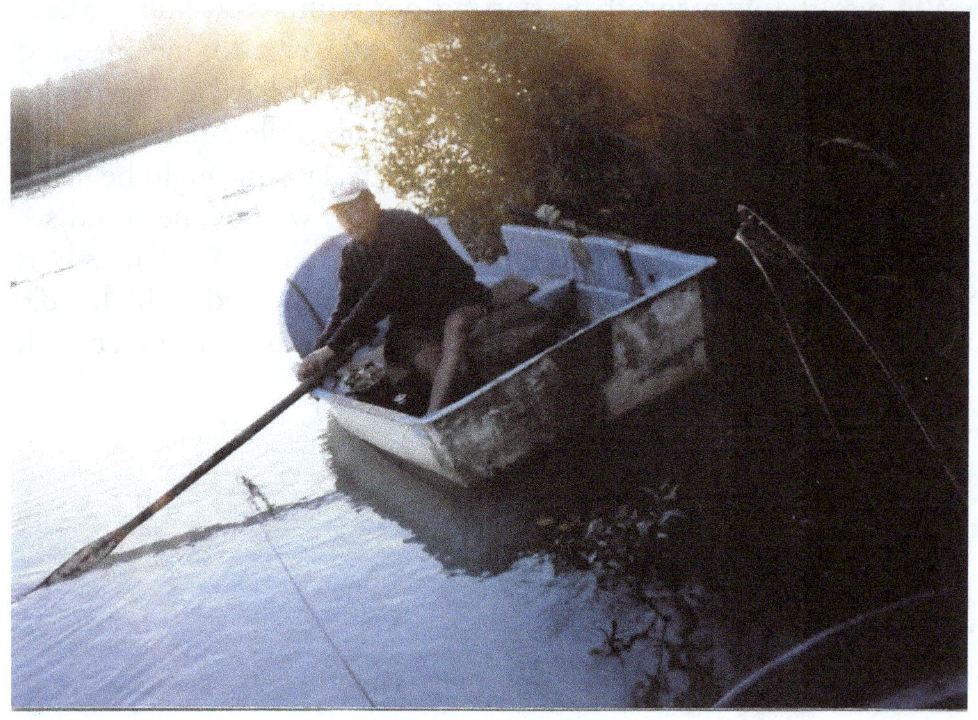

DENNIS "BEX" BEXELL:

Clyde in his boat, "Fang." You can see it's pretty beat-up. This wasn't the boat he disappeared in though. That was a canoe-type. In a way, I think "Fang" was the safer boat.

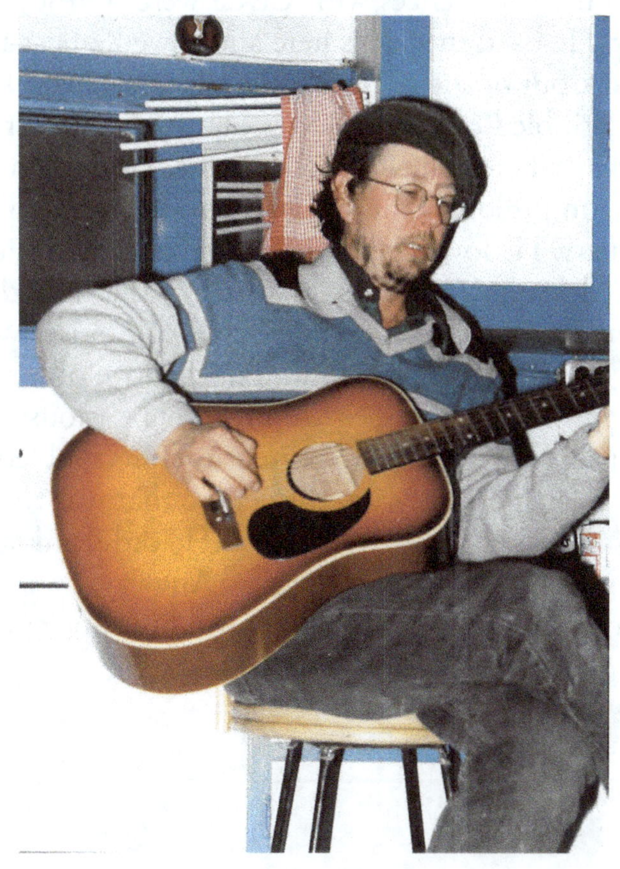

DENNIS "BEX" BEXELL:

The guitar he is playing is also called "Fang." For some reason, he had Fang on the brain. The guitar weighed a ton.

Fang photos by Bex.

DENNIS "BEX" BEXELL:

Most of my experiences with Clyde were on the north fork near La Conner. He lived in shacks here and rowed a beat-up, old dinghy with a chunk out of the stern he called Fang. As you know, he was a poet who scribbled out short verses on any handy scrap of paper to be given away wherever he happened to be. He'd roam town for days, sometimes, on prolonged drinking binges before heading back to his river sanctuary. He loved folk music and had a gigantic, heavy guitar he also titled Fang. We'd often jam out in the inky darkness of the river singing Bob Dylan or Ian and Sylvia or Louise. We'd laugh a lot too for he had a great sense of humor. The love of his life was Ruth, a devoted painter, who he helped out in her various pursuits. Clyde would help out anyone who seemed lost or troubled. He believed himself to be a Bodhisattva, and I believe that was true. He touched many lives. It wasn't all cherries either. He did drink a lot and could be annoying, especially in his last years. Anyway, I was only one of his many companions. He was prodigious in his associations.

RUTH:

There was a group of us, I was the newcomer. We'd all go to the town tavern, or up on the hill.
I was taking care of cabins and he came there.

JANET SAUNDERS:

The only significant girlfriends I recall are Ruth Beckel and, if only for the name, a woman called "Bonnie" who Clyde met on "the spit" just off the Swinomish Slough. Sounded to me like it was hot romance for a while, but ended up being mostly great fun due to the names.

i love the girl
who loves Sante fe —
a muse incorporates
it's findings,
Lo, lo, to the muse.
He~~r~~ at the other
end of the wind,

Clyde's poem for Ruth.

RUTH:

Oh, my heart…The first thing that comes to my mind…"What's for lunch?" He was comedy, the sweetest, capable of incredible love. He saw past. Because he had allowed himself to be himself, he could see in others, their authentic self. And if they were at all willing, he could meet them there. I just consider my time with him one of the biggest gifts I've ever had. We had so much fun. We would walk down the path, we were in the woods, and there were several cabins there, it used to be a commune then. What he would do that I loved—instead of just walking someplace, he would be standing and I would be facing the same direction and I would stand on his feet and we would walk together like that. He was a wonderful cook, he loved food. He loved people, he loved every single person. And the more disliked or outsider the person was, the more he lavished his own love on them. Because he understood what it meant to be outside. Many people didn't see him the way I'm describing. So he had to deal with some disfavor from others. And he was so sensitive, I think he felt it. But that was part of his life. He was not able, and also he insisted on being himself. Often the environment didn't necessarily hold that safely for him. I loved that guy and it's wonderful to talk about him.

DENNIS "BEX" BEXELL:

That's a great and perfect picture of Clyde from Ruth. I don't think I could improve upon that. What she said is what I saw also. They were totally in love and totally transcendent kind of people, ready to throw themselves out there no matter what the situation.

Painting and Poem by RUTH:

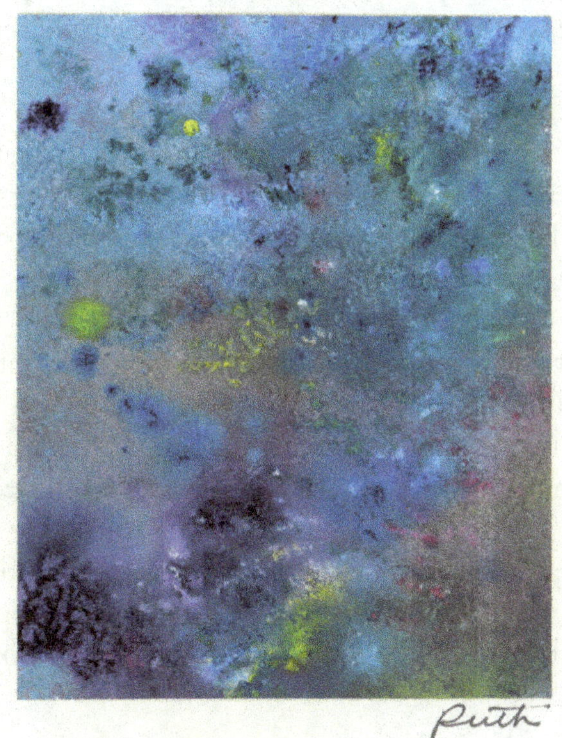

yes, I wonder about *How*
      running thru the streets
           carrying paintings
                like kites?

coloring air
      and wearing it
           for one's deliberate cloth

thinking of oneself
      as a transformational machine
           eating experience
              producing art

NOT JUST BEAUTY
BUT THE WHOLE THING

RUTH:

What he would always say, in this slow kind of way, "What's--for--lunch?" It says so much about him: the humor, the reality and the truth.

He was such an original person, and our time together was not rosy and la-di-da all the time. We had hard times. But that was the good of it too, because we were both allowing ourselves to be our strong selves. Neither one of us gave in to the other.

He was an artist. We didn't have any money. We got a lot of our food from the dumpster. With all that stuff, he would make soups, really good soups. He was a wonderful cook. I think he liked to be on the nourishing side—he was so much the receiver, because of how he lived, but he was truly so generous in his spirit. He lived his life according to what he thought. It was rather unusual and that was his main quality. It was his authenticity. And he made people mad, and some people really didn't like him. But then he had those of us who loved him.

He was such a beautiful person. I'm so grateful that I had anything to do with him, even though it was rough a lot. I think it's true that we must have really loved each other.

He was always the joker though. He could never go too far in sentiment, he would make a joke out of it.

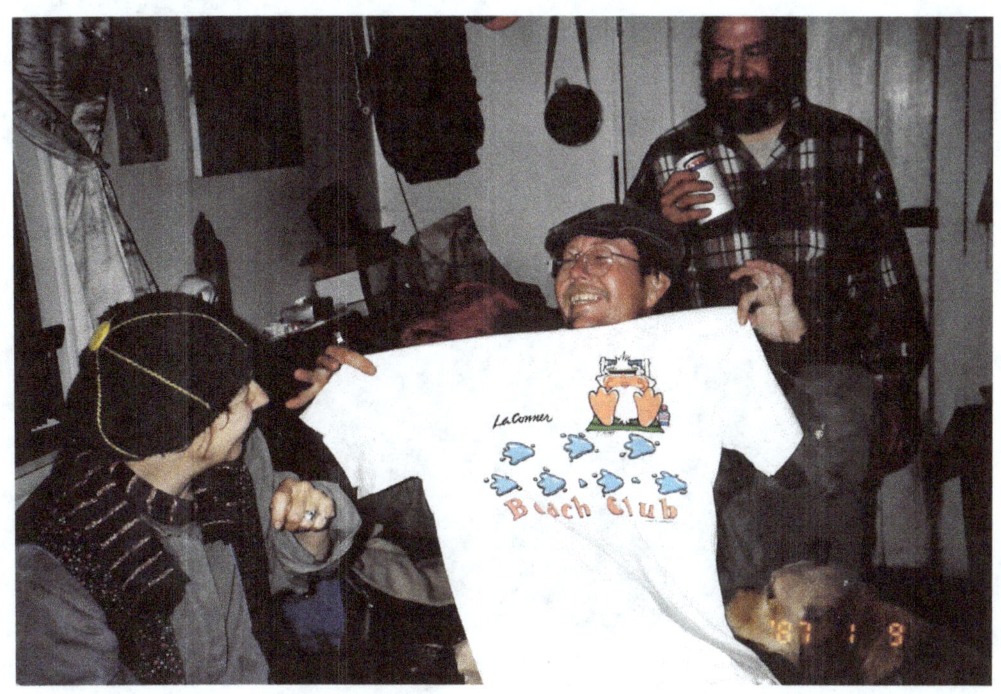

Joanne and Jimmy Zabik give Clyde a present: a La Conner Beach Club t-shirt! Photo courtesy of the Zabiks.

Happy Holidays,
or Seasons Gratings.

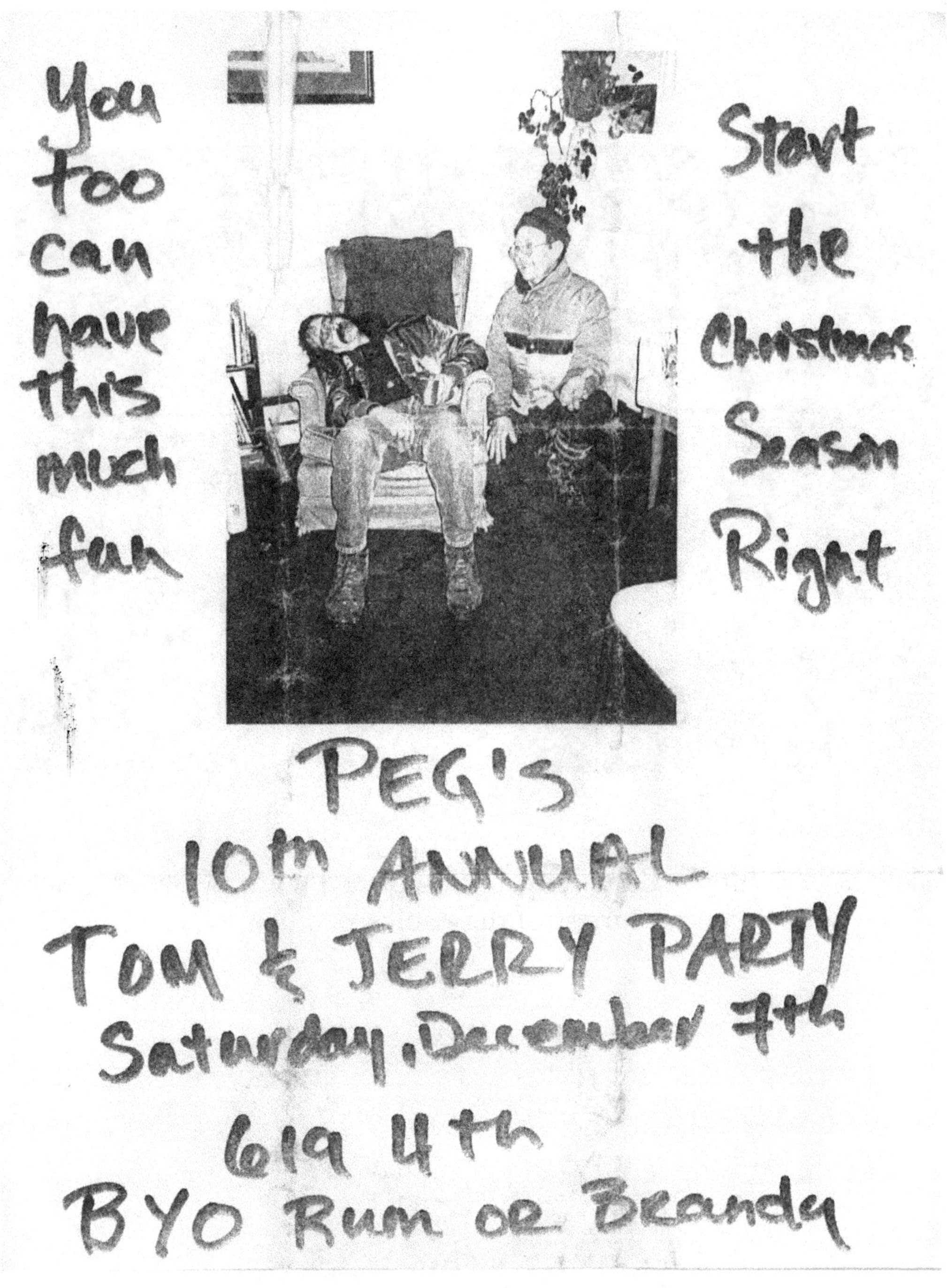

MICHAEL CLOUGH: Clyde loved those parties. They were hosted by Peggy Smith. She was the proprietor of Cafe Pojante a coffee shop in La Conner: art shows, poetry readings, a hangout. Her Tom and Jerry parties were legendary.

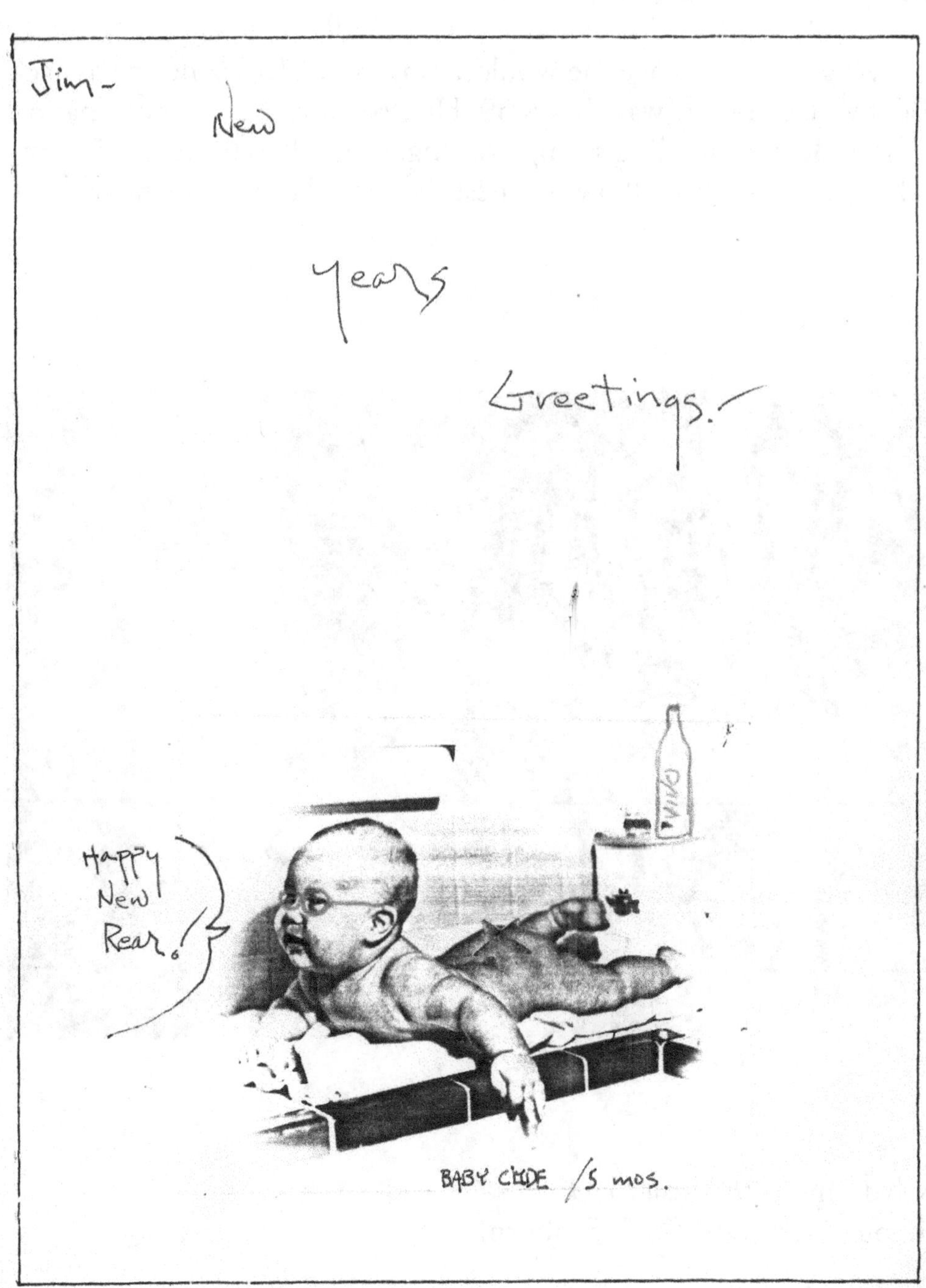

Clyde's card to Jim Smith.

MICHAEL CLOUGH:

When asked his age, he would always say, "The same age as Jack Benny." Jack Benny was always 39. He also did a good impersonation of Jack Benny. Standing saying nothing; head tilted to side; chin rested in palm; crooked elbow on chest. Perplexed or in a quandary.

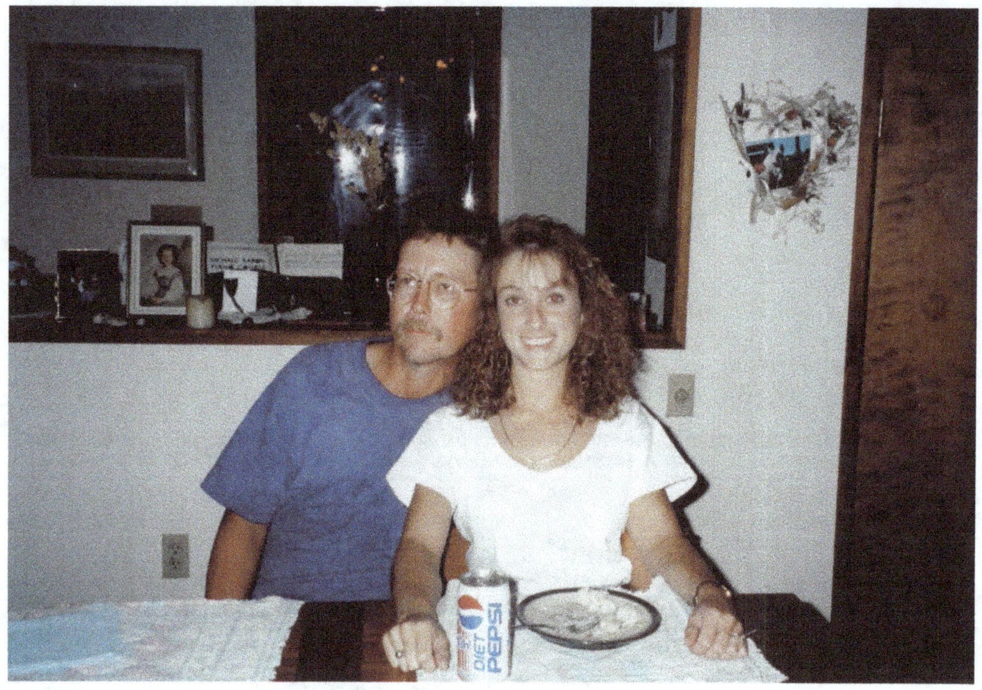

Clyde and niece Susie, 1993.
Photo courtesy of Sarah Sanborn.

MICHAEL CLOUGH:

Here are a couple of Clyde jokes:

Daffy Duck went to the drug store to buy some ChapStick. The pharmacist asked, "Are you paying with cash today, Sir?" Daffy said, "Just put it on my bill."

Clyde: "Would you like to hear a Zen joke?"

You: "Uh, ah yeah sure."

Clyde:

CHARLIE KRAFFT:

Clyde called me up in Seattle once drunk. He introduced himself and then put "The Button-Down Mind of Bob Newhart" LP on a record player wherever he was calling from, with his phone receiver beside it, and just walked away. After about 10 minutes of that I got tired waiting for him to come back to the phone and say something so I hung up.

TIM MCNULTY:

I do recall one of Clyde's poems Robert Sund passed on to me. Clyde wrote it after Robert told him about some of us on the Peninsula who thought that Hood Canal should be renamed Twana Fjord—to honor the native people who lived here and give lower 48's only fjord its due.

Clyde's "Twana Fjord," with calligraphy by Robert Sund.

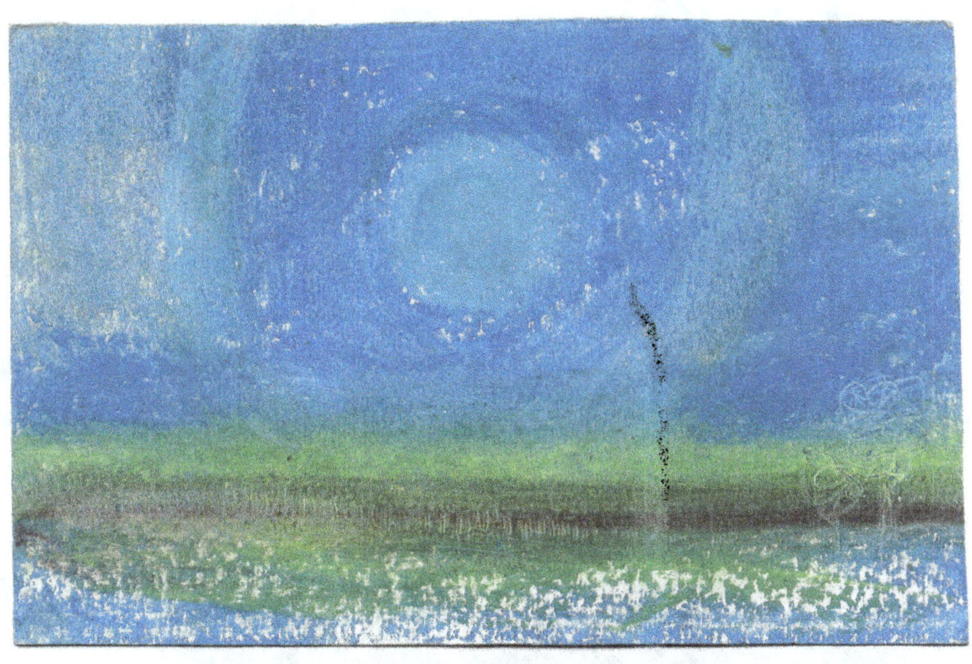

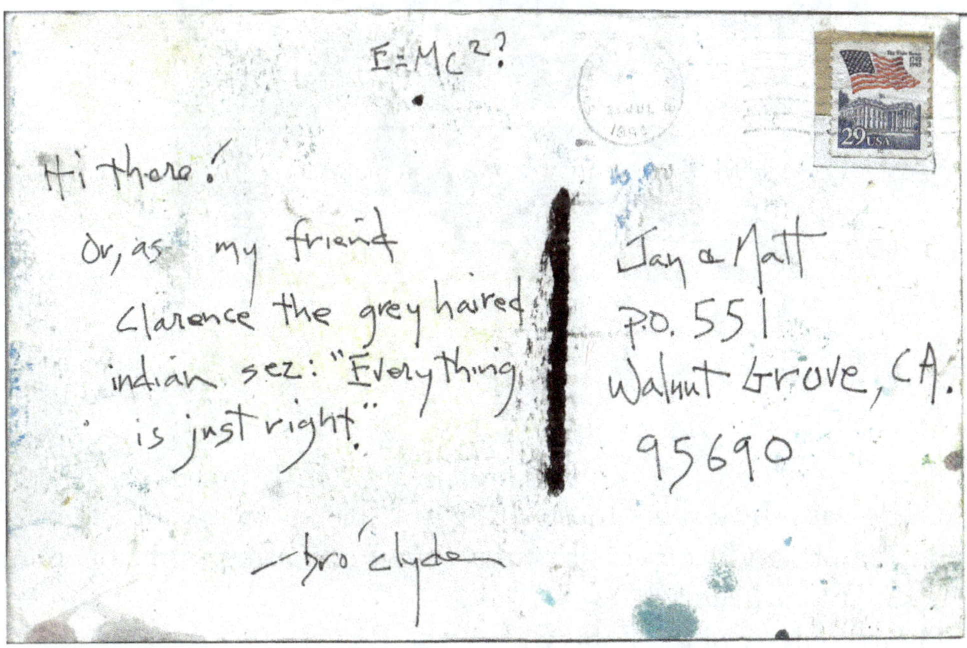

Clyde's painted postcard, front and back, courtesy of Jan Sanborn, from July 1994.

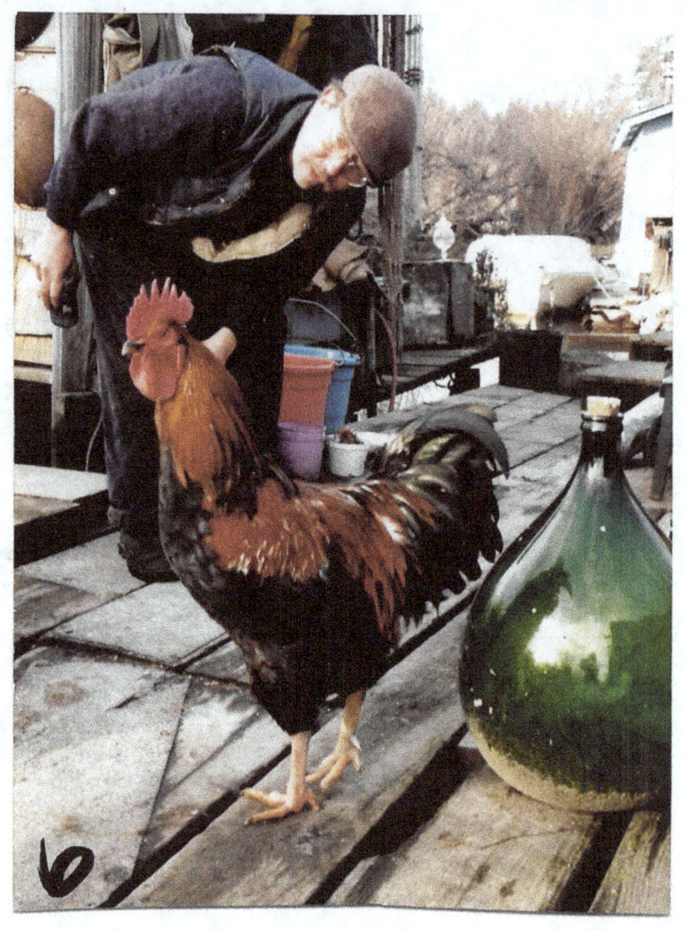

Clyde with the Zabik's rooster, Leggy. "That rooster would come in our house and lie down next to our stove and listen to the opera on Saturday. Clyde loved Leggy."
Photo courtesy of the Zabiks.

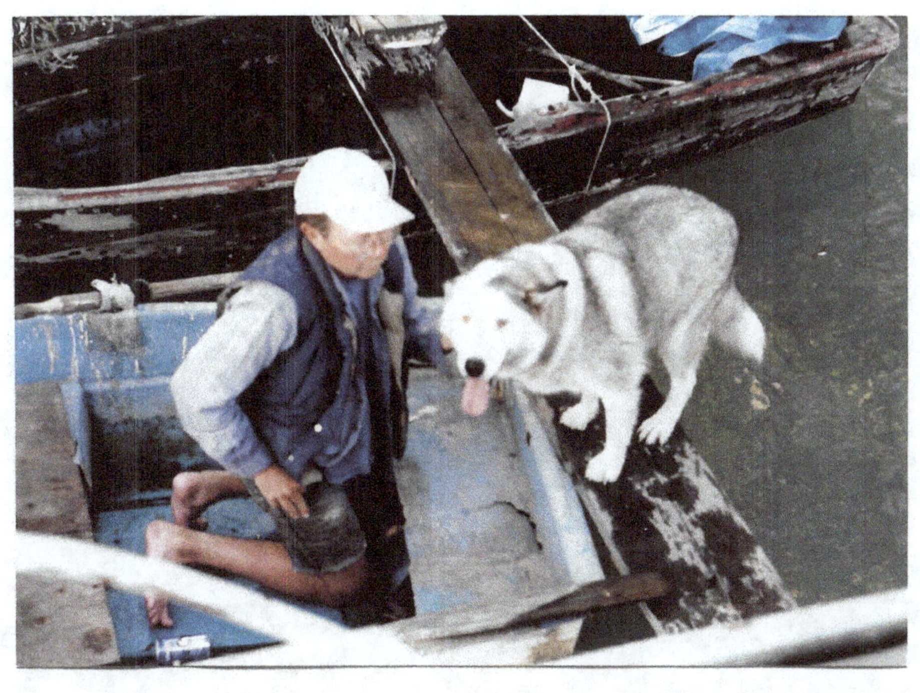

Clyde with Jim and Sue Lundberg's dog, Hoser.
Photo courtesy of Zabiks.

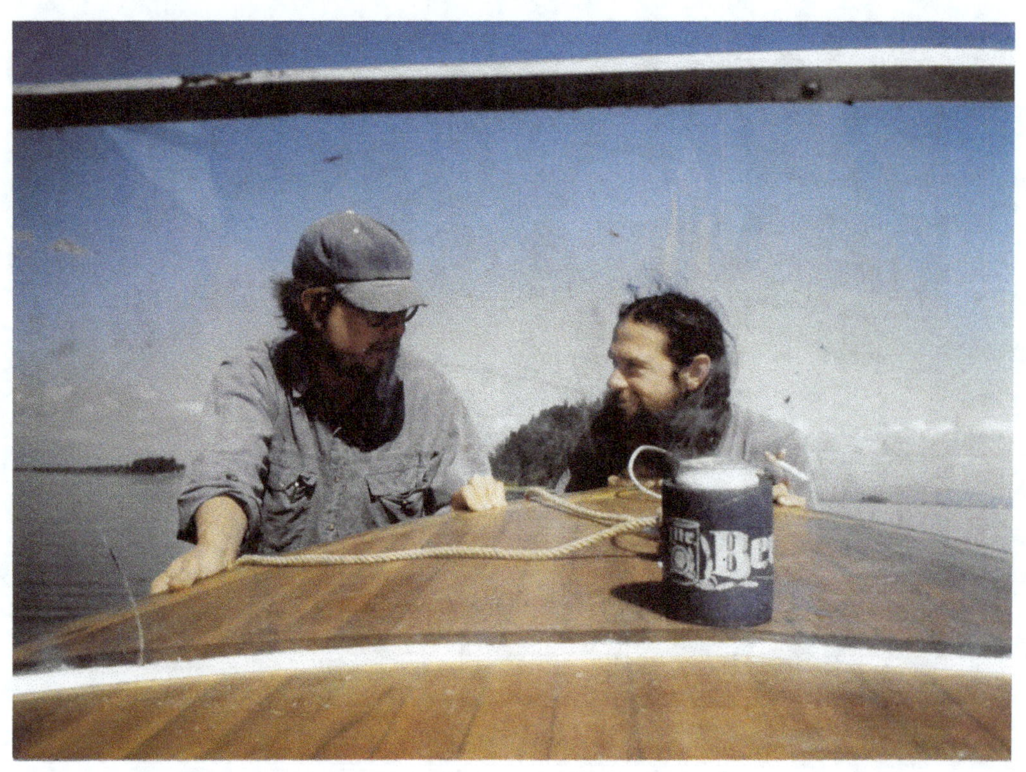

Clyde and Jimmy Zabik on the river.
Photo courtesy of Zabiks.

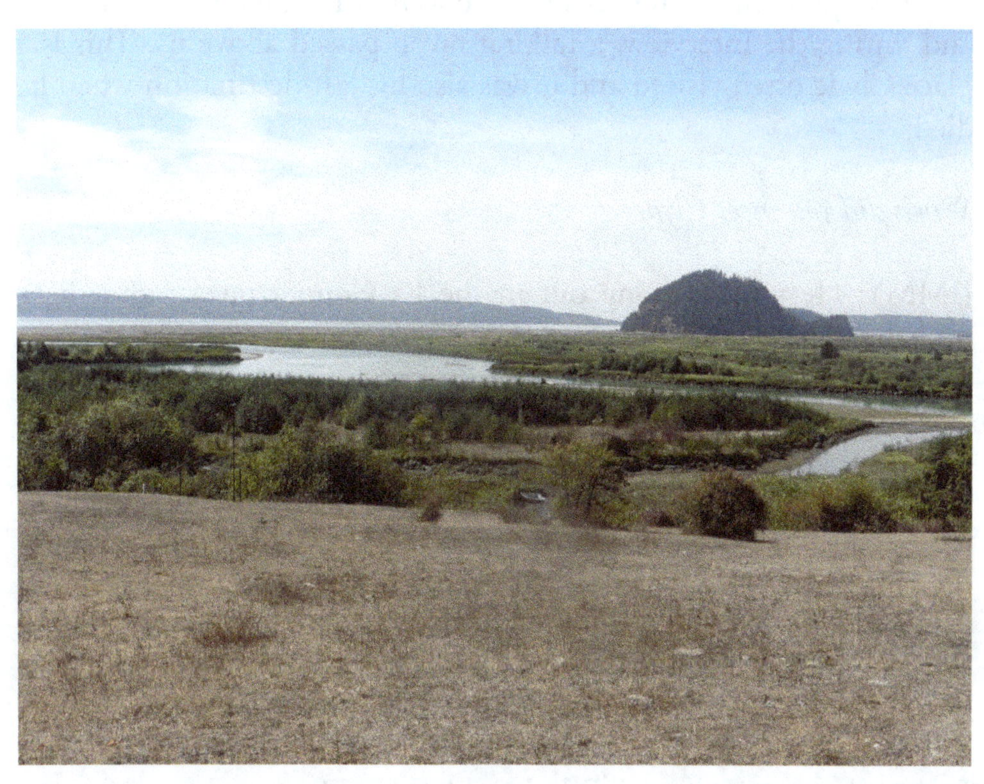

View that Clyde knew.

INTERVIEW WITH JIMMY & JOANNE ZABIK:

EDITOR: The Zabik's house rests on water, on a very beautiful and peaceful spot along the Skagit River. We sat in a garden by the channel slough, next to a blossoming mock orange. The other flowers Joanne is growing are protected from the deer by fishing net. Despite the Navy jet flight path overhead, we were surrounded by bird songs and during the interview, a talking raven passed above us. This is a place Clyde often visited and it was also his last destination when he died.

When did you meet Clyde?

JIMMY: He used to hang out in the La Conner tavern and that's probably where I met him.

When did you know he was writing poetry?

I knew it right away. Clyde's poetry was a spur of the moment thing to get a beer. So he would carry toilet paper around in the bar, or a napkin, and write a poem on it and then give it to somebody and they would give him a beer.

It's too bad his poetry was never collected when he was alive.

Because he gave it all away. It's the old artist thing: you're not famous until your dead.

We were really good friends. I worked all the time and would come home for the weekend with a bunch of beer and a gallon of wine for Clyde, and after he passed everybody out, he'd take the gallon of wine and go to town.

We lived down river, a place we called the sandspit, on McGlinn Island. You go under the bridge in La Conner, there's a dirt road that goes out. If you go all the way to the end of that dirt road, it cuts to the left. There was one shack on the left and Clyde was living there then. There were at least three or four other shacks on the boardwalk, float houses, and a dock right on the edge of the water. A lot of the Indians would come out there to go fishing and we'd use a wheelbarrow and haul their fish back out to their cars for them.

Then Clyde hooked up with this lady Linda and they moved, and that's when I moved into that house. He got a job in Big Lake. He worked for DSHS. Clyde would scoot around on his office chair with wheels. I don't know what he did there. I don't think he did a whole hell of a lot.

He moved back out to the sandspit, into somebody else's house that somebody moved out of. That house ended up getting burnt. My house got bulldozed down.

JOANNE reappears: I just found the bat. He's hanging in the front of my shop. But that's the shady side at least.

Do you have any stories about Clyde that spring to mind?

JIMMY: We were talking about his job.

JOANNE: He used to scoot back and forth. He liked his chair. It had wheels.

He loved animals. Clyde was really good to animals. He treated them better than people. When we moved into Fishtown, Jimmy brought his dog up from the sandspit and Zeke got fleas really bad and I can remember Clyde standing there and he pretended he was Zeke and said, "Come on people. You're supposed to be smarter than I am. Can't you figure this out?"

Was the sandspit the first place Clyde moved to?

JIMMY: No, there was a place called the ghetto, in downtown La Conner which they tore up. That used to be an old slummy part of La Conner. It was just old shacks on pilings.

He always liked to live in a shack.

JOANNE: It's easy.

And sometimes a tent.

JOANNE: Tents are okay.

JIMMY: He lived in a tent on Chocolate Lilly Hill, on Sullivan Slough. Clyde lived in a cabin right across the slough from Barge Island. That cabin came from Shit Creek, where Robert Sund's cabin is. Clyde had a boat on Barge Island for a while, a boat with a cabin, a cabin cruiser. It didn't have a motor in it. And he went away and the tide went out too far and it sat down on a log under the water and punched a hole and sunk it. I tried to resurrect it, but it didn't work.

JOANNE: But then he had Jim and Janet [Jim Smith and Janet Saunders]. They lived right next door to the old firehouse. So it was really convenient for him in town. He could wander over there and crawl into his personal space.

JIMMY: He had a lot of places he could crawl into.

JOANNE: He'd go from place to place. When Jimmy lived at the sandspit, he was there all the time.

JIMMY: And I had food and beer most of the time. I'd see him walking across the sand in the morning. My bed was right even with the window. And I'd wake up and look out the window and I'd see Clyde coming over the hill. He'd go down through the gulley and come back up and he'd stop. He'd stand there and look around, look down at the ground, and bend over and dig and pull up a beer, crack the lid. He'd grab my beers and hide them in the sand.

JOANNE: I remember another story. You were on crutches, you couldn't walk and you lived down out at the sandspit.

JIMMY: Nobody could drive in to get me. They put a gate up to keep us out, but we lived there anyway. I was stuck at the sandspit, so when

I did get to town I went overboard. I got really drunk and crazy and took the whole bar on with crutches. One day, me and Clyde were walking home. I was on a bicycle. I could ride the bicycle with one foot and not use my other foot. And I get up in the morning and I don't have any crutches. And Clyde comes over and I said, "Well, Clyde, you're supposed to be walking my crutches home." And he told me I pissed him off and he threw the crutches in the channel.

JOANNE: I know that they pushed you into town in a wheelbarrow.

JIMMY: They tried. That didn't go over so well. I had the money, so they hauled me all over the place. When I had my broken leg, I got my $165 a month so we'd go to town once a month and stock up.

How did you two meet?

JOANNE: It's all Clyde's fault…I was living on Barge Island with this guy and I moved out. It was Paul Hansen's old cabin. I went out rowing down Steamboat Slough and there's Dave Foote's house.

JIMMY: Then me and Clyde showed up and Clyde made her cry.

JOANNE: He was insulting as ever, the louse, really humiliating. He said, "Oh that accent. You sound like a waitress." And on and on… Just contempt…I started crying, burst into tears. And Jimmy was so kind, he hands me a tissue to wipe my eyes, and he said, "Clyde, don't be such a jerk. Shut up. Don't make her cry."

JIMMY: Then we got married about a year later. And Clyde was our best dog, and my dog was our best man.

Clyde became friends with you.

JOANNE: Oh right away actually, he got over it. When a girl gets involved with a guy, there goes your meal ticket. Clyde was a little bit jealous at first. He was not nice. He was very protective of Jimmy, his meal ticket.

Everybody knew him. He was so quiet, he never offended anyone, unless he was loaded or had a hangover. He didn't mess with anybody. You couldn't help but like him.

A few people have mentioned that anytime they saw Clyde he'd have mud all over his boots.

JIMMY: Coming from the river someplace.

JOANNE: There was no way around it. I've seen him in tennis shoes. And he wore that shirt that was totally shredded. The whole back of it was holes. I hated that shirt. But better than no shirt.

JIMMY: He always had broken glasses, because he couldn't afford glasses, so they were taped together all the time.

How would he get around? Did he have a boat?

JIMMY: He had a rowboat. He got around. That's what killed him too.

JOANNE: Not that boat.

JIMMY: No, it was a different one. It was kind of a canoe-kayak mix. We weren't here, but he was coming up to see us.

JOANNE: We had a friend housesitting for the three months we were gone. And we got a call to tell us that Clyde had died and the cops had been there questioning everybody, trying to find out exactly what happened to Clyde.

JIMMY: Clyde borrowed a pair of pants from Les Holmes because he fell in previously. And Clyde was coming back to return the pants and to visit us and he didn't make it.

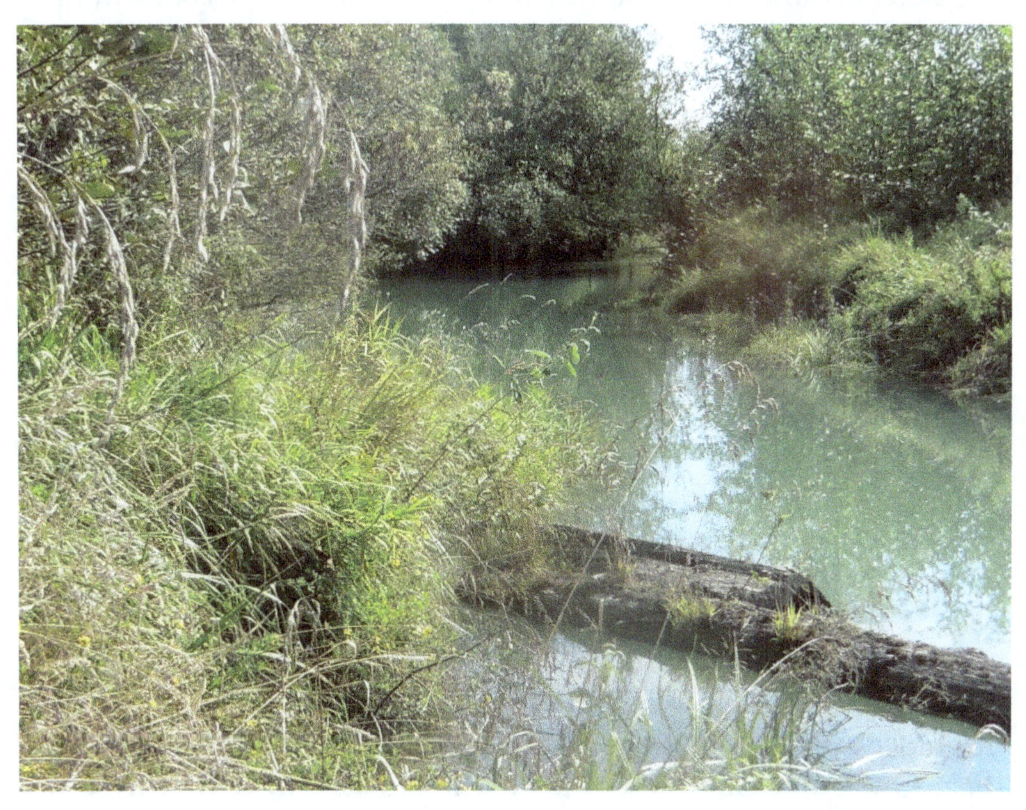

The water at the Zabik's where Clyde would arrive.

LES HOLMES:

I was surprised to hear about it that Monday morning when it was in the paper. He was wearing a pair of my jeans, and I gave him my lifejacket because he used to run around in that damn kayak without a lifejacket. He'd come in my cabin and he'd say, "Well, Les. I'll write you a poem if I could have a beer." And I'd say, "You start writing and I'll give you a beer." He was my pal. He had glasses that looked like coke bottles. They were so scratched up you'd think that they went through a sandpaper machine. I tried to fix those glasses so many times. I don't have any of his poems any more but he used to say, "The Ocean is just a bigger bend in the river." And he would play my guitar and sing Bob Dylan, "Everybody must get stoned" over and over.

From JANET SAUNDERS: Below is a little story about Clyde that his older brother Roger Sanborn just sent me. (A little background first: Gwen and Oz were Clyde's mom and stepfather who lived in Lodi, California. Sarah is Clyde's niece. Clyde was quite close to his mom and niece. Roger was living in southern California somewhere).

ROGER SANBORN:

Clyde came to stay when Gwen and Oz went to Kauai. He tuned my guitar and sang Bob Dylan. I recall the "Walkin' Atomic Blues." He danced some ballet steps with Sarah. They sailed my small boat, and he was able to sail it upwind to the dock. Sarah pushed him off into water. He lost his thick-lens glasses and was not able to drive back to Lodi. I had a diver client go down for them, and (then) we sent him and the dog away. I think that was the last time we saw him.

MICHAEL CLOUGH:

There were times when I didn't see much of Clyde. I had my life on the South Fork. Relationships, stuff to do. I'd go to town for some social life, but Clyde was 86'd from the watering holes. So I would run into him at parties, poetry readings, art shows etc. He would ride his old bike from La Conner to Edison to an art show and have some trouble finding his bike the next morning. Jim Smith kept tabs on him. And Jim was the one wondering when Clyde wasn't around. As he was usually in La Conner during the day on his bike or sitting on a park bench, perhaps he'd do some dumpster diving. I'm pretty sure he didn't go to California that winter. I don't know why. He was staying in a sinking float shack on Sullivan Slough, pretty close to town. Maybe the last time I saw him was in La Conner. He was on his bike, I stopped to chat. He said "He-lo Mich-ael, how are you?"

Poem for Clyde by DENNIS "BEX" BEXELL:

What the Light Takes Back

He was dead, from a friend I was told.
"Found on the river with his glasses
and life vest on and his naked feet
shining in the cold."
I fell numb thinking of how strange
life passes.

Like a dream when he stood on the
weathered dock
pricking the pimples of anger with
tipsy laughs
in the slim March sun where the great
Mallard flocks traced their celestial
paths.

Then paddling off from my drowsy
shape,
until, aroused, I jumped to my naked
feet
and yelled down the slough at his
shrinking fate.

"Hey, where you going?" He turned
in his seat.
"I'm going upriver and let you rest
awhile."
Saying with no scorn or disapproval,
without a hint or semblance
of guile,
as though he was merely submitting to
his removal.

And now I sit unable to move or speak
feeling as if shrunk by a rare

magnificent feat
that dwarfed my petty ego down to the
deep
while my friend slumped in a corner to
weep.

Poem by CLYDE SANBORN:

You sit alone in your room and cry
Looking out the window
I sit on a cloud
and listen

Clyde 4-3-82

CHANNEL TOWN PRESS

35¢

VOL. 21, NO. 5   LaConner, Washington   Wednesday, March 20, 1996

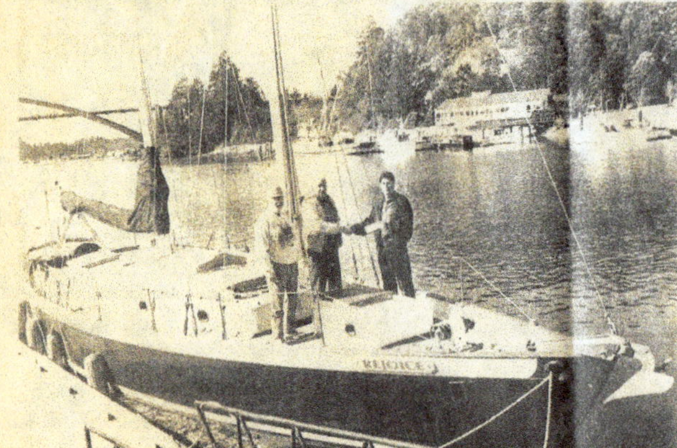

REJOICE — LaConner Rotary Club President, Matthew Paul (middle), presents Guy Hupy of the LaConner Sea Scouts, a check for $750 aboard the Scout's sailboat "Rejoice". Doug Jones, the Rotary chairman for the Smelt Derby (left) enjoys the view from the boat. The Rotary donation will be used by the local youth program for several projects.
—Photo by Jeff Elkins

Swinomish to begin HUD financed housing projects

The sounds of hammers and saws will soon be heard from across the channel as the Swinomish Tribe launches a $2.4 million housing renovation and home construction project this summer.

Funded by a HUD grant, the Swinomish Housing Authority will build nine single family homes at scattered sites on reservation lands.

"The land is owned by individuals. New home owners will enter into a lease with the Housing Authority, who will build the house and sell it back to the family," said John Petrich, General Manager of the Swinomish Housing, Utilities and Facilities, who explained that the project grant totaled $1 million.

Money collected from the new homes would be recycled into more construction projects later on.

In a second venture, funded by a $1.5 million HUD grant that was received last fall, the 95 houses under the control of the housing authority would be renovated. These would include rented as well as home buyer dwellings.

"We'll inspect each home and determine what it needs. We'll replace roofing, siding and vinyl floors," said Petrich.

Interior renovation would also include kitchen and bathroom refurbishing.

"We will be phasing out the wood burning stoves for heat," said Petrich. "We would like to replace it with natural gas but gas lines don't cross the channel. Our other option is propane," added Petrich, who explained that air quality was the key issue.

The project would also include replacing single pane windows with double pane, and adding

Continued on Page 7

Local man discovered dead on sand spit

Site for totem still undecided

The tree cutting controversy in Pioneer Park was finally put down. She grew concerned that with then Mayor Dan O'Donnell,

Local man discovered dead on sand spit

The LaConner Fire Department and the Swinomish Tribal Police recovered the body of 47-year-old LaConnerite, Clyde Sanborn, on a small spit of land between McGlinn Island and Bald Island late Saturday morning.

A kayaker discovered the body at around 11:30 a.m. and contacted a tour boat in the area, who in turn contacted law enforcement via CB radio.

According to Skagit County Coroner, Bruce Bacon, the cause of death was drowning. There [was] local speculation that [Sanbo]rn had succumbed to [hyp]othermia.

"He did take in some water at the time of the incident," said Bacon.

According to authorities, Sanborn was wearing life jacket and a backpack, and was in the water less than 24 hours. They were not sure where he had gone into the water.

Clyde, his bicycle and his backpack, were a familiar sight in and around LaConner. He supported himself by mowing lawns, doing odd jobs, and working as a poet and painter.

His family and many friends will gather at 5 p.m. in Pioneer Park today, March 20, for a memorial and potluck to celebrate his life and mourn his passing.

STP reviews plans for road construction

Several local road improvement projects will be on the agenda at the Skagit Council of Government's (SCOG) public meeting, Wednesday, March 20.

The Skagit Transportation Program (STP), a sub board of SCOG, will discuss three projects slated for LaConner area, at the meeting, which will start at 4 p.m. at the Bayview Regional Airport.

The Skagit County Regional Transportation Program distributes federal dollars to eligible agencies in Skagit County. The STP board selects transportation

• Obituary •

CLYDE LAYTON SANBORN, JR.

Clyde Layton Sanborn, Jr., 47, of LaConner, died Friday, March 15, 1966 near LaConner.

Born on April 21, 1948 in Oakland, California, he was the son of Clyde and Gwen Sanborn. They later moved to Castro Valley and at age 12 they moved to Stockton. He graduated from Amos Alonzo Stag High School in 1966.

Following his graduation he entered the United States Navy. He served during the Viet Nam War and was discharged in 1971.

He returned to Stockton and then moved to Seattle. In 1976 he moved to Skagit County where he lived a Zen minimalist life on the river.

Mr. Sanborn was a poet and a painter.

Survivors include his mother, Gwen Smith of Lodi, Calif.; a sister Janet Sanborn and her companion, Matthew Maiden, also of Lodi; a brother and sister-in-law, Christopher and Ruthe Sanborn of Soquel, Calif.; a half-brother and his wife, Roger and Deanna Sanborn of Santa Rosa, Calif.; nieces, Bethany Burns and Angela Pope both of Lodi, Sarah Sanborn of Utah and Suzie Bachman of Calif.; nephews, Brendan Sanborn of Stockton, Calif.; and Timothy Sanborn of Santa Rosa, Calif.; an aunt, Merilee Collier of Stockton, Calif.; and special friend, Ruth of LaConner.

A celebration of the life of Clyde L. Sanborn, Jr., will be held on Wednesday, March 20 at 5 p.m. with a potluck dinner at Pioneer Park. Arrangements are in care of Hawthorne Funeral Home in Mount Vernon.

• Obituary •

JANET G. ROBISON

Mrs. Janet G. Robison, 58, a Shelter Bay resident, died at her home Monday, March 18, 1996. She was born in Hoonah, Alaska, October 4, 1937, the daughter of Robert and Elsie Johnstone Greenewald, the youngest of 14

Local SHIBA
available by

New Senior Health Insurance Advisors (SHIBA) volunteers Esther Karlstrom and Douglas Gaines, both of LaConner, will be available from 1-3 p.m. Tuesdays at the LaConner Medical Center. They will assist local people of all ages navigate through the maze, answering questions about Medicare, long term care insurance, Healthy Options, the Basic Health Plan (BHP), and medical billing in general.

SHIBA is a Washington State Insurance Commission program,

• Letter •

Dear Clyde,
River Brother
Beloved Gadfly:

There's a hole here where suddenly you are not.

We huddle in small groups and we grieve.

Love, Paula

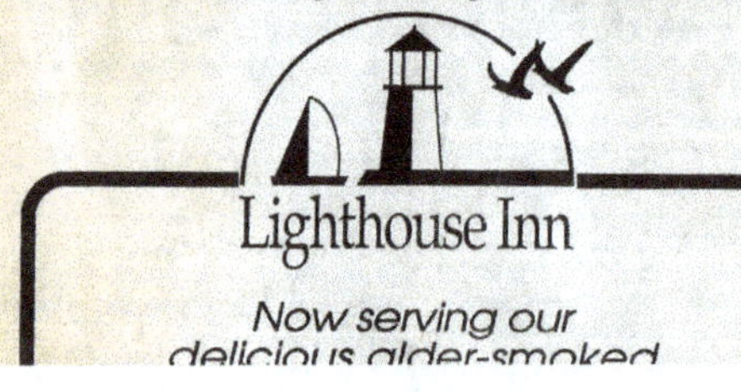

In This Issue	Braves' Sports Reports Pages 4 & 5	Letters to the Editor Page 2	CTP's Own Un-classifieds Page 8

Channel Town Press

35¢

VOL. 21, NO. 7 — LaConner, Washington — Wednesday, March 27, 1996

First Street changes to one-way traffic Friday

Because of a large influx of traffic for the Tulip Festival, First Street will once again become one-way southbound at 12:01 a.m. this Friday. In past years, two-way traffic was allowed up to Washington Street. This year the directional revision will start at Morris Street. Washington Street will remain two-way.

"First Street will stay one way, at least until the end of the Tulip Festival," said LaConner Police Chief Larry Yonally, who explained that Town officials will play it by ear as to when to change the street back.

Dealing with crowds, cars, trucks and buses won't be easy for law enforcement or locals. According to Yonally, at least five officers will be on duty to direct traffic during the day. Motorcycle patrolmen from Island County and the Washington State Patrol will be in the area. Skagit County Sheriff's Deputies will also be out in force.

"We are expecting a lot of people," warned Yonally.

To stop congestion downtown, truck traffic will be diverted from Second Street. Trucks will be required to use Caledonia Street to Maple. Tour buses will be routed towards the Marina.

To help local residents reserve space for their own vehicles, the police department has a limited number of free "no parking" signs available at Town Hall to place near their driveways or usual parking spots. The signs are available on a first-come basis.

Anyone planning to pick up their mail at the post office is

Party leads to students' suspension from sports

The roar of an admiring sports crowd will be a mere memory for several members of the LaConner High School softball

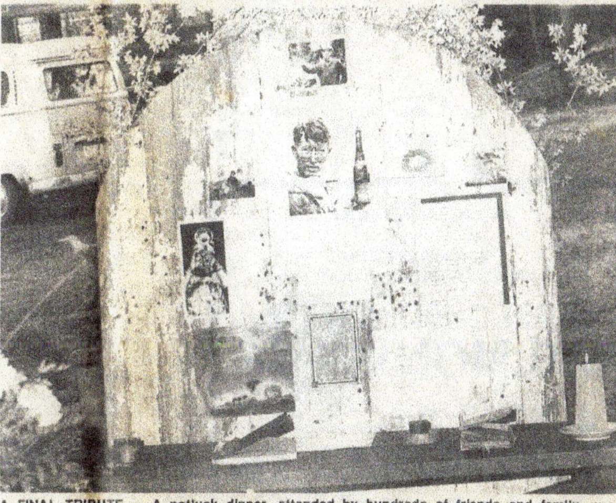

A FINAL TRIBUTE — A potluck dinner, attended by hundreds of friends and family, was held at Pioneer Park last Wednesday evening in memory of Clyde Sanborn. A remembrance board displayed some of his artwork, family photos and a sampling of the many short poems for which he was so well known.
—Photo by Jeff Elkins

Community gathers for Sanborn memorial

Community gathers for Sanborn memorial

Cars, vans and bicycles crowded into every available parking spot in and around Pioneer Park on Wednesday, March 20, for a memorial potluck for the late Clyde Sanborn.

Sanborn, 47, was found dead Saturday morning, March 15, on a sand spit near the south end of the Swinomish Channel. He was the victim of an apparent drowning accident.

Tears filled the eyes of many of the hundreds of mourners, others laughed and talked about pleasant memories of Clyde. Artwork and poems, written by what many locals believe was the last "River Rat" in LaConner, were on display.

One mourner brought several poems written by Clyde. The cherished gifts, written many years ago, were handwritten on yellowed scraps of paper. They were given tearfully to Clyde's mother, Gwen Smith, who attended the vigil with several other family members from Califiornia.

Clyde, a poet and artist, was known to always have had an interesting tidbit to add to any conversation.

He once wrote: "One should always carry a pen. One never knows when one may run into a poem."

According to his close friend, Jim Smith, the Skagit County Sheriff's office is trying to determine Clyde's whereabouts in the days prior to his death. A daily visitor to town, he had not been seen around recently. Anyone who may have seen or spoke to him in the days preceeding his death is asked to contact the Sheriff's office at 336-9450.

ders future
rd boats

vide moorage for ten or more boats.

• Letter •

...itor,
...ople lost the battle for ...all as a community cen-...next battle will be over ...g called "mixed use" in ...h industrial area. This ...Moore-Clark and ...r Pier, and it will per-...s and shops in what has ...en an industrial area. ...al vote on adopting a ...reline Master Plan has ...taken, but already there ...s in it that will author-...d use. Once this is ...by the Town Council,

then the area will be rezoned from industrial to mixed use. This will legitimize what BP America (owner of Moore-Clark) tried to do via the Growth Management Hearings Board, costing the Town about $24,000 in attorney fees and other costs.

Our 1993 visioning survey clearly indicated that the people wanted to maintain an industrial base and promote living wage jobs in this Town. If you still feel that way, then you should attend the Council meetings and

participate in this very important decision.

Dan O'Donnell,
LaConner

• Letter •

To all of Clyde's dear friends,

The depth of love shown by you for our dear Clyde at the recent gathering in his honor at Pioneer Park surpassed our greatest imaginings. It is impossible to put into words our gratitude for your sharing of his presence in your lives. The fact that you came to join in the celebration (and many of you from long distances) was a real comfort to us.

We would love to hear from any and all of you who may have other memories to share, would like copies of photos of him from us, or anything else that comes to mind.

Love and peace,
Clyde's family
Gwen Wilson/Jan Sanborn
1436 W. Elm St.
Lodi, CA 95242

• Letter •

Dear Clyde,

You are gone but not forgotten. You cannot see or smell the flowers, but we will do that for you.

I will cherish the gift of your jackknife that you have given me.

If there is another life in this world we will meet again.

Miss you, love you,
Chico & Nellie
LaConner

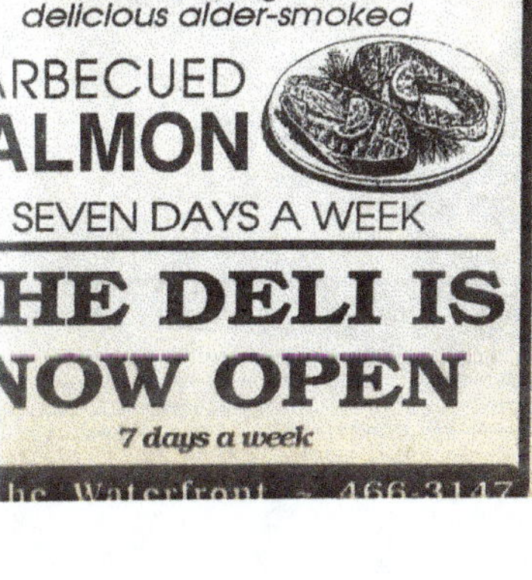

~IN MEMORIAM~

The Funeral

The last time I saw Clyde, he was in a temporary container. Or maybe I should say that he was contained within this container. Or perhaps that he was the contents of the container.

The Temporary Container. A brown cardboard box, a bit bigger than a shoebox. TEMPORARY CONTAINER in large black letters printed clearly on the sides. A sensitive touch of the funeral directors.

From the Temporary Container Clyde passed into the hands of his loving mother. A small slender woman of great emotional strength. I heard her say softly, Clyde you've shrunk.

From his mother's hands Clyde passed into the the river. Gray ashes merging with green water, surrounded by floating daffodils tossed in by friends and family, the tide slowly moving, carrying through a back eddy, and out again toward the bay and on.

I thought of keeping the Temporary Container, knowing Clyde would have appreciated the final Zen joke, the Temporary Container, the transitory nature of life.

But instead we burned the Temporary Container in the old fire pit of Clyde's summer camp, up above his floating flowers and flowing ashes. His camp on the river. His cup remains empty.

Ashes to ashes. Dust to dust. Water to mist. Clyde too will be missed.

Early spring '96
—Michael Clough

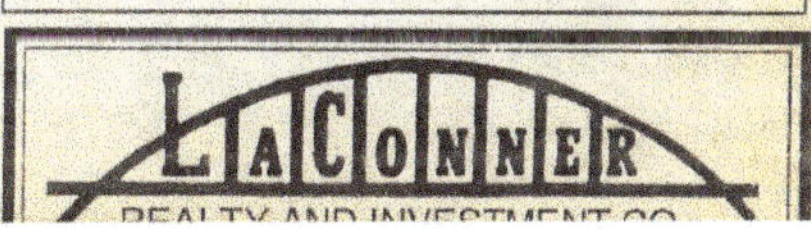

MICHAEL CLOUGH:

Clyde touched many people from both sides of the Channel. Not in a hurry to go anywhere, he would have a few words on the street with strangers and locals alike. I was amazed at how many people showed up at his memorial.

CLYDE SANBORN MEMORIAL RECORDING:

EDITOR: Clyde's memorial took place at Pioneer Park, La Conner, on March 20, 1996. We're very fortunate that a video recording was made. Among the memories and music, jokes, laughter and sadness, many of his friends and family spoke. The following are some of the highlights:

JIM SMITH begins with reading from Ecclesiastes, "All the rivers run into the sea, yet the sea is not full. Unto the place from whence the rivers come, thither they return again." Jim continues, "The last time I saw him he was out visiting my place in order that we might go to see *Waiting for Godot*, Clyde's favorite all-time play. I'm reading this for Clyde, "Do not despair, one of the thieves was saved. But do not presume, one of the thieves was damned."

PAUL HANSEN opens the pages of *The Diamond Sutra* and explains, "There's a time when people get so stupid that Buddhism disappears from the Earth," and he reads the Buddha's response: "Yes, even then there will be beings who when these words of the sutra are being taught will understand this truth. For even at that time, there will be Bodhisattvas who are gifted with good conduct, gifted with virtuous qualities, gifted with wisdom and who, when these words of the sutra are being taught, will understand this truth."

Paul's dog Nero even appears for the reading of Clyde's poem "Nero Woof."

Paul also reads his poem "Did You Know Clyde?" to much audience appreciation:

> Years from now
> a couple of us who are left
> will be creaking down the sidewalk
> and some tourist will ask
> Do you live here?
> Did you know Clyde?
> And when we answer
> will yell to his buddy
> Hey, come here! These old guys
> knew Clyde
> and you know
> he was enlightened.

KEVIN PAUL:

I was one of the first people out there who found him. It took me all day to shake off that feeling of loss of a good friend and brother. Our people view the loss of a loved one in a different way from the white world. In our world there is no death, there's no such word as death, there's only a change of worlds. So when we sing on the drum, these memories we have of our loved ones who have gone on to the other side always come back to our hearts and we think of them. We may never forget Clyde, but I can assure you this, he will never forget you. Just as our ancestors have passed on to the other side, they still watch over us, they still walk with us, they still dance with us when we sing our song. They protect us. We view the spiritual world as something very real and very alive. And for the rest of your lives somewhere along the line, somewhere along your path, Clyde is going to be giving you a message. He'll be with you in spirit.

KAREN HACKETT:

"A Memorial in Memory of Clyde"

There is a bridge connecting Heaven and Earth—it is called the "Rainbow Bridge."

Just this side of the "Rainbow Bridge" is a park called Pioneer. It's a place where we are gathered now in memory of you. Beyond the park there is a land of meadows, hills, valleys and mountains with lush farmers' fields, daffodils, tulips and irises. It is a land where you are now, where there is always food, water, and perfectly warm spring weather—where the frail are young again, where in your past life you've shared a poem, given freely, always with a smile, and indulged in intelligent conversations. There's only one thing missing now— you are not on earth and we cannot see you. You'll be with us, Clyde, certain times, certain places—for those who were touched by you. You'll be missed!

You have been seen and when you and your special friends meet again, then they too shall cross the "Rainbow Bridge," never again to be separated. Now at peace, your memory shall remain.

Goodbye for now, friend.

ROBERT SUND:

The thing about Clyde I think that we all will remember is his voice. For the last several days I've had conversations with Clyde. Just before I stepped up here, there was another one and he said to me [imitates Clyde's manner of speaking]: "Robert read the one about the bee."

> A bee thumps against the dusty window,
> falls to the sill,
> climbs back up, buzzing;
> falls again;
> and does this over and over.
> If only he would climb higher!
> The top half of the window is
> open.

We want to put together a book of Clyde's poems. Five or six years ago, I persuaded him at long last to type up the ones he thought were best. He did. He brought them to me and it's here and the manuscript is also in your homes. So we'll put a notice in the paper about where to send these. And we're going to set up Clyde's Book Publishing Fund.

ALLEN SCHERMERHORN [interrupting]: Everybody here, go through every closet and drawer and book to try to get those old little poems from Clyde—pieces of toilet paper, napkins, we've all got them!

ROBERT SUND [continuing]: I have a lot of them. As a matter of fact, Clyde's first reading was at a bookstore years ago on Main Street and we read together. I was going through some books trying to find something appropriate. I'm working on a piece myself on Clyde as a poet, what his voice meant. For instance, one day he rode downriver

to my shack on Bald Island and he asked, "Have you written any po-
ems?" I said, "Well, I'm writing all the time, Clyde, but I really don't
know whether it's poetry or not." And Clyde said, "Ohh! That's the
beginning of style." So we will gather this book. We all have the pages
of it here and there. [Robert closes with two poems that Clyde liked,
beginnning with Sund's own, "Spring Poem in the Skagit Valley"]:

> The birds are going the other way now,
> passing houses as they go.

> And geese fly
>   back
>   and forth
>   across the valley,
>   getting ready.

> The sound of geese in the distance
>   is wonderful:
>   in our minds
>   we rise up
>   and move on.

[And Robert concludes with a poem from Japan's 13th century
Zen master, Dogen]:

> Midnight,
> No waves
> No wind, the empty boat
> Is flooded with moonlight

[Holding a flapping scrap of paper, Robert vanishes with a line
from *The Bhagavad Gita*, "He alone sees who sees all beings as him-
self."]

ALLEN SCHERMERHORN:

We threw a big party. It's just my friends and river friends out there on a sandspit on McGlinn Island. So I ran a string from La Conner, and this ran about a mile and a half from La Conner, and you could follow the string and go through McGlinn Island and up to the sandspit and here's this party, happening on the beach. The party started around 8 o'clock in the morning, but by midnight what's left are sitting around the campfire and here comes this guy following the string line. And he didn't come empty handed. He had a bucket full of crabs. And we said, "Who are you?" and he said, "I come from Seattle." And that's how we met Clyde. He came in with a bucket of crabs, followed the line for about a mile and a half. Lots of us have been lost out there. He had enough sense to grab the string line.

SARAH SANBORN:

Ever since I can remember, my memory of Uncle Clyde is with a guitar and a harmonica. He'd sit and play these tunes with such a likeness to Bob Dylan that we were always surprised he could make his voice sound so like Bob's. It wasn't until I reached adolescence that I realized that Clyde was not just a talented musician but a special person who maybe didn't follow the rules of the rest of society. In some families the child's life is planned and then at a certain age he or she goes off to college and becomes a person who they want to become. Clyde was the kind of person who felt that he didn't need to go off to college, but that his college was all around him: the sunshine glistening on a blade of grass in the morning dew, a slight afternoon breeze that ruffles calmly the leaves of any tree, and the teachings of his own spirit, and the fellow friends here in La Conner and beyond.

One evening in our home in Kenwood, California, our Aunt Jan Sanborn and Uncle Clyde Sanborn came for a visit. It was always extremely exciting as well as entertaining to enjoy the company of these two creative, loving souls with their instruments—Jan with her flute or penny whistle and oh so classy jazzy voice, and Clyde with his guitar, harmonica and that rough and fun voice of his. I'll never forget how Jan and her brother Clyde made me feel. Clyde, I hope they're keeping up with you on the other side. You will be surely missed. Love, your niece, Sarah Sanborn

MIKE HEATON & JIM SMITH:

No poet could have lived his poetry more faithfully and naturally than Clyde. His natural spirit made us mindful of the failings of the modern age.

Yet life for an eccentric around La Conner can have a hard edge to it. As the town moved toward conformity and became more conscious of its image, riverrats became less appreciated and Clyde was no exception. Still, Clyde was unrepentant. His life was often hard, but he was free.

The freedom of earlier days is rarely seen in La Conner anymore, and Clyde's passing marked the end of an era. His memorial service in Pioneer Park during the spring equinox was attended by the largest number of people ever to gather in the park. Clyde's free and gentle nature touched many lives.

By playing a Zen character, Clyde often tested our patience and our capacity for taking ourselves seriously. Now he's gone, leaving these poems behind to remind us of our proper place in the universe.

JAN SANBORN:

It was a fantastic gathering, about 400 people attended. I really appreciate everyone who participated in presentations, and the outpouring kindness and caring of all the people who came. Who would have thought an old river rat would have touched so many lives? But that was Clyde. He had a way of connecting with people on a level that mattered to them.

MICHAEL CLOUGH:

Shortly after Clyde died, Jim Wilbur (a member of the Swinomish tribe) said he saw Clyde out in Dunlap Bay sitting in a washed up chair. Just like Clyde to spot an empty seat and stop to try it out.

It is important as I have always thought that Jim had a seeing Beyond; the way some of the Natives do.

JIM SMITH AND JANET SAUNDERS:

We did some of the memorial planning, then it evolved with lots of people jumping in. (As Jim put it, the plan for a memorial happened spontaneously as the news of Clyde's death swept through town.) Food, flowers, mementoes for display, speakers, paper plates, firewood, etc. all came together quickly and generously, as we recall. It was a big warm heartfelt event that went on into the night. The next day Clyde's mom and family and a few of us friends took his ashes to the River and let him go.

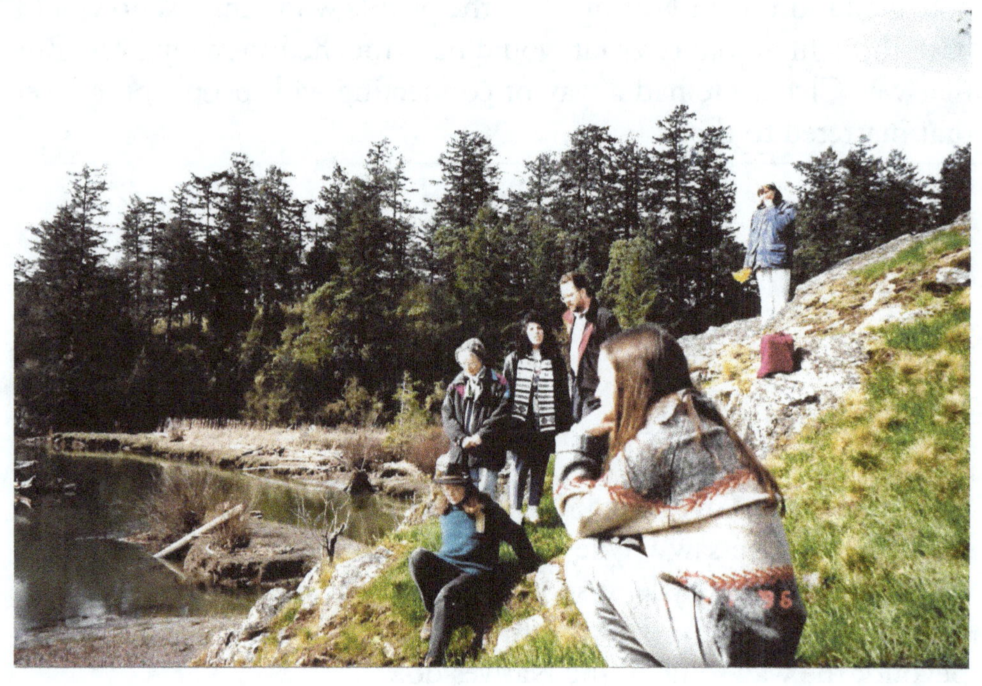

JAN SANBORN: Standing, my mother, Gwen, on the left, Chris' wife Ruthe in the middle, and my brother Chris on the right. Janet Saunders, top of hill with daffodils. In foreground is Sarah. In the green sweater is me (crawling down the steep part of the hill, to get to the point where I scattered the ashes. The photo is deceptive, it doesn't look like we are very high above the water, but we were quite a few feet up).

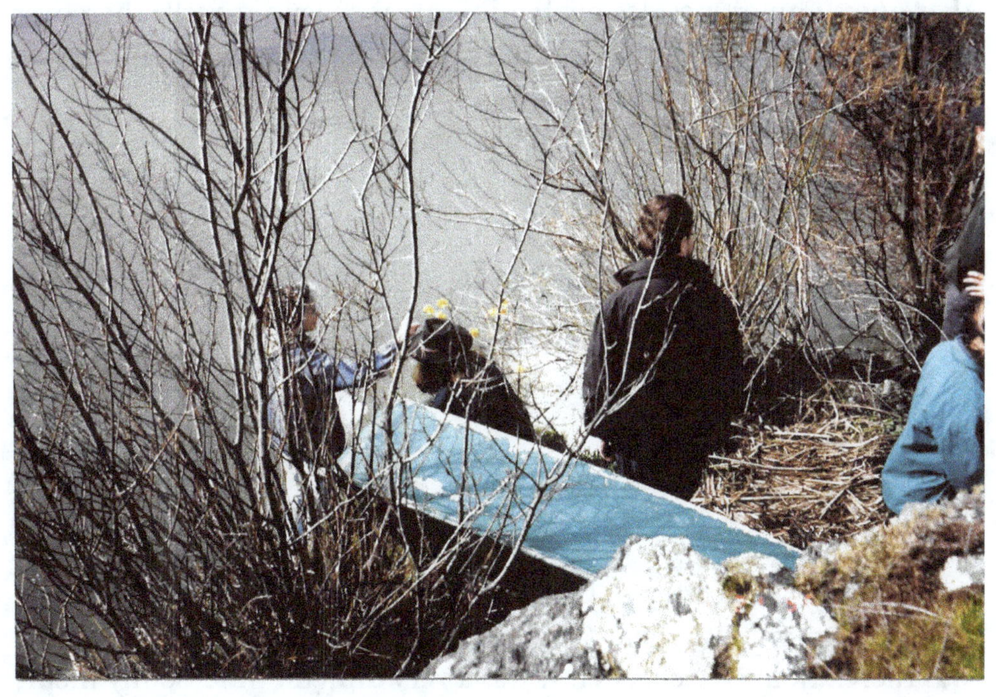

JAN SANBORN: My mom tossing in some daffodils after the ashes. Me, in the black hat. My brother Chris, in the black jacket.

MICHAEL CLOUGH:

We scattered Clyde's ashes in Sullivan Slough. A walk across Sam's field, down the dike to the rock near where Clyde pitched his tent that one summer. Besides his family members and myself, there was Jim Smith and Schaefer. His mom was with us. She said something like, "Have a great trip, Clyde."

JAN SANBORN:

The day we scattered Clyde's ashes into the river...Yes, I was there. My mom was there, as was my niece, Sarah. Michael Clough was there... Johnny Schaeffer. It was a very difficult time, so my memories are sketchy, there was so much emotion blocking my perceptions. I remember that my mom was going to scatter the ashes, but didn't seem to want to. I asked her if she would like me to, and she said yes. We were on a high spot next to the river, there was a rock promontory I walked out on to spread the ashes. Sarah walked out with me. She asked if I could sing Clyde a song, and I wanted to sing the one he was always getting me to perform at parties and gatherings—"Twisted" (I learned Joni Mitchell's version, although I don't think she wrote it.) It begins, "My analyst told me that I was right out of my head, the way he described it, he said I'd be better dead than live..." Well, I just couldn't quite bring myself to sing it at that juncture. Sarah just smiled, hand on my arm, and said, "That's okay, he heard it anyway." I threw the ashes, and she, a large bundle of daffodils.

Someone told me later that some of the flowers washed up where his body was found. I don't know if it's true or not.

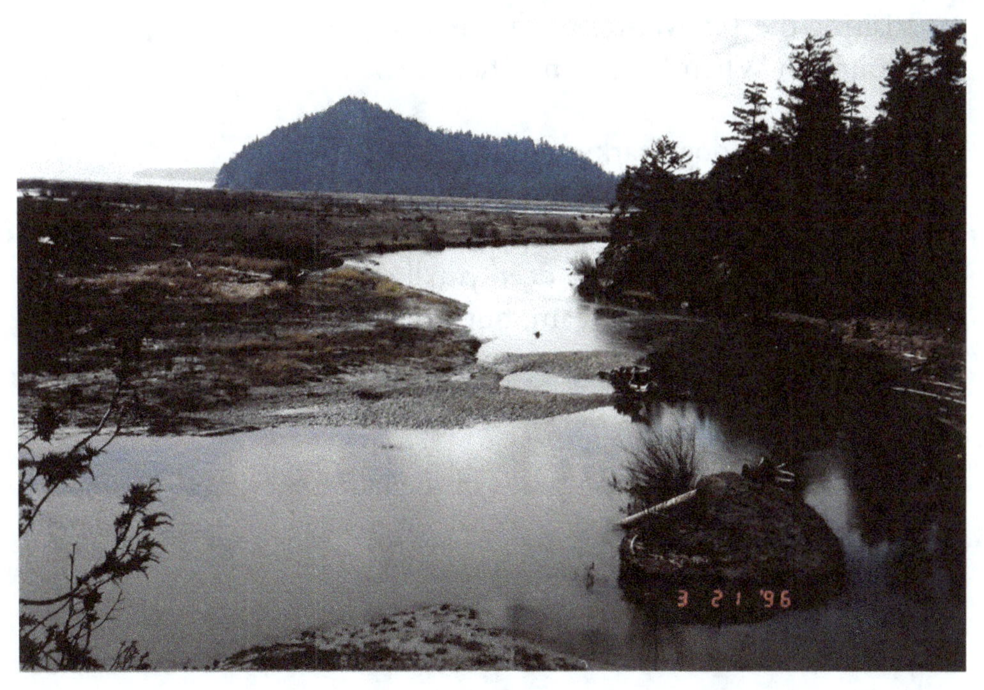

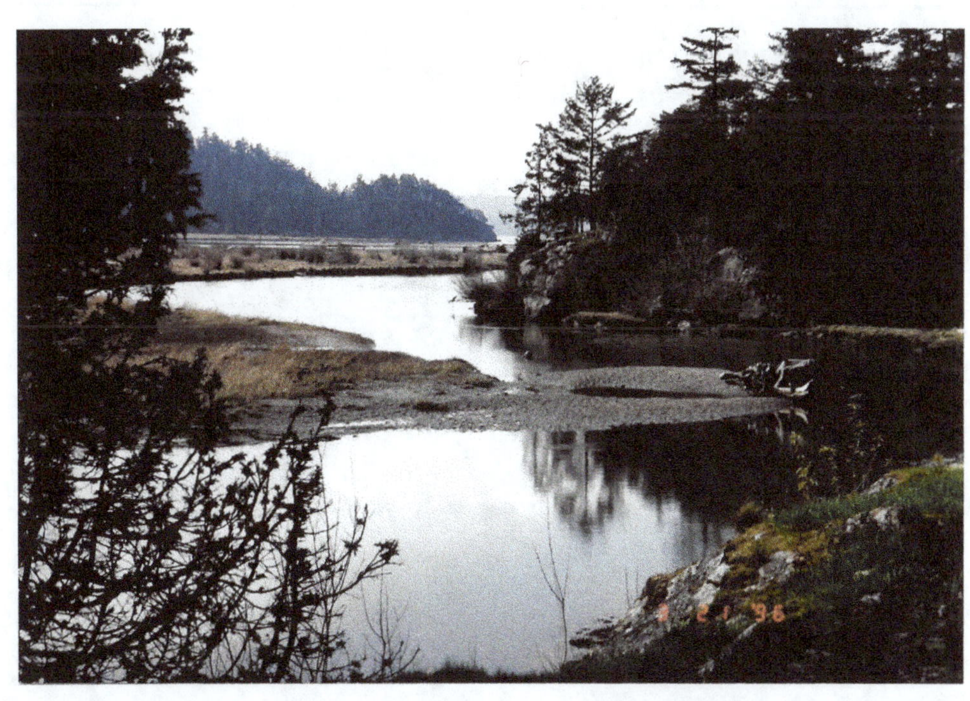

LI PO:

Visiting the Tao Master of Tai-t'ien
Mountain When He Wasn't There

You can hear dogs barking in the sound of the
    water here,
and peach blossoms sparkle from the rain.
Where the trees are really deep you'll see a deer.
No one's here by the stream, but I can't hear the
    temple bell.
Wild bamboo slices through the sky's bright
    white-clouded blues,
and the cascade tries to fly free of the jade-blue
    peak.
Nobody knows where you've gone.
A sadness like Autumn: I lean on a pine here, a
    pine there.

PAUL HANSEN:

At the Grave of Li Tai-Bai.

i. Encountering
The Late Clyde Sanborn

for Clyde and his friends

Near Li Bai's
Grave the constant
Crow and murmur of chickens.
Two young women wash eggs
In the small pond. Behind a bare
Shoulder-high wall, weeds stand fresh
Yellow-green on earthen mound: twisted pines,
Bamboo, dark circle of cypress. Crossing a high
Threshold to enter the temple and bow before
The immaculate white statue of the great
Tang poet, I suddenly sense Clyde,
Strolling in behind me, in slurred
Tones he utters
A short poem

All I can catch is,
When will that taxi driver
Bring in the wine?

ii. The Butterfly's Dream

Walking around
The gravemound, new bamboo,
Mushrooms: hidden birds sing sweet.
A butterfly flutters by, white as Li Bai's image
In his shady temple. I wonder, has the spirit
Of the exiled immortal dropped in
For a quick look?

iii. Farewell to Clyde

I pace around
The round gravemound
Again and again, never so reluctant
To leave a tomb, feel spirit
Fingers touch softly
My sleeve.

Leave
Me here, my friend,
I'll stay awhile.

iv. For Li Bai

On the way
The unpaved, rugged road,
Truly hard to travel. A youthful
Mother nurses her baby at the door
Of a tiny store. A bare-assed tyke clings
To his daddy's back: scenes you knew so well,
And in your sense of self perhaps, suspected even
That after this bakers' dozen of centuries, lonely
Foreigners would trek five thousand miles to watch
A butterfly flit by, taste the stillness
Of your grave and listen
To a dead friend's
Poem.

Quingshan, Anhui
April, 1998

MICHAEL CLOUGH:

A Pseudo Chinese Poem for Clyde and Li Po

Like the ancient Chinese poet Li Po
The poet Clyde loved,
The moon in the river, words, wine.
They both died of occupational hazard.

When Li Po died his remains were stored in
An earthen urn.
When Clyde died his ashes came in a cardboard box
Marked TEMPORARY CONTAINER.

A last worldly joke played on Clyde by the
times and funeral directors?
Li Po too would have laughed at the irony!
The Temporary Container.

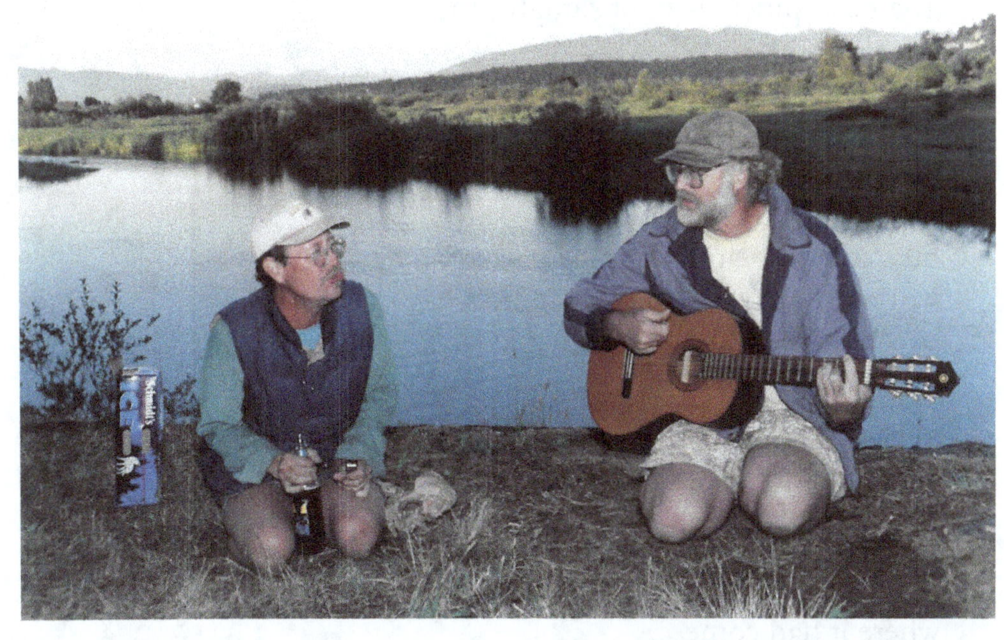

Clyde and Bex up on Brown Lilly Hill on Sullivan's Slough, 1995. "He had a tent up there for his last few years. It was somewhere, anyway, he could be alone for periods. In the winter, he usually came up with other options."   Photo courtesy of Bex.

DENNIS "BEX" BEXELL:

Brown Lilly Hill

He's still hanging out on the hill
sipping beer.
There's a spidery web of sloughs, the
Bay's smooth sheer.
His hat's a little cockeyed and the
twisting smoke of a cigarette
rises into the flower scented air above
the smooth rock face where he sits.
He's contemplating life, the patterns
woven like the breeze-stroked tide
sweeping in along the soft banks of
marsh willows and daffodils thinking,
"Life's like the catspaw faces and figures
that appear momentarily upon the
moving water
for our changing eyes to see." For,
he was thinking of his own life and
where it had come
to a backwater slough of intermittent
revelation.
All the shacks once alive with bodies
and souls
now empty, abandoned, or bulldozed
down by the landlords in a tirade
about freeloading vagabonds having it
made.
While he had stepped off the treadmill to
digress
upon all these matters, sip a beer, wait
for friends or lovers
and good cheer. Now all gone or too
busy to care.
"So, what's the use," he reflected. "Of being

anywhere." as he crushed a beer can
standing high on this hill beneath the
sweeping madrone limbs
gazing over the grassy marsh to
where the Bay begins,
hoisting his pack and off down
the path
leading to the dike and over Sam's
field of glowing green peas
to the barn where his old bike sat.
Down the drive he rode towards town,
his front wheel wobbling as he glanced
at the ground,
but paying no mind as he rode the
astral winds
to where friendly smiles greeted
and the light poured in.

SUE & JIM LUNDBERG:

To Clyde,

We met Clyde on what we call "Margaret's Hill"
Chatting with Clyde was always a thrill.
A twinkle in his eyes, a beer in one hand.
At times we could not understand
what he was getting at (it usually took a long time)
and we wondered if it was us, the beer or the wine!

A great sense of humor, a caring heart,
A love for the river, birds, sunsets…all of this part
of a dear friend we wish was still here
to talk to, laugh with and share a beer.

We find ourselves looking up the hill and hoping to see
Clyde walking down with his bike…but guess it is not to be.

So now there is not a sunset, a bird flying by or
    the changing of tide
that we don't think of you…our good friend: Clyde.

Sue Lundberg: As a Hospice nurse for 15 years, Clyde's poem is very
dear to me. It shows his understanding of the work I do.

Dear Sue

Helping people die is a grace.
    Even on bad days, it
        takes a gentle touch.
Two birds flew over, when

2

you weren't looking.
    They said, happy
        birthday too.

Poem by RUTH:

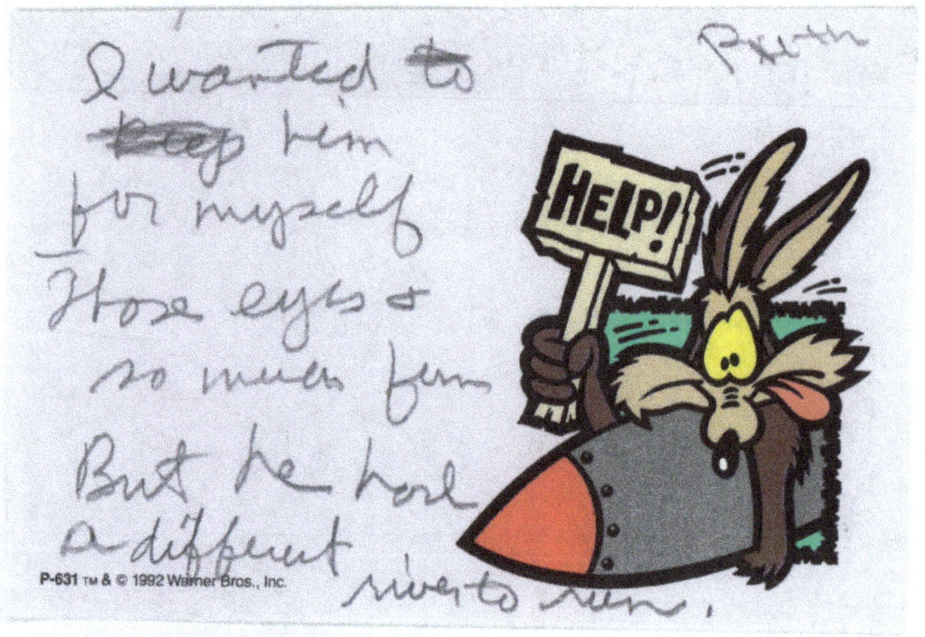

I wanted him
for myself
Those eyes and
so much fun
But he had
a different
river to run.

JIM SMITH:

A Tribute to Clyde Sanborn

Poet Clyde Sanborn left his mark on LaConner. A large circle painted and decorated by local artist Maggie Wilder on the parking lot between the Crossroads building and the Museum of Northwest Art is inscribed with his minimalist Zen thoughts. No run on sentences in Clyde's life.

The poetry circle is a tribute to Clyde who lived a simple life in float shacks and cabins on the north fork of the Skagit River for two decades and hung out in LaConner on his days off. He came into town for supplies and to write poetry for his friends on scraps of paper, napkins and bar coasters. He drowned nine years ago after his boat capsized in the swollen Skagit River. When Clyde's body floated ashore in log-clogged Dunlap Bay he was wearing his trademark pack and rubber boots.

It was a sad day as the news of his drowning spread through town. The bereaved curious soon gathered at Pioneer Park for a celebration of Clyde's life. Clyde's mother, brothers, sister, nephew and niece came up from California for the memorial. Afterwards, his brother Roger said he'd never been to an affair like it in his life. He said it combined all the elements of an Irish wake, Methodist potluck dinner and spiritually-laced Asian funeral. Clyde was a well-rounded character in LaConner.

Hundreds of LaConnerites attended this wake/potluck/funeral. Representatives of the Dysfunctional Sons of the Pioneers were there. Fishtown resident Avocado Richard and river rascals Ivan, Peter and Red Dan stood around the blazing fire in the shelter's stone fireplace until mid-morning the next day talking about life with Clyde. Old timers Clem Thein and Pat Good came. Constable Larry Yonally stood outside the circle of revelation and redemption as river grown passed among local reprobates. Town mayor Dan O'Donnell was one of Clyde's friends and came to pay his respects. Writer Tom Robbins, a benefactor of Clyde's town life, was there. Robert Sund came and spoke eloquently to Clyde's friends. Chinese translator Paul Hansen read from a Tibetan text. Yes, existentialist Jean Paul Sartre was right, "…and the dead are prey for the living."

It was quite an occasion. Skagit County Historical Museum curator Pat Doran attended and spread the picnic tables with white bed sheets, arranged bushels of daffodils and set candles.

Amateur funeral director Karen Hackett (Gargoyle Lady) placed lighted torches at the entrance to the park. She told the crowd that Clyde always reminded her of an enlightened preppie in his layered river clothing. She also distributed packets of wildflower seeds to be spread in remembrance of him.

John Kaguras recited a one-line Clyde poem from memory. The tribute to Clyde went on and on in front of a Bo Miller floodlighted altar salvaged from the flotsam on the waterfront displaying pictures of Clyde and samples of his calligraphed poetry.

Jimmy Wilbur and Kevin Paul played drums and sang a prayerful Swinomish song of remembrance for Clyde. Clyde's niece read a poem she had written. Bex played a Dylan song on his guitar. There were serious moments and spontaneous eruptions of applause and laughter which would have pleased Clyde.

Clyde's girlfriend, Ruth, hung her painting "Under the River" above the fireplace. A few LaConner river women spoke of their fondness for Clyde before leaving the park early to attend an exorcism in another part of town. There was something meaningful for everyone who gathered in the park.

A few days ago at Gretchen's Café Culture, I was telling a newcomer to town, "Nora from Anacortes," a Clyde story. These stories will surface a decade after Clyde's passing. He made that much of an impression. I told Nora that Clyde's mother, Gwen, used to come up from Stockton to visit him. She stayed with Janet and I during her visits, when we lived on Morris Street next to Joanne's Grocery dumpster where Clyde scrounged for past-due yogurt. I told Nora that the only thing that changed in Clyde's life when his mother visited was that he drank premium beer instead of Rainier Ale while she was in town.

Gwen had a mother's unconditional love for Clyde. Everyone else merely tolerated him, not turning him into a local hero until he was gone.

A year after his death Clyde's poetry was published in a book entitled "Flash Flood." Soon, an expanded second edition of the book will be coming out. If you have a Clyde poem which you would like included, please send it to me, at P.O Box 614, LaConner, WA 98257.

TO: SKAGIT VALLEY HERALD
FROM: J. Saunders
      466-2066
DATE: MAY 3, 1996

CLYDE'S POETRY SOUGHT

Plans are under way to publish a collection of Clyde Sanborn's poems. The LaConner poet, who did most of his writing on cocktail napkins or coasters which he subsequently gave away, died recently in an accident on the Skagit River. People who have poems by Clyde are urged to make a copy and put it in the drop box at Cafe Pojante in downtown LaConner or send it to Ben Munsey at P.O. Box 1158, LaConner, WA 98257 <munsey@sos.net> as soon as possible.

JIM SMITH:

Clyde's Last Encounter
(the first Republican Dharma Bum)

Clyde Sanborn died two years ago in a drowning accident in the Skagit River. He had lived on the Skagit River for nearly 20 years after moving here from Seattle in the late 1970s following an honorable discharge from the Navy.

On the river he lived a simple life. He camped out on Brown Lily Hill above the entrance to Sullivan Slough during good weather and found shelter in abandoned cabins and on half-sunken boats along the river during the rainy winter months. It was not an easy life. The quest for enlightenment is not for sissies.

Clyde made daily trips into town where he did what he called the "Food Stamp Shuffle." He would buy fruit with a dollar food stamp at one grocery store and then walk to the other and buy a quart of beer with the change.

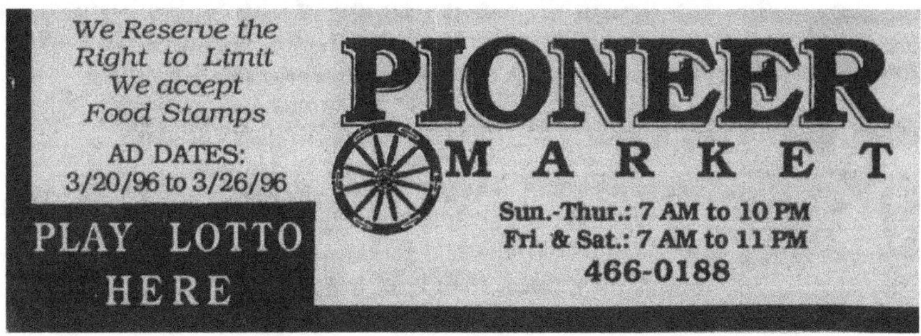

He also met his simple Zen needs with the money he earned mowing lawns and doing odd jobs around town. Using his food stamps for beer forced him to make up the nutritional deficit by gathering past due food from dumpsters behind the grocery stores, an activity he referred to as "dumpster diving." Clyde was generous and kind. Often he would prepare creative meals with this dumpster food at his friends' houses in town or on the river. His biggest dumpster score was a freezer full of meat from the dumpster behind the Pioneer Market which he stashed in Chico and Maude's freezer at the Wagon Wheel Motel. He would bring this meat to cook outs.

Clyde also made the rounds of the bars in La Conner. His

favorite was the Lighthouse where he entertained the patrons with his poetry written on coasters and napkins in exchange for a drink. He was 86'd from the LaConner Tavern when he was caught rolling a "smokie-wokie" at the back table one afternoon. His expulsion was permanent, although occasionally he would sneak in when there was a large crowd distracting the bartender. During his last visit to the Tavern, he was seen standing next to the pool table reciting one of his poems to United States Senator Slade Gorton who had come into the LaConner Tavern with some of his Young Republican supporters.

Following his recitation, Clyde asked Slade a typical Clyde-Zen question, "What's more powerful, love or war?" The Senator backed away from Clyde, his toothy politician's smile replaced with a more contemplative expression. It was obvious Slade was wondering if he was being put on. But Clyde was serious.

The Senator was one of the last to see Clyde in top form. For this reason Flash Flood is dedicated to Senator Slade Gorton who has been seen in rags, gaunt and haggard standing at Clyde's campsite on Brown Lily Hill waiting for Clyde to return from town with a quart of Rainier Ale and pondering Clyde's question.

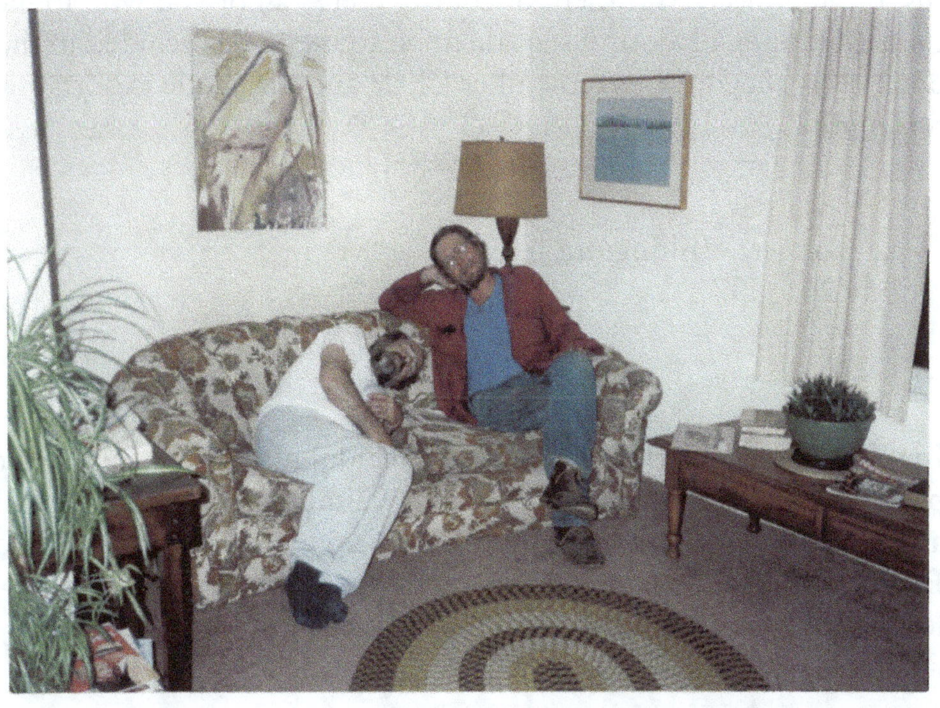

Jim Smith & Clyde Sanborn.

EDITOR: After the publication of *Flash Flood & Other Poems*, BEN MUNSEY began "Project Clyde on the Web." As Ben explains online: "The first edition of *Flashflood and Other Poems*, published by Project Clyde in 1997, is sold out. We want to thank all of the keepers of Clyde's poems who brought them to us for inclusion in the book. If you're a friend of Clyde's and still have a poem of his you'd like to share with the world, you can still be a part of Project Clyde on the Web. Just send the poem on to Ben. Who knows? There may even be a second paper edition someday."

Ben added a paragraph after the original book's introduction:

When Clyde's death came—suddenly, like a flash flood—the need arose to try to salvage some of the flotsam and jetsam of his poetry. I want to thank the many people who did so much to help bring these poems together. Some—like Robert Sund, Paul Hansen and Clifford Burke—gave valued advice. Others—like Jim Smith and Steve Herold—donated hours of skillful work. Clyde's family— Chris, Roger and Jan Sanborn and Gwen Wilson—provided impetus to the project. And then, of course, there's all of you who found these gifts from Clyde and sent them on to me to be included in this book. May they help us remember Clyde and his gentle exhortation to simplify.

Ben Munsey
La Conner, Washington
July 26, 1997

In its online incarnation, *Flash Flood* includes nine poems not in the printed book. The first of these, "Sandy Climbed" fits naturally right after the book's poem, "Sailing." The poem "Crashing at Meg and Ben's" was added before "86'd," and the other seven poems followed. Here are those additional poems:

Sandy Climbed

Sandy climbed the rigging,
   the sky, he climbed —
And finally got back
   to himself.

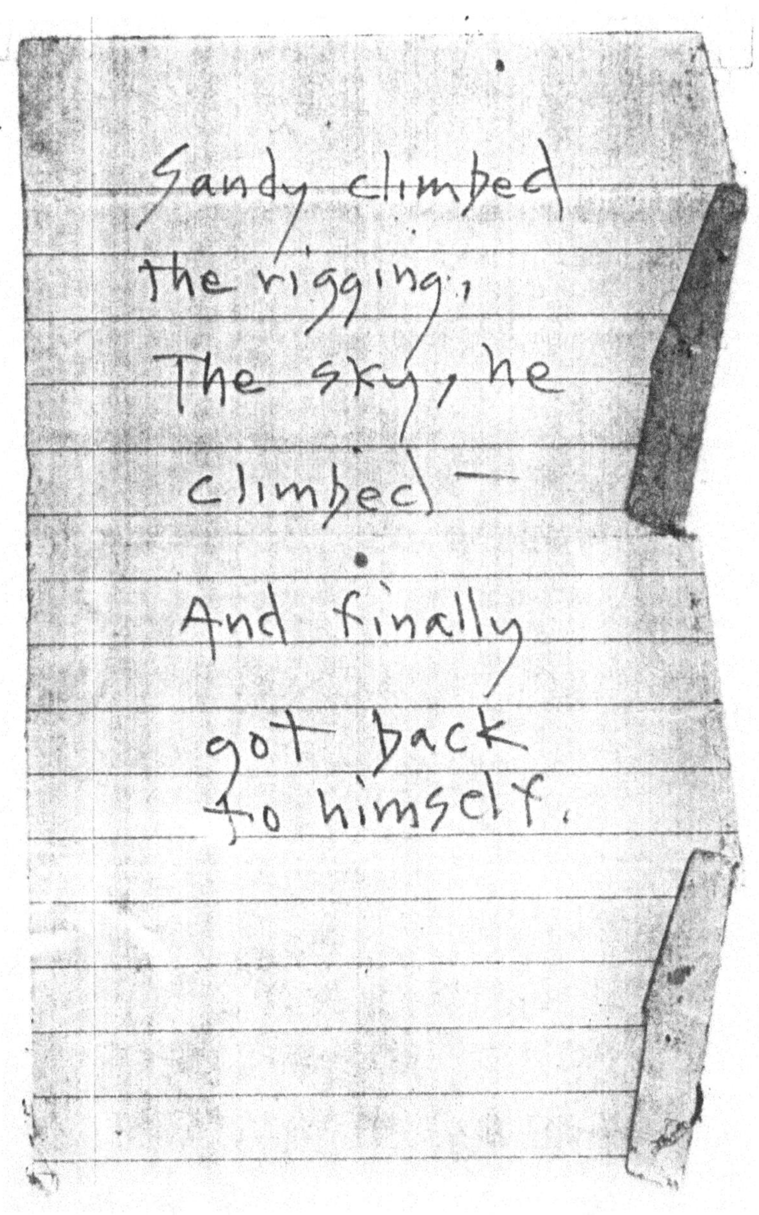

Crashing at Meg and Ben's

After Ian and I
swept the floor
    I go outside and find
    a raw cow head
    next the Realty sign
    in the frontyard,
with a dog chewing on it.

There is nothing quite so
sweet this morning
as looking into a dead
cow eye, in the
early morning sunshine.

And by the way, where is Drucilla?

Beyond a Holy Dream

Beyond a holy dream,
    a leaf of the autumn
became a diamond
    in my hand.

-O-

I place a piece of wonder
    in your hand
with the loudness of a single
    snowflake in the meadow
that lives and dies without a name.

Grinning Under Starlight

Grinning under starlight
   under a thousand
      silent exploding suns

with the woman golden
   on the outside and inside.

That hair, those fillings,
   a regular Katzenjammer
      of a girl,

singing silver songs to herself
   and the moon and me.

For Randy and Debbie's Wedding

The heart of love is simple
    and absorbs the complex.
Love is the field of goodness
    in the meadows of the child.

"Jed, the rings please."

This day is the day
    of all things as they are.
So rejoice in the beauties
    that already exist.

Now let us party for the
    union of two that we love.

6/2/79

Allia

When I saw the hamburger
    you brought me
    eighteen years ago
       I fell in love.

I fell in love with you.

Now, I'll tiptoe to Oregon,
    I'll be singing 'Allia'
    in Oregon,
I'll bounce to Oregon —
    that old hamburger
    has yet to be digested.

Clyde in Fishtown at Bo's House

At first, mother and father swallow
    did some squawking, their new ones
    just now flying. And twenty or thirty spiders
    contemplated catatonia, in little brown balls
        before moving on
Ah, Solitude at last! Then the conspiracy began;
    a contest between boat motors and jet motors.
    One jet came so close, the jet fuel made
        rainbows in my tea.
I asked the pilot if he wouldn't mind changing
    course a few degrees and how the war was going.
He said he'd like to bring his boat out to do some
    fishing after work.
On Thursday two fishermen park downstream about
    thirty feet.
They talk about the "nice fish"
    that one of them lost, while fishing the straits.
I asked them if they'd seen Big Butch Hazard,
    the Skagit's toughest, smelliest, meanest, biggest
    fish, a former Olympian swimmer, who could bend
    a crane hook straight just by starin' at it hard.
No, he said, and asked me if I'd seen Buddha.
    They brought the beer
    I brought some wine.
        We told "fishing stories."

In the Blue Boat

In the blue boat
    my boots stand still,
    moving with the tide.

The moon is full
    but not up.

The stars dream of shining
    under blue.

One oar holds my boat.
    An upward finger
    holding earth and sky.

Lifting the cup
    I slosh on my bare chest,
    and rub wine into my heart.

Revision

When I started revising this poem,
    there were more words.
Now, the more I think of it,
    there aren't so many.
Pretty soon there won't be any left.

Paintings by CLYDE SANBORN:

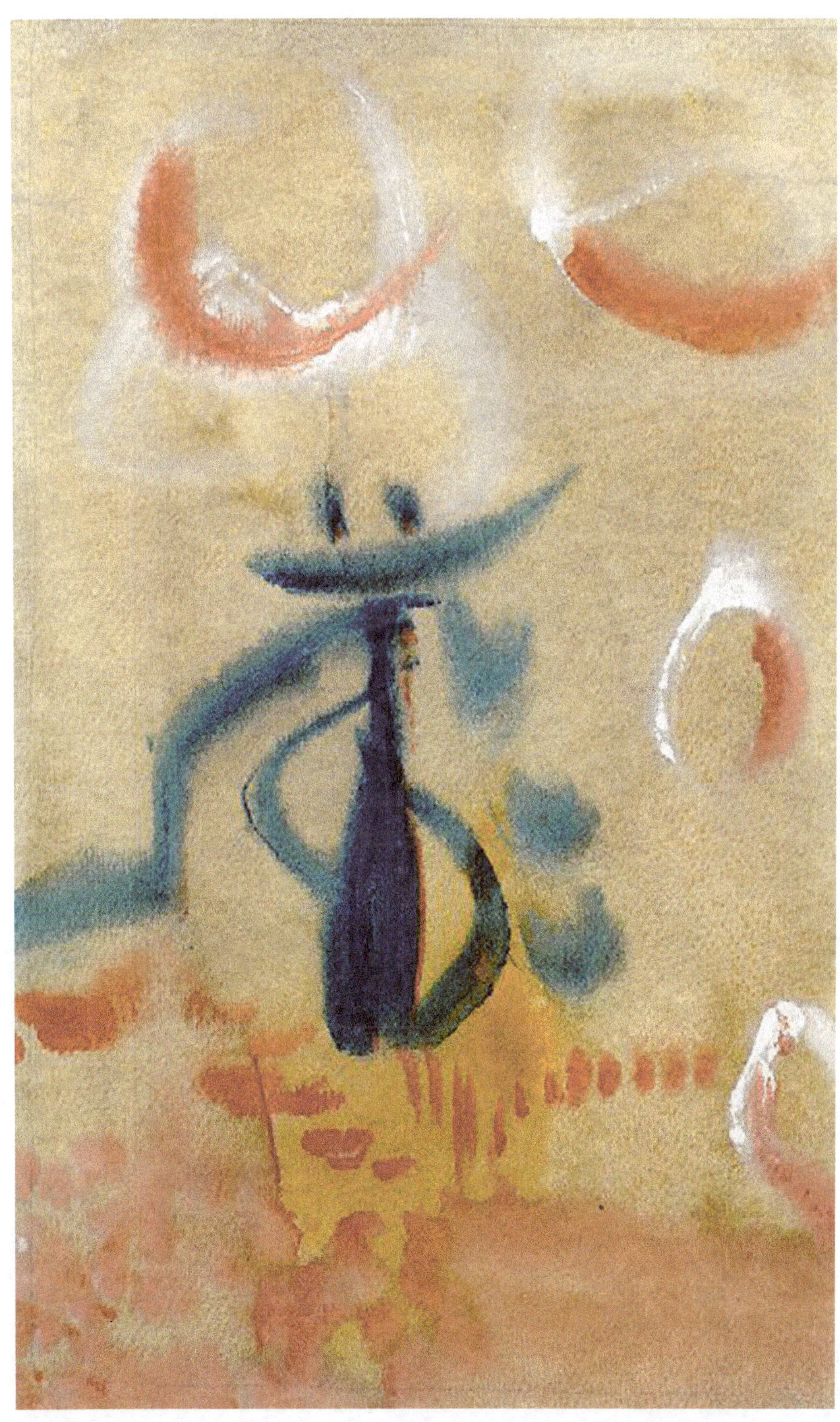

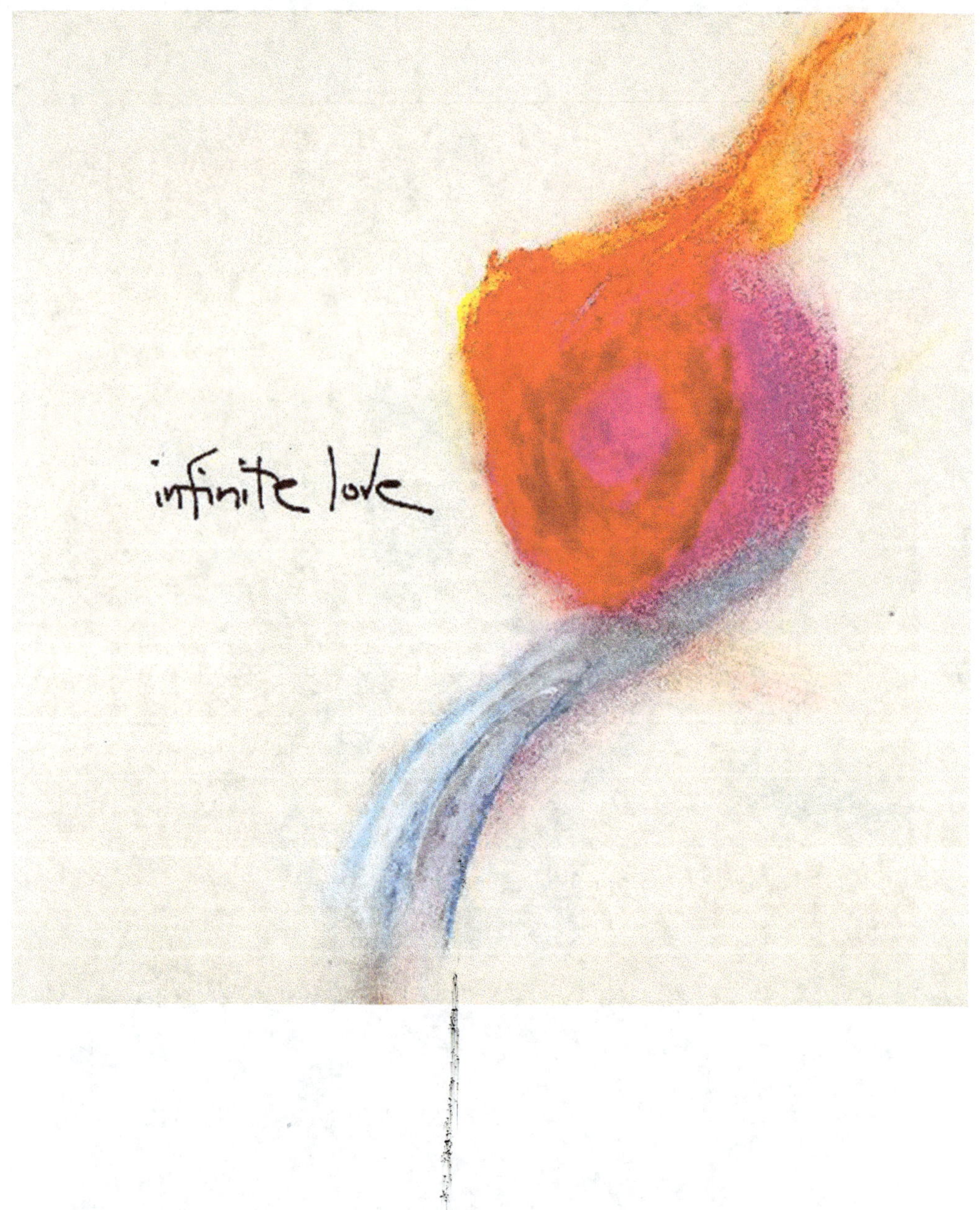

infinite love

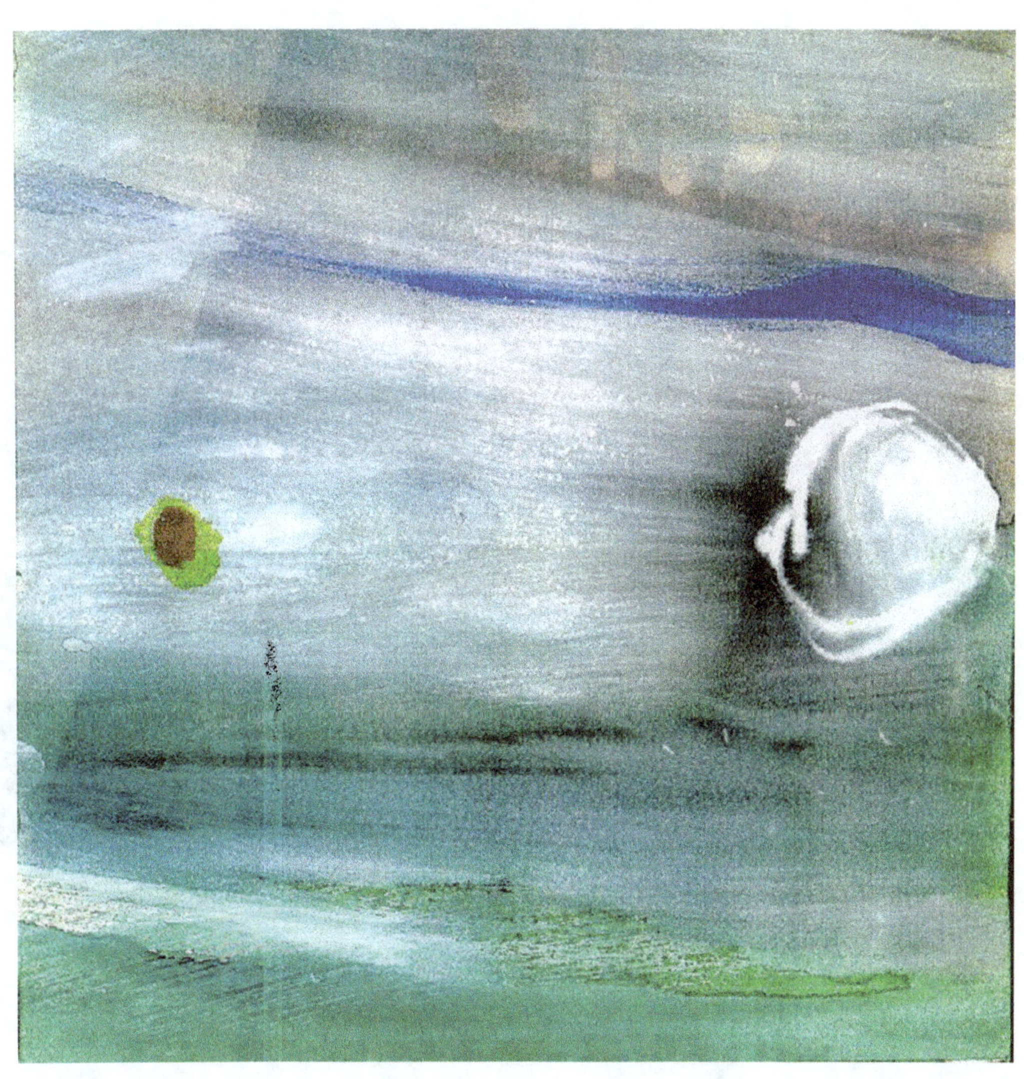

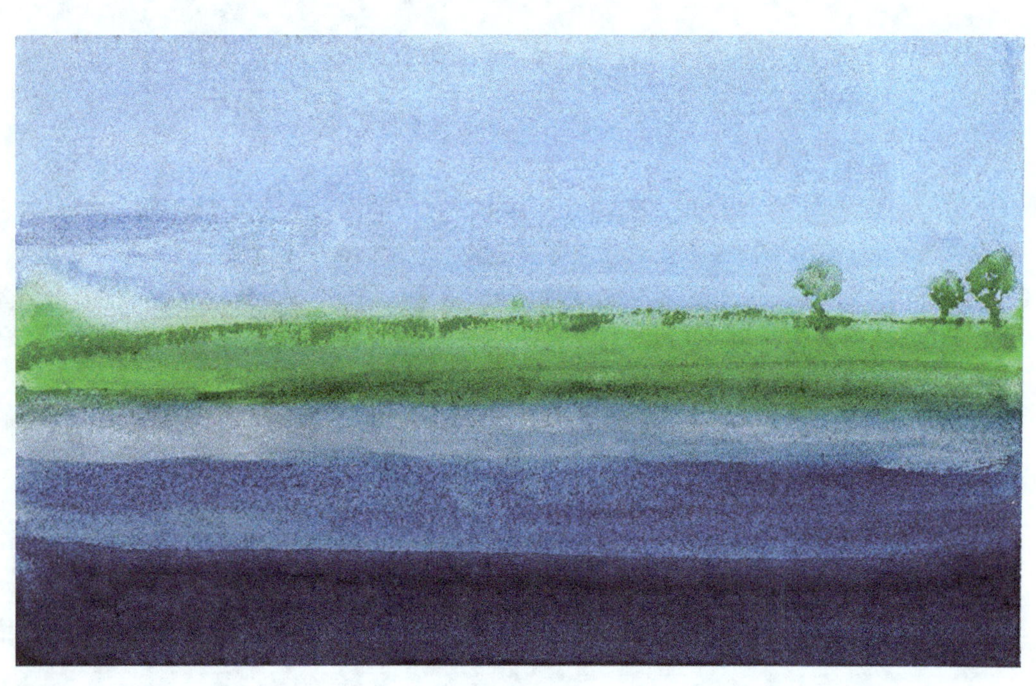

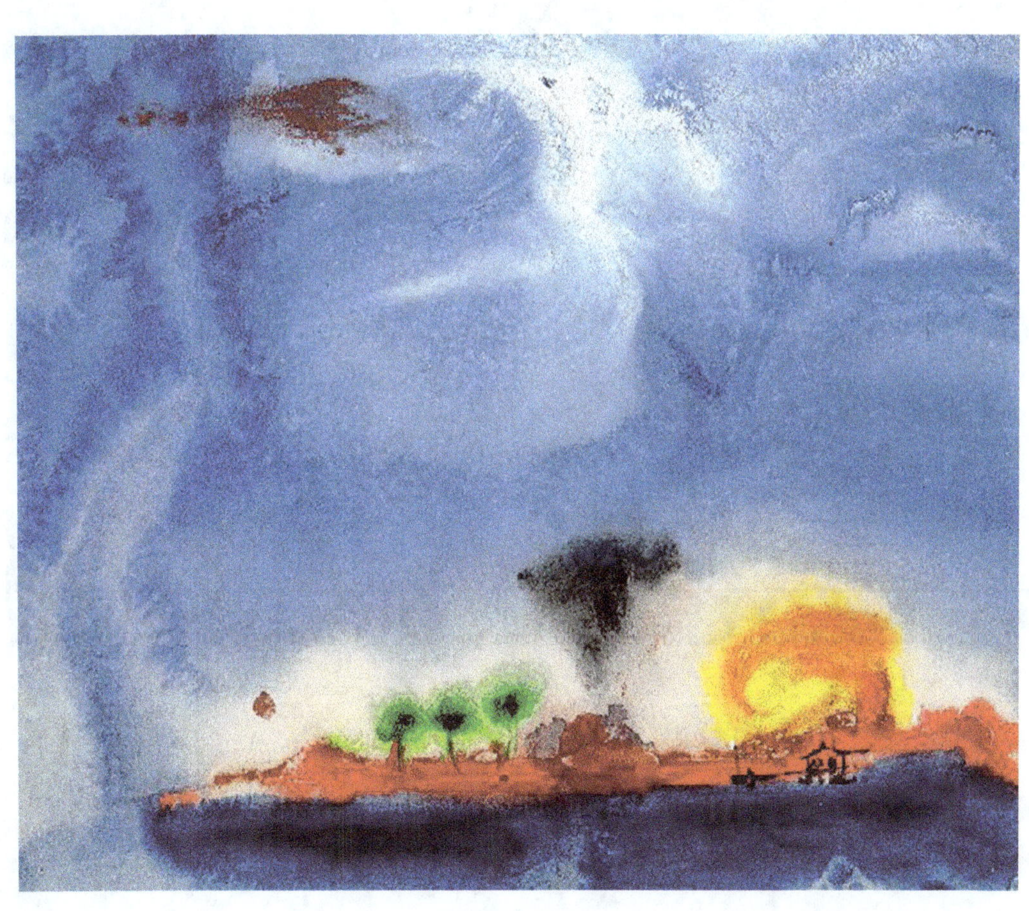

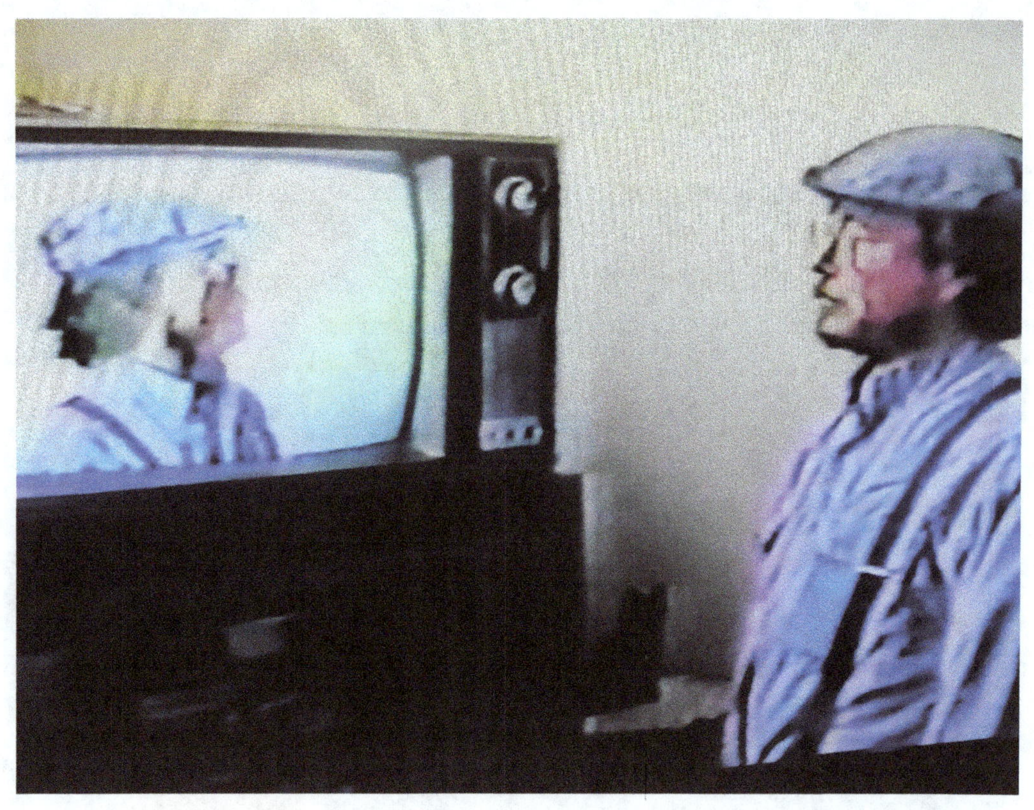

CLYDE INTERVIEWING CLYDE (Stockton, California):

EDITOR: This is from an old unmarked video cassette. As Michael Clough remembers, "The interview was recorded at his mom's. It must have been the year before the year he died because he didn't go to mom's that winter. Maybe the first time ever. Clyde would bus to California, Greyhound or sometimes the Green Tortoise, the hippie bus. I think it was a tough winter for him. I only saw that interview once. I think it was after his death."

[The video begins with a close-up of Clyde.]

"Good afternoon, ladies and gentlemen. Today's question is—who is the real Clyde Sanborn? And we have with us today Clyde Sanborn to answer that question."

[The Camera pulls back to reveal that the Clyde who was talking is actually on TV. And standing beside the TV set is Clyde Sanborn, watching himself.]

TV: "Clyde…"

"Hi."

TV: "Welcome."

"Thank you."

TV: "Clyde, where are you from?"

"Uh, from the Pleiades. I can't say exactly what star system."

TV: "I see, I see. Uh…How do you feel?"

"I feel fine."

TV: "That's good. Um, can I ask, how did you drive to planet Earth?"

"Oh I got a Type 3 hyperfoil with modified singularity and modulator."

TV: "Gee, that's very interesting. Well, I hope you enjoy your stay here on Earth."

"Thank you. That's very kind of you."

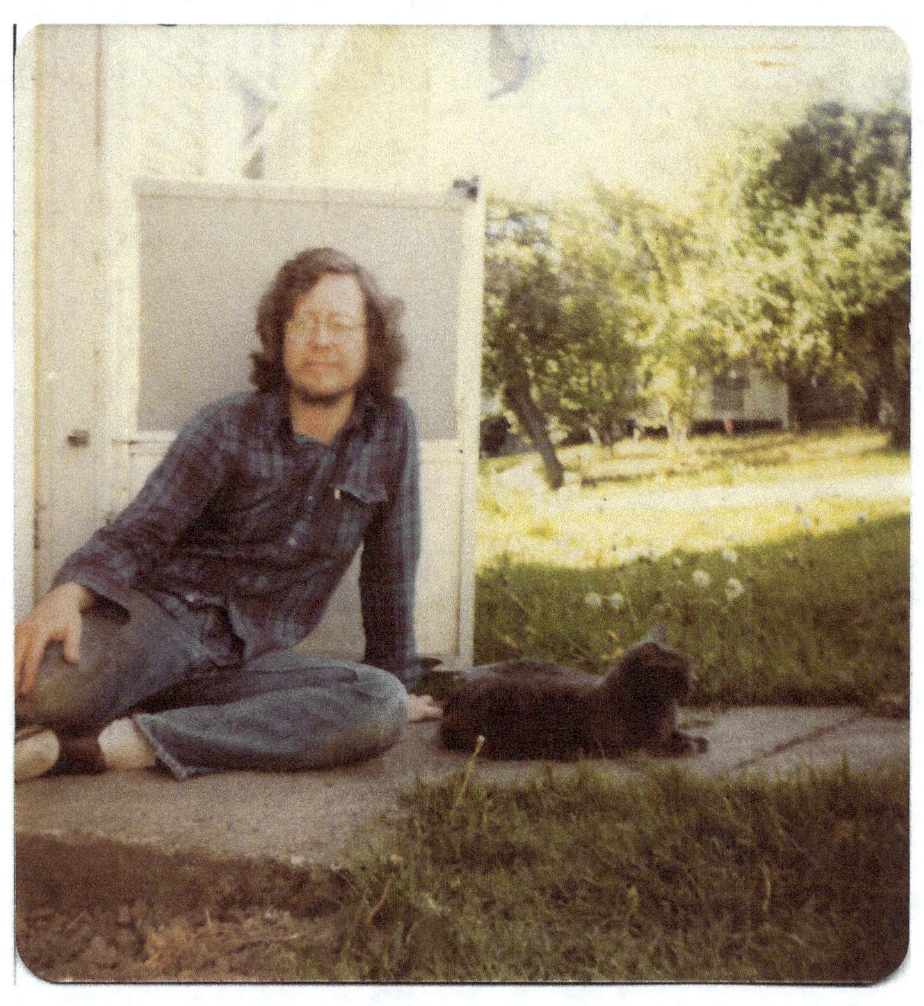

Clyde and his cat, when he lived in Mount Vernon.
Photo courtesy of Jan Sanborn.

Poem by CLYDE SANBORN:

Siesta

The cat seems simple in the sun
that is passing through the candle,
    touching the edge of the board.

    It comes in waves.

The cat seems ample in the lukewarm
afternoon I begin to doze in.

The cat is suddenly a grinning bird merchant,
selling his whistle.   The teeth are extra.

He hands me a mirror with the moon inside.

The cat and I, we somersault and
somersault.

    Stumbling a moment
    up eternity.

CONTRIBUTORS:

ERIK AMBJOR:

Erik Schweiss Ambjor, met Clyde in the late seventies in La Conner and Seattle through his friendship with Robert Sund. His photography has been featured in several of Robert Sund's books of poems, including Ish River and Notes from Disappearing Lake and most recently in A Flutter of Birds Passing Through Heaven. He currently resides in San Francisco and is the owner of Sonoma Forge, a specialty producer of designer faucets.

RUTH BECKEL:

Ruth is an abstract artist whose paintings are full of life and color and beauty. She was born and raised in Seattle, lived many years in Bellingham with her family, then Clear Lake and La Conner where she met Clyde sometime in the late 1980s. Ruth fit right in with Clyde's off-beat, charming, minimalist style and soon they were an "item" around town.

Ruth lives now in Truth or Consequences, New Mexico, still making paintings as well as poems. And, she says, still missing "Ol' Clyde."

DENNIS "BEX" BEXELL:

There was not a freer individual I'd ever met in life than Clyde. He drifted from shack to shack to leaky boat to tent, his sole possessions an ancient, gigantic Royal typewriter and a tank of a guitar. The Skagit River delta was his refuge as was mine. We spent many a time sitting on the back deck of my sailboat, Rahoola, or up at his tent site on Brown Lilly Hill downing beers and dissecting various facets of life. But the river world was only one element of Clyde's life. He relished town, also, and being among people. There he could be found crashing in Jim Smith's basement, sleeping under a bush by the Yacht Club, or hanging out at anyone's home or bar that allowed him in. Wherever he might be, one could always expect one of his incisive, short poems as a parting gift. He was a genuine hermit sage in the style of a Han Shan or Li Po. He was also a steadfast, loyal friend who bailed me out on more than a few occasions.

MICHAEL CLOUGH:

Back in the "Before Times" as Clyde labelled them, 1970s; the concept of Karma was often bandied about. Fate, actions, reactions, consequences, past, future; a preordained path or the results of Life's choices. A mystery I don't know if my years of friendship and knowing Clyde was Karma, his or mine; but it was definitely a TRIP! From a chance meeting in San Diego 1969 when we were both in the Military; Clyde Navy me Air Force. Later in Seattle. As roommates, neighbors, sharing the same friends, jobs, good times. When I moved to La Conner and then to The River, Clyde soon followed.

There seems to be some bond that connected us. Perhaps it was all those Psychedelic drugs that we took.

JOAN CROSS:

I enjoyed Clyde's one-liners that carried humor in their brevity. I'd see him at the old 1890's Tavern in La Conner and he'd look me in the eye and think of a phrase that he'd write on a napkin and give it to me as a gift. His gifts were always seeing the world from an unpredictable perspective. He'd stop by my house on his way back from town to his river shack calling me his 'black-eyed Susan' as I work in my yard. He was a big part of La Conner art/poetry scene in the '70s and '80s.

CHUCK EASTON:

Jazz guitarist Chuck Easton grew up in Mount Vernon. He spent a couple of years in the US Army, with a year in Korea, and some time in Boston going to music school, but has lived most of his life in the area bounded by Seattle, Bellingham, and Port Townsend, with La Conner in the middle, or, with a nod towards Clyde, inside the triangle formed by the Blue Moon, the Kulshan and the Town Tavern, with the 1890's in the center. Alas, the Kulshan and the Town Tavern are no more; the 1890's has either moved or the name has been changed. Fortunately, the Blue Moon lives on.

Chuck lives south of Chimacum with his wife, Autumn Scott, and two cats. He teaches a variety of instruments at Crossroads Music in Pt. Townsend and gigs locally on guitar, bass and occasionally flute, saxophone, trombone and even Eb tuba. He still likes to down a few beers.

SHEILA FARR:

Sheila Farr participates in the Northwest arts scene as a poet, author and arts writer. Her books on artists Fay Jones, Leo Kenney, James Martin and others are published by the University of Washington Press. She served as art critic for the Seattle Times from 2000 - 2009.

PAUL HANSEN:

In Clyde's life there was Zen, comedy and a tragic thread. After twenty years I suspect I will always miss him.

CHARLIE KRAFFT:

A native of the Pacific Northwest Charles Krafft moved to La Conner in 1967 from San Francisco where he'd gone looking for the San Francisco Poetry Renaissance remnant and became immersed in the emerging psychedelic counter-culture. After the Diggers' "Death of Hippy" funeral and before "The Summer of Love" he returned to the Skagit Valley where he pursued a career as an artist and part-time poet until 1980. Krafft met Clyde Sanborn in The Deluxe Tavern in 1975 during a year spent living off Broadway St. on Seattle's Capitol Hill. Sanborn worked in the kitchen there and often passed out hot baked potatoes to friends waiting outside for him at the backdoor after the bar closed. When Clyde moved into the Frank Allen/Oscar Hambre fish camp on the sandspit just outside La Conner a few years after Krafft returned, he and Sanborn resumed their friendship and carousing. Krafft's poem about hitchhiking to Port Townsend to attend a poetry reading given by Gary Snyder at the Fort Warden State Park sums up the sort of mischief they enjoyed getting into together.

JEFF LANGLOW:

Clyde presented me this poem [p.158] one afternoon in La Conner. We were pretty accustomed to each other and not infrequently 'single.' My life is a story every minute. I'd say Clyde might agree.

TIM MCNULTY:

Tim McNulty is a poet, nature writer, and friend of a number of Skagit river rats. Tim's few encounters with Clyde were always enjoyable, often puzzling, sometimes wondrous. Clyde left him feeling afterward as though he had just encountered a wise old Zen master on the skids.

FRED OWENS:

I contributed to this book about Clyde because he was a good friend. I can picture him now, sitting on the front porch of Jim Smith's house on Morris Street, holding a half gallon jug of red wine. Clyde had a deep, slow voice and you could hear him talk even if he said nothing. He died in 1996 and hundreds of people came to his funeral. We still remember him. I am supposed to be writing about myself here, but I only want to say I was his friend.

TOM ROBBINS:

Tom Robbins is the author of nine best-selling novels, a collection of short writings, and a memoir. Published in 22 foreign countries, his books have been adapted for film and stage. Born and raised in the South, Robbins has lived in La Conner, Washington since 1970.

JAN SANBORN:

Clyde was my brother, senior to me by 11 years. In many ways, he was more like a dad, being responsible for introducing me to many ideas, philosophies, etc. since I was a little girl. He taught me to love nature, and as his poem says, have "more respect for insects and stones." He went into the Navy when I was seven, and those were a long four years without him. He let me listen to his prodigious record collection though, which helped pass the time. His time in the service changed him, though he never wanted to talk about that. He was absent a lot as we got older, but he was always there for me when I needed a wise ear. I loved him greatly. I miss him, but am reminded of him every day, in some little way, as I do my best to reflect back into the world the best of what he taught me. A huge thanks to Allen for taking on this Clydish project, and to all his friends and loved ones who contributed to the effort.

SARAH SANBORN:

Clyde had an amazing ability to know things about people, situations, he was a seer, and could see through you, it was truly a gift. Many people now are waking up to this kind of ability within ourselves, our Buddha nature within. Clyde would want us all to be able to listen to that within ourselves, and pay attention to that. He knew how to meditate, and I think he lived his life as a waking mediation in Zen consciousness. As his niece, his influence in my life has been very profound, and I find that getting back to nature, living close to it, within it, or being in it daily is important if you live in the city. Clyde taught me and still continues to teach me about living in the moment, downsizing my life, so that my stuff doesn't own me; as in if you have lots of stuff, belongings, the stuff begins to own you. He has inspired me to want to live as he did, with music, poetry, art, close to nature, in a community of friends and family. He was a river rat, they call it, and my dream is to live in a community of tiny house village, where people are close by, regularly or daily communicate, reach out and support each other, especially for our elders and retired generation, they need to be with others, to have social contact. Follow your thoughts, and observe where the mind goes, focus it moment by moment, or it will control you. Clyde certainly taught me how to find peace, through inner meditation, and by instead of following the crowd, follow my heart.

JOHN SCHAEFER:

John Schaefer is a native Northwest artist originally from Olympia, WA. He worked at The San Francisco Museum of Art from 1972-1973 before relocating to the Skagit Valley in 1975, where he lived until 1989 in a cabin that was only accessible by boat on the South Fork of the Skagit River, outside of Conway, WA. He moved Clyde Sanborn from Seattle to La Conner and introduced him to Jimmy Schermerhorn, then occupying a cabin on the sandspit outside of town that Clyde eventually took possession of. Schaefer currently lives in Port Townsend, Washington, where he continues to produce meticulously rendered geometric paintings reminiscent of the late work of his friend and mentor Leo Kenny. He has exhibited at The Foster White and William Traver Galleries in Seattle and more recently with Charles Krafft at the Lucinda Douglas Gallery in

Bellingham, WA.

JIM SMITH & JANET SAUNDERS:
Neither of us remembers exactly when we met Clyde, but we're pretty sure it was in the '80s and definitely somewhere in La Conner. Maybe it was at the gas station where he often leaned his bike against the pump while he purchased his beer ration for the day. At any rate, Clyde became a regular visitor at our house on Morris Street, sometimes bringing gifts of flowers, a fresh poem or an odd edible to add to lunch (looking suspiciously like a dumpster product) and once a homeless cat who lived out her long life with us. He mowed our lawn, played his harmonica for us and (sort of) helped Jim fix up our new old house after we moved to Pull and Be Damned Road. Always entertaining, always a little Zen, always a little kooky. That was our friend Clyde. When he disappeared one day, we missed the old boy. And sometimes still do.

ROBERT SUND:
Poet and artist Robert Sund lived in the Ish River Country, and was Clyde's friend and neighbor. In 2016, Good Deed Rain published *A Flutter of Birds Passing Through Heaven: A Tribute to Robert Sund*.

JIM WOODRING:
Jim Woodring is an American cartoonist.

JOANNE & JIMMY ZABIK:
"We miss his company."

CREDITS:

Alan Watts quote from *Cloud Hidden, Whereabouts Unknown: A Mountain Journal*, Pantheon Books, 1968.

Clyde Sanborn, *Flash Flood & Other Poems*, Edited by Ben Munsey and Jim Smith. Book design and production by Steve Herold and Books AtoZ, 1997.

Jay Carpenter provided all the photographs of Clyde's Navy days.

Clyde in The Deluxe kitchen, photograph courtesy of Paul Dorpat Seattle Now & Then: Broadway and Roy and The Deluxe: https://pauldorpat.com/2016/11/05/seattle-now-then-broadway-and-roy-and-the-deluxe/

rainbow city: a deluxe coloring/poetry book, Alley Graphics, Seattle, WA 1975.

1890's photo by Rustle Frost.

Thank you to Sherry Thostenson from The La Conner Pub & Eatery.

Robert Sund, "July 19, 1979" and "September 13, 1981," *Notes from Disappearing Lake: The River Journals of Robert Sund*, edited by Glenn Chip Hughes and Tim McNulty, NY: Pleasure Boat Studio, 2012.

Thank you to Tom Robbins for the letter.

Fred Owens, "Clyde's Bicycle" excerpted from Frog Hospital, http://froghospital911.blogspot.com/2016/01/clydes-bicycle_14.html

"The small flower gazes at moon light" courtesy of Janet Saunders.

"SPLASH" courtesy of Janet Saunders. Thank you Janet for all your generosity!

Jan Sanborn provided all the early family photos of Clyde.

Clyde's Interview cassette and Memorial DVD courtesy of Janet Saunders.

Paul Hansen, "At the Grave of Li Tai-Bai," from *Ramblings of An Unfrocked Mandarin*, Watermark Press, Anacortes, Washington. 2001.

"Overnight with a Friend" and "Visiting the Tao Master of Tai-t'ien Mountain When He Wasn't There" from *Bright Moon, White Clouds: Selected Poems of Li Po*, edited and translated by J. P. Seaton, ©2012 by J. P. Seaton. Reprinted by arrangement with The Permissions Company, Inc., on behalf of Shambhala Publications Inc., Boulder, Colorado, www.shambhala.com.

Robert Sund, "A Bee Thumps Against the Dusty Window" and "Spring Time on the Skagit Valley" used with permission of the Robert Sund Poetry Trust.

Jimmy & Joanne Zabik interview with editor, August 29, 2016.

Channel Town Press newspapers from March 20, 1996 and March 27, 1996.

Jim Smith, "A Tribute to Clyde Sanborn" from *Channel Town Press*, June 29, 2005.

For "Clyde Interviewing Clyde" thanks to Michael Clough who remembered seeing this videotape at Jim Smith's, and with Janet Saunders' help was able to unearth it. Michael mailed it to me in a bag with his bound box copy of *Zen Flesh, Zen Bones*.

Thanks to Larry Smith for proofreading suggestions and enthusiasm.

Many people helped create this book, through emails, letters, interviews, and phone calls, passing the word on to others in a great chain of sharing. Clyde Sanborn knew hundreds of people and left a ripple that continues to spread.   Thanks Clyde.

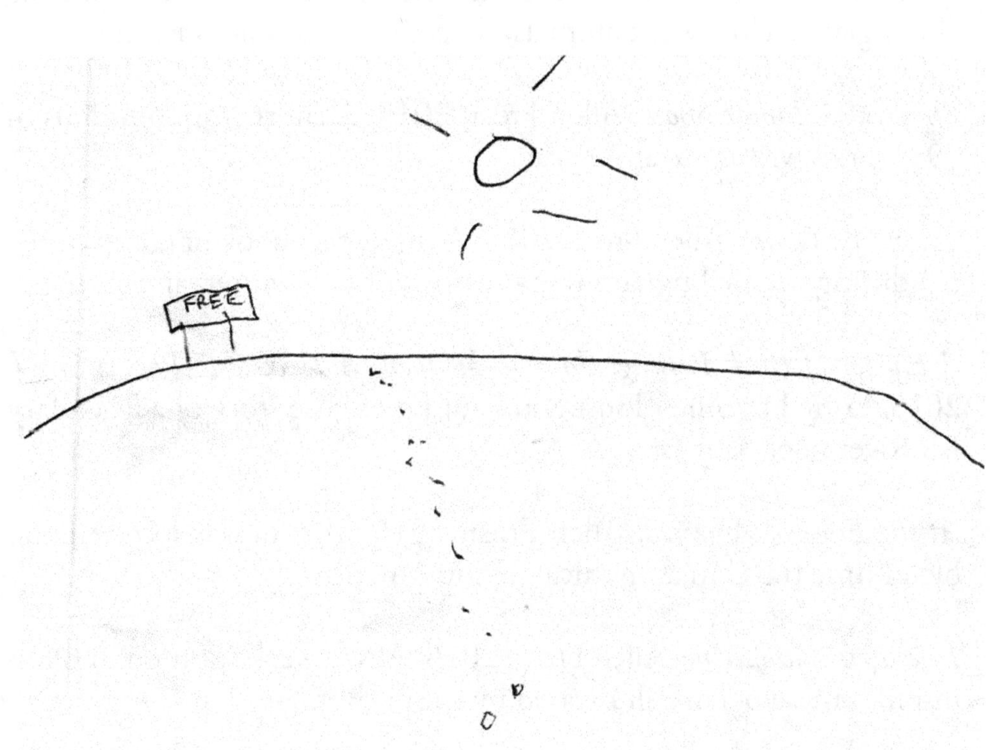

FREE

Saint Lemonade, Allen Frost, 2014. Two novels illustrated by the author in the manner of the old Big Little Books.

Playground, Allen Frost, 2014. Poems collected from seven years of chapbooks.

Roosevelt, Allen Frost, 2015. A Pacific Northwest novel set in July, 1942, when a boy and a girl search for a missing elephant. Illustrated throughout by Fred Sodt.

5 Novels, Allen Frost, 2015. Novels written over five years, featuring circus giants, clockwork animals, detectives and time travelers.

The Sylvan Moore Show, Allen Frost, 2015. A short story omnibus of 193 stories written over 30 years.

Town in a Cloud, Allen Frost, 2015. A three-part book of poetry, written during the Bellingham rainy seasons of fall, winter, and spring.

A Flutter of Birds Passing Through Heaven: A Tribute to Robert Sund. 2016. Edited by Allen Frost and Paul Piper. The story of a legendary Ish River poet & artist.

At the Edge of America, Allen Frost, 2016. Two novels in one book blend time travel in a mythical poetic America.

Lake Erie Submarine, Allen Frost, 2016. A two week vacation in Ohio inspired these poems, illustrated by the author.

and Light, Paul Piper, 2016. Poetry written over three years. Illustrated with watercolors by Penny Piper.

The Book of Ticks, Allen Frost, 2017. A giant collection of 8 mysterious adventures featuring Phil Ticks. Illustrated throughout by Aaron Gunderson.

I Can Only Imagine, Allen Frost, 2017. Five adventures of love and heartbreak dreamed in an imaginary world. Color & illustrations by Annabelle Barrett.

The Orphanage of Abandoned Teenagers, Allen Frost, 2017. A fictional guide for teens and their parents. Illustrated by the author.

Different Planet, Allen Frost, 2017. Four science fiction adventures: reincarnation, robots, talking animals, outer space and clones. Cover & illustrations by Laura Vasyutynska.

Go with the Flow: A Tribute to Clyde Sanborn. 2018. Edited by Allen Frost. The life and art of a timeless river poet.

This is Allen Frost's 21st published book.